THREE SIGMA LEADERSHIP

OR, THE WAY OF THE CHIEF ENGINEER

Leadership Skills for
NASA's Corps of Chief Engineers

STEVEN R. HIRSHORN

Published by the National Aeronautics and Space Administration.

The opinions expressed in this volume are those of the author and do not necessarily reflect the official positions of the United States Government or of the National Aeronautics and Space Administration.

National Aeronautics and Space Administration
Washington, DC

This book is dedicated to those who bravely accept the challenge of incredibly difficult, never-before-solved problems and routinely find elegant solutions to those problems. To the hard-working, always dedicated, endearingly passionate, occasionally quirky, and everlastingly resourceful and competent NASA engineers. *Ad Astra.*

CONTENTS

Acknowledgments		vii
Author's Note		ix
Greetings from the NASA Chief Engineer		xi
Preface		xiii
Introduction		xv
1	Demonstrating Emotional Intelligence	1
2	Representing the Voice of Many	13
3	Being the Box Top	25
4	Getting a Mentor/Being a Mentor	37
5	Demonstrating Knowledge of Systems Engineering	49
6	Being the Adult in the Room	59
7	Acting as the Lead Technical Integrator	71
8	Negotiating Solutions	83
9	Dealing with Engineering Change	95
10	Showing Enthusiasm	105
11	Learning Continuously	115
12	Serving as a Technical Authority	125
13	Maintaining Fairness	137

14	Managing Yourself	147
15	Employing Sound Engineering Judgement	157
16	Being Good at Both Tactics and Strategy	167
17	Maintaining an Awareness of Cultural Differences	177
18	Showing Accountability	189
19	Becoming a Master of Risk	199
20	Promoting Innovation	211
21	Building a Team	221
22	Having the Agility to Adapt	231
23	Ensuring Technical Excellence	241
24	Having Fun and Showing It	251
	Epilogue	259

APPENDICES

1	Principles of Naval Leadership	263
2	Chief Engineer's Desk Reference Material	269

ACKNOWLEDGMENTS

My thanks and gratitude need to be acknowledged for David Mobley, former NASA Chief Engineer at Headquarters (HQ) in the 1990s, for the peer review he conducted of this book. His perspectives—extracted from decades of experience and the wisdom drawn from it—and the validation of the ideas and propositions throughout enabled this book to ascend into the realm of "just possibly quite helpful." His hours of review and honest feedback and contributions gave me confidence that I maybe had hit the mark. What's more, included in this book are a few tidbits of wisdom directly from Dave, for which I am extremely grateful. Even today, I can still learn from the masters, and Dave is emblematic of one.

I also wish to acknowledge Rob Manning, Chief Engineer of the Jet Propulsion Laboratory, for his eloquent, heartfelt, and perfectly appropriate Preface to this book. I can think of no one more qualified or respected to have authored this book's Preface, and I am extremely honored to include Rob's words.

To both of you gentlemen—thank you so much!

My sincerest gratitude also goes to Keith Maynard and Jennifer Way, whose editing expertise converted this book from the dry, technical wit of a rocket engineer into eloquent prose that's understandable to the general public, and to Courtney Hampton, whose artistic interpretations on the front and back cover exceeded all my expectations and which appropriately convey the character and ambiance of the book's content. This effort simply could not have been successful without all of your contributions! And lastly, my sincerest gratitude to Michele Ostovar, for her leadership in shepherding this book through the publishing process.

AUTHOR'S NOTE

At NASA the terms "Chief Engineer" and "Lead Systems Engineer" are sometimes used interchangeably. They both can represent a project's technical leader. Throughout this book I use the term "Chief Engineer," but if Lead Systems Engineer is your title and your responsibilities are synonymous with those normally carried by Chief Engineers, then this book is written for you, too.

Disclaimer

The content herein does not in any way reflect official policy of the NASA Office of Chief Engineer. All opinions, perspectives, and guidance offered in this book are those of the author.

GREETINGS FROM THE NASA CHIEF ENGINEER

As a technical organization, charged with performing groundbreaking and pathfinding challenges on a daily basis, NASA has long valued the role of its Chief Engineers and Lead Systems Engineers. Although it takes a team to accomplish our missions and no members are unimportant, the Chief Engineers and Lead Systems Engineers who we look to lead our technical teams are critical to the success of our endeavors. It is this corps of dedicated, experienced, and passionate problem solvers and leaders who battle the technical headwinds that face every project, finding often hidden solutions and overcoming seemingly insurmountable obstacles to create paths to success. Furthermore, it is that indomitable spirit of ingenuity and perseverance that defines the Agency.

Developing our Chief Engineers and Lead Systems Engineers is a commitment of the NASA engineering community, and one of our tenets for excellence. This development ensures our corps of engineers obtain the depth of technical acumen that they require, first as discipline engineers and then as Chief Engineers and Lead Systems Engineers, but also the associated management skills and experience to ensure they can interact with the rest of the project team and with program, Center, and Agency leadership. What's more, this development also ensures that NASA Chief Engineers and Lead Systems Engineers proficiently serves as leaders of their own technical teams, and that's what this book is all about.

These technical leaders are critical to successfully implementing the three safety tenets we inherited from the Apollo program. These include the following:

1. Strong in-line checks and balances. This means that engineers check their fellow engineers, and that no one checks their own homework.
2. Healthy tension between responsible organizations. In NASA today that is the programs and the three Technical Authorities (Engineering, Safety, and Health and Medical). Each organization has to be on equal footing with separate but equal chains of command to allow issues to be raised independently and provide the healthy tension to create organizational checks and balances.
3. "Value-added" independent assessment. "Value-added" means you bring in outside technical experts to peer review critical issues. Having a fresh set of eyes on a problem can provide a different perspective, leverage different experiences and result in more robust solutions.

NASA arrived at these three tenets through considerable blood, sweat, and loss, and our commitment to them is now inscribed in our Agency governance. As Chief Engineers and Lead Systems Engineers, your role in this is paramount, and achieving excellence in this is an expectation of your job.

Serving in this role is not an easy task, but it is a tremendously rewarding one. You are the leaders of your technical teams, owners of the technical baseline, standard bearers of engineering best practices, decision makers, risk mitigators and problem solvers. You are Chief Engineers and Lead Systems Engineers, the title of which should say it all.

—Ralph R. Roe, Jr.

PREFACE

When I was young, I used to think that the machines that NASA engineers lofted into deep space were "out there" and stood alone as a thing. Many even call these machines by their names, as if they were living things with minds of their own. I have even seen engineers treat and talk about these as if they were somehow separate from the humanity of their creation. While I have also been guilty of that, sometimes the innate complexity of our creations leads to their appearing to develop minds of their own. Despite many of them being hundreds of millions of miles from home, I no longer see these machines as being alone in their part of the universe.

Instead I see the faces and hear the voices of the creators of these wonderful machines. When I see Spirit and Opportunity's housefly solar panels, I think of Kobie and Dara. When I see pictures of Curiosity's descent stage that lowered the rover to the surface of Mars in our "skycrane maneuver" I think of Ben and Carl. As I imagine samples being dropped off on Mars, I can hear Louise's voice cautiously explaining her team's new Mars 2020 sample caching system. I see Prasun's white knuckles when I imagine the Phoenix lander entering Mars using the first interplanetary knuckleball. When I see those glorious images from Mars Reconnaissance Orbiter, not only do I see Alfred, but I also imagine the calm smiling faces of the two can-do Tims from Lockheed Martin, confidently explaining their nadir guidance approach. I see many more. So many faces. Every subtle nuance in the primary structure, every curve, every mechanism, every wire, every electronics circuit board, every chip, every software module, every thermal blanket, every nav filter and heat pipe. Alan, Jackie, Keith, Ann, Pradeep, Howard,

Al, Chris, Ian, Denise, Mike…. The list of talented faces and names go on and on. They all have their story.

I can no longer separate the "thing" from the people. They are one. When Opportunity was finally declared dead after an intense dust storm, I didn't mourn for our lost rover. While I was sad for the ops team that tirelessly squeezed every last drop out of an amazing and an amazingly lucky mission, I was proud for the many engineers around the world who made these rovers come true. It's the people. The people behind Opportunity, the people behind Cassini, the people behind the International Space Station (ISS), and the people behind the James Webb Space Telescope (JWST) who make these machines real and the missions come true.

It's that important detail that is so often overlooked. Instead we give people group names—like Ball, Goddard Space Flight Center (GSFC), Jet Propulsion Laboratory (JPL), and Lockheed Martin Astronautics—that strip off the humanity from their handiwork and hide the fact that their fingerprints are all over these missions. Your job as Chief Engineer is to not fall prey to that kind of thinking. You must integrate not only the machine, but the entire human enterprise behind that machine. Your mission is to help many artists integrate each of their parts of the painting into a massive single working piece of art.

Steve Hirshorn's excellent new book will remind you that Chief Engineering is not about being the best engineer. It's not about being a technical boss. It's about enabling a lot of talented people to win and for their and your mission to work. You will win, too, if they and the mission come before you. Being a Chief Engineer is an intensely human enterprise and humbling experience. Read what Steve has to say. You will be better, and your team will be better for it.

—Rob Manning
JPL Chief Engineer

INTRODUCTION

Why am I writing this book and for whom am I writing it? Those are really good questions—thanks for asking them!

At the time of this writing I have spent almost three decades (29 years, to be exact) supporting our great Agency in the pursuit of our Nation's space exploration, aeronautics, and technology development and having the opportunity and honor to serve in a number of capacities from technical to managerial to leadership. NASA is at its foundation a technical agency and, as such, the majority of those in our leadership positions arose from technical backgrounds. These leaders are engineers and technologists, scientists and technical discipline experts, who have either volunteered or were "volun-told" to become managers and leaders. Some of them may have even desired and strived to attain the position of Chief Engineer. If the same is true of you, this book is for you. You have set your sights on that job, working for years to build the experience and reputation that someday would pay off with that longed-for call from the boss. You've made it, congratulations! But now that you're here, what is expected of you, and what does it mean to be a Chief Engineer and a leader?

Leadership is as necessary an ingredient in the cocktail of being a NASA Chief Engineer as any other. Some would say it is the most important ingredient. All of us who bear the title of Chief Engineer have spent the majority of our careers learning the trade of our technical discipline, working on projects, succeeding and sometimes failing (hopefully for the right reasons), but all the while learning, gaining the experience and the wisdom that come along with those successes and failures. We live, breathe, and eat the technical jargon that accompanies our trade, whether in formal life-cycle reviews, more informal technical discussions, or one-on-ones between colleagues. We perform trades, we assess suitability of designs for a given mission, we balance risk with reward, and in the end, we do everything within our ability to ensure that the spacecraft, aircraft, or demonstrations that carry the NASA logo are successful. These parts of the Chief Engineer job are familiar, and our careers have provided us the background, training, and experience to conduct them with confidence and accuracy.

But now you've been handed the additional responsibilities of leadership and the equation shifts somewhat away from the purely technical, from the experience that gives us engineering judgement, and toward the new responsibilities of leading people. There is wide anecdotal evidence that more projects fail not because of technical shortcomings but from organizational failings, from the inability of leaders to ensure the excellence and potential of their team. This organizational failing is, to be honest, not limited to NASA but can happen to any endeavor in which people are the critical element. It proves that leadership is as necessary to ensuring success at NASA as is technical acumen and rigorous engineering processes.

But what does it mean to be a leader in the role of a Chief Engineer and how do you prepare yourself for those responsibilities? There are some Agency-wide courses available and a few NASA Centers have career development frameworks that provide elements of preparation for the responsibilities to come. And the value that mentorship brings to those recently elevated to the position cannot be underestimated. But in my experience, we mostly just insert newly appointed Chief Engineers into the breach and have them learn on the job what it means to lead. I think we can do better.

Leadership is, at its core, about people—understanding people, motivating people, resolving conflicts with people, and encouraging people to move in the same direction. That may not be something we engineers/scientists/technologists feel particularly comfortable with. We prefer to work with hardware, with software, with mathematics and physics, with requirements and design, with verification and validation (V&V) and with hazard assessments and Monte Carlo simulations. But when it comes to focusing on the people (remember, a critical element of success), we shy away and retreat to those more familiar technical surroundings.

An inescapable fact is that it is immeasurably more difficult dealing with people than it is with the systems and vehicles we develop. You cannot insult a vehicle. You cannot irritate a vehicle. Vehicles don't need to be motivated. They simply perform as designed and operate within their capabilities and certifications. There is variability with vehicles, but it's quantifiable. Not so with people. And that, perhaps, is what makes dealing with people so difficult. They're not quantifiable.

A Chief Engineer has to master people skills. They also have to be technically proficient, understand the engineering method, be both flexible and decisive, and have vision. They have to listen well, have the ability to manage themselves, and be a continuous learner. These are all attributes of effective leaders that now fall to you as lead of the project's technical team. Where do you start? Well, hopefully, one place you can start is with this book. If you look back over your career, you can very likely pinpoint a handful of circumstances that you recognized as poor leadership from your supervisors or managers. Think about it right now, I'll wait as you cringe in the memory. And while examples of poor leadership are tremendous teachers, it's probably more difficult to identify circumstances that characterize good leadership. Hopefully, that's where this book can help, to identify, describe, and explain what constitutes good leadership and to establish the bar of expectation of leadership as demonstrated by NASA Chief Engineers.

In this book you will find scenarios that help explain good leadership in the context of NASA's technical and development work. Some of these are theoretical and others more practical, taken from my career. They are offered as windows into potentially confusing and nebulous topics, which I hope should become clearer and more familiar. Before we get into all of that, and speaking of my career, a little about me.

A LITTLE ABOUT ME

Each of us is composed of a kaleidoscope of experiences, the collected set of our previous jobs and responsibilities, our interactions with managers, engineers, researchers, and leaders, and the lessons we have learned over the arc of our careers. Add into that the life experience we pick up outside the fence of NASA and "poof," we become individuals. These experiences constitute much of what makes us who we are and helps (or sometimes hinders) our decisions, perspectives and judgements. Sometimes we can actively navigate our path and which experiences we gain, other times those experiences are thrust upon us. But collectively, the trajectory they outline all lead to great wisdom. Here's what my trajectory looked like.

Space Shuttle Mission Control Flight Controller (1990–2001)
Mission Operations Directorate (MOD), Johnson Space Center (JSC)

Hands down, this was the best job ever! What an experience, fresh out of graduate school and thrust into a pressure-fed environment where you are responsible for a multibillion-dollar national asset and the lives of the astronauts residing within her. What responsibility! For 11 years I worked in Johnson Space Center's Mission Control as a Space Shuttle flight controller, sitting at the same revered consoles that my predecessors occupied during the early space program and missions to the Moon. Believe me, an entire book could be written about this experience, replete with anecdotes both humorous and tragic. Over those years on console I directly supported 55 Space Shuttle missions, overseeing the Orbiter's electrical systems, managing consumables, and helping to ensure the success of those spaceflight missions.

What I learned about leadership from that experience:
- Teamwork is important for accomplishing complex and complicated tasks.
- There are many subtleties to effectively leading a small team and creating bonds within that team.
- Pressure can both positively and negatively affect performance.
- There are many idiosyncrasies to being an authority.
- Maintaining a systemic perspective is necessary.

Technical Assistant for Shuttle (2001–2006)
Systems Division, MOD, JSC

After 11 years on console I was elevated to Technical Assistant for Shuttle, a technical management position within the Systems Division, which supplied the Mission Control flight controllers (this division was responsible for the Shuttle hardware and software systems). In this capacity I provided insights and interpretations to the Division Chief on technical issues occurring on the Shuttle, which necessitated considerable interaction among all Division personnel, as well as coordinating and integrating inputs from across the Division in preparation for each mission's Certification of Flight Readiness (CoFR). This position also included the responsibility of representing the MOD to the Orbiter Project Office, necessitating me to sit in on all of the Configuration Control Board meetings when we were not flying and all of the daily Orbiter situation meetings when we were flying.

What I learned about leadership from that experience:
- I learned how to integrate internally and represent externally an entire Division of almost 300 people.
- There are both good and bad things about Center-level leadership.
- Decision-making is hard.
- The boss isn't always right.
- Offering unpopular positions is both scary and empowering.
- Having the ability to change your mind due to new evidence is mandatory.
- If you don't take care of yourself first, you can't be successful at anything else.

MOD Lead Engineer for Constellation (2006–2011)
Flight Director's Office, MOD, JSC

Having attained a reputation for having technical acumen and good integration skills, I was brought up to the Flight Director's Office and from there served as the MOD Lead Engineer for our Constellation program development. This focused largely on the control center and mission simulator development occurring inside the Directorate. In this position I chaired a technical panel for the first time, was responsible for coordinating and integrating technical development, and also was looked upon to provide vision and leadership in ways not required by my previous positions. I did so from an envied perch—the Flight Director's Office—where I witnessed the natural variations within an office composed of nothing but A-team players. The job also required me to be the Mission Operations representative to the Constellation Systems Engineering and Integration organization, from which I had an insightful view of the entire program.

What I learned about leadership from that experience:
- Leading a panel (or decision board) is a gratifying but sometimes lonely job.
- Technical development is all about systems engineering.
- A spectrum of leadership capabilities is evident even in a group consisting entirely of leaders.
- Dealing with difficult people is time-consuming, but necessary and possible.
- Perception sometimes replaces reality, but you have the ability to overcome that.
- Empathy is a mandatory leadership skill.

Systems Engineering and Integration Manager (2011–2013)
Integrated Systems Research Program,
Aeronautics Research Mission Directorate (ARMD), NASA HQ
I transferred to HQ, where all the great decisions are made! Not really. Well, maybe a few. In this position I served as technical integrator, risk manager, and third in command of an aeronautics research program. My responsibilities were fairly open, and I was utilized for any number of ad hoc tasks by the Program Director. At the time the program managed two large research efforts, one investigating and maturing high-potential aircraft technologies to improve environmental friendliness and the second seeking to lower the barriers of incorporating

Unmanned Aircraft Systems (UAS) into the national air space. I spent the majority of my time focused on oversight of these two projects and on support to the program for HQ-type activities (such as budget proposals, congressional interactions, developing strategic goals and objectives, writing the program plan).

What I learned about leadership from that experience:
- People skills are very important. Successful leaders have them, the unsuccessful ones don't.
- Politics can get in the way of doing the right thing, so stay the course ethically.
- Personal relationships are important, but don't allow them to interfere with working with others
- There are differences between the roles of up-and-out vs. down-and-in.
- Organizational dysfunction can affect all levels.

ARMD and STMD Deputy Chief Engineer (2013–2015)
Office of Chief Engineer, NASA HQ

I accepted a one-year detail in the HQ Office of Chief Engineer as Deputy Chief Engineer to both the Aeronautics Research Mission Directorate and the Space Technology Mission Directorate (STMD). As can sometimes occur with one-year details, the job was so much fun that I transferred permanently. Because both of these Mission Directorates were relatively small compared with NASA's two other Mission Directorates (Science and Human Exploration and Operations), they shared one Chief Engineer. Most of the responsibilities focused on oversight and independent evaluation; however, given the large number of projects in both of these Mission Directorates, there was a lot of territory to cover. As a Mission Directorate Chief Engineer (OK, deputy), I also got tasked with periodically presenting our office's independent evaluations of programs and projects to the Agency's Baseline Performance Review, which is chaired by the NASA Associate Administrator and attended by Center Directors and HQ Office Chiefs. In addition, I was asked to take over responsibility for NASA Systems Engineering policy (NASA Procedural Requirement [NPR] 7123) and guidance (*NASA Systems Engineering Handbook*), both of which fall under the purview of the HQ Office of Chief Engineer. Opportunities also presented themselves to provide leadership on a few Agency-wide teams on a few other tactical activities, such as determining criteria on how we should assess research and technology development projects at the Agency-level.

What I learned about leadership from that experience:
- Agency senior leadership are just people—higher paid and higher in the Agency hierarchy but ultimately just people.
- Acting positions have all the responsivity but none of the authority of their associated permanent position.
- Chief Engineers can have influence.
- When people talk to you, listen—even if they are just venting (maybe especially when they are just venting).
- There is great value in having a good mentor.

ARMD Chief Engineer (2015–Present)
Office of Chief Engineer, NASA HQ

And here I am, Chief Engineer for all of aeronautics at NASA. It's a great gig, really. It allows me to provide both oversight and evaluation for a wide variety of programs and projects and to continue with the systems engineering policy as I had before. But being the full-blown Chief Engineer now offers me some roles that I didn't have as deputy, such as interacting with other Center Chief Engineers and being a member of the ARMD Directorate Program Management Council. I get involved with the roles and responsibilities of Chief Engineers across the Agency and play a leadership role in a variety of special studies, such as determining governance of NASA's piloted X-plane projects and assessing how we use Technology Readiness Assessments. I interface with other Government agencies like the Defense Department, the Government Accountability Office, and the National Academy of Sciences. I'm allowed latitude to attack problems where I see them, like the lack of leadership training for NASA's Chief Engineers (my solution is what you're holding in your hands right now).

What I learned about leadership from that experience:
- Competence combined with humility can get you far.
- Technical Authority (TA) is a vital part of how NASA stays successful.
- Policy is important, but how it gets implemented is more important.
- I can use my position and influence to better the Agency.
- Luck is a part of success.
- I'm still learning and will continue to learn—even after almost three decades in the business, I can still improve myself.

So, there you go, that's my trajectory, the path I took from wet behind the ears new hire right out of graduate school to Chief Engineer for Aeronautics at HQ. This trajectory is unique to me, as yours is to you. There are many paths you can take from entry level to senior leadership and one is no better than another. But more important, it's not the positions and jobs I've performed that have prepared me for my present position but all the lessons I've picked up along the way. It's not the stops I've made during my career but the experience that I've accumulated. Those bits and pieces, collectively, make me who I am and not the titles I have held.

I look at this book in the following way. If you're familiar with J.R.R. Tolkien, in the opening volume to the *Lord of the Rings* you'll recall that Sauron, the main antagonist, created rings for others in Middle Earth. With these rings and the ring he forged for himself (the "One Ring"), he could control all of the land and all who resided within it. To accomplish this, within his One Ring, Sauron was noted to have "poured his cruelty, his malice, and his will to dominate all life."[*] Relax, I don't have any cruelty, malice, or will to dominate all life, but I do have the desire

---

[*] "One Ring To Rule Them All," *The Lord of the Rings: The Fellowship of the Ring*, directed by Peter Jackson (2001, Los Angeles: New Line Cinema, 2002), DVD.

to help prepare NASA's Chief Engineers for the jobs ahead of them. As such, into this book I have poured my experience, my wisdom, and my beliefs in the hope that they can provide a useful guide on what we expect from our Chief Engineers and the behaviors we expect them to demonstrate. I hope this volume will be a useful source of guidance and inspiration, submitted from the perspective of one of your own and offered not as direction but as a mentor offers coaching and support.

Please note that the 24 behaviors outlined in this book won't provide you all you'll need to know to be an exceptional leader. It would be a mistake to assume that you can simply read through this material, put it down, and clear the bar. It's not quite that easy, I'm afraid. This book provides a start, a foundation for effective leadership, but there's a lot more to learn. I encourage you to continue the learning process even after finishing this book. Read more. Attend lectures and presentations on leadership. Watch and observe and note to yourself what works and what doesn't. Here, you can start right now! You may note that I appended some brilliant material to the end of this book (aka, Appendix 1). It's list of expected leadership behaviors created by the U.S. Navy. Although I won't go over them in detail in this book, they remain for me the very finest short and concise encapsulation of leadership I have ever found. I have this list laminated and hanging over my desk at NASA HQ and I reference it almost daily. Take a look, it's quite insightful.

Why did I select *Three-Sigma Leadership* for the title of this book? Three sigma is a statistical calculation, commonly used in engineering analysis, that refers to data within three standard deviations from a mean. Three sigma also refers to processes that operate efficiently and produce results of the highest quality. At one standard deviation, or one sigma, the operation will succeed around 68 percent of the time. Two standard deviations, or two sigma, result in 95 percent success. At three standard deviations, 99.7 percent of the operations assessed are successful. When engineers assess whether a system or component will perform as designed, they will run hundreds, sometimes thousands, of analyses manipulating a host of variables. When the analysis results indicate that success occurs at three sigma, or 99.7 percent of the time, we call it good enough.

Leadership can be imagined similarly. No leader will get it right 100 percent of the time. But if leaders can be effective to a three-sigma level, we'll call it good enough.

We are about to take a journey together, a trek through the nature of what it means to be a NASA Chief Engineer. I hope the journey will be enjoyable for you, that you get to laugh once or twice, but more importantly to reflect on the awesome responsibilities you now own and how you can be the best you can be.

Ad Astra!

CHAPTER 1
DEMONSTRATING EMOTIONAL INTELLIGENCE

Never let it be said that NASA Chief Engineers recoil from tough challenges, so we'll start with a biggie but a toughie. To be blunt, we in the NASA technical community generally don't do well with emotional intelligence. Whether it's because we as a community are right-brained and logically oriented, or maybe it's because historically our leaders have tended to be male (some for whom emotional intelligence doesn't come as naturally) or maybe it's for entirely different reasons. Emotional intelligence is undervalued as a dominant and requisite skill for leaders in engineering. In fact, focusing on emotional intelligence in the conduct of our work is often ridiculed and denigrated by our peers. Engineers are taught to value technical competence, to be logical in our thought processes, and to rely on data and repeatable phenomena—to think and not to feel. Emotions are not part of engineering, we're told, and emotions are a distraction from the high-risk, time-critical work that we routinely do.

Unfortunately, whether we are developing a spacecraft, an aircraft, a technology, or conducting research, there is one component that all of those areas have in common. If you guessed the hardware/software or the extreme environments in which these systems will be operating, you'd be wrong. The one component common to everything that NASA does is that projects are composed of people, and the performance of those people is as critical to the success of the project as is the performance of the technology. The performance of our project personnel can spell disaster and failure just as acutely as the performance of the things we build. History has noted that more projects fail because of organizational dysfunction or lack of effective leadership than due to hardware exceeding certification tolerances or operating outside of the expected environment. It's easy, in fact, to perform rigorous testing to ensure operational hardware and software performance meets requirements and to repeat that testing to provide confidence in the results, but it is very difficult to test an organization's personnel performance and that performance may not always be repeatable. Organizations and people are highly non-deterministic.

If we as technical leaders are oblivious to the performance of our people, then we are failing just as we would fail by ignoring out-of-family technical performance. But while we may be attuned to recognizing when the hardware is talking to us, we frequently are not attuned to the messaging we get from our team. As engineers, many of us miss the subtle hints buried within their words, their tone, their selection of wording, their pauses and the occasional silences that say as much as words (and sometimes even more). Recognizing these hints and being attuned to the motivations and forces influencing our team is what emotional intelligence is all about.

While we receive lots of training over the course of our careers, we rarely receive training on how to understand what a team member is really saying when the message is filled with subtlety, or when the messenger is hesitant to give all the information. We deal with facts and the tangible, not in subtleties and the subjective. That doesn't compute for most of us. But it needs to when you are a leader responsible for a team, as Chief Engineers are.

How do we do this? How do we pay attention to the emotional state of our team, or even care about it? It's a difficult task, and to become proficient it is something that has to be practiced and refined, like any skill. Psychologically, as people grow up, they develop differing levels of emotional intelligence, and even those with strong inherent capabilities still need to refine those skills over the course of their professional career. There's no simple answer, but there is a starting point. When discussing technical matters with your team, get used to paying attention to the emotional state, the nonverbal cues and the feeling you get from your people. I know, that sounds antithetical to who we are as engineers—we pay attention to the data and facts. But it's not antithetical to who we are as leaders.

When someone yells and gets red in the face, we know they are angry. That's not so subtle. But when someone is hesitant, or somewhat fearful or uncomfortable, their style of communication is much subtler. Pay attention to that. Pay attention to where they point their gaze, to the cadence of their voice, to the use of or lack of hand gestures. All of those indications are giveaways to a person's emotional state and windows into their true feelings.

Here's an example. One of my jobs had been as the Mission Operations representative to the Space Shuttle Orbiter project. In this capacity I would participate in the weekly Orbiter Configuration Control Boards, where we discussed all of the sustaining engineering required to keep the Orbiters flying safely and successfully. These board meetings were highly technical, covering issues on subsystems, assemblies, components, and even piece parts. We discussed certification, qualification, technical performance, design changes, material processes, and all the matter one would expect at a Configuration Control Board.

On one occasion, prior to the formal Board, we were having a preliminary discussion with the deputy manager of the Orbiter project on an out-of-family condition on one of the Orbiter's Auxiliary Power Units (APU) on the previous Shuttle mission. In this case, prior to reentry when the APU was started its turbine speed was within certification limits but outside of historical performance (the vehicle, of course, landed safely). Through this discussion we were considering whether it was acceptable to fly the APU as-is on the Orbiter's next mission. The alternative was to direct Kennedy Space Center to remove and replace the APU.

The APU subsystem manager, the person responsible for these components, was discussing his thoughts. Let's call him Larry. Larry went through the telemetry of the out-of-family event, discussed the potential causes of the behavior, and reviewed all the acceptance testing and flight history of that particular unit. He didn't have any hard data that indicated the exhibited performance could result in a failure of the APU, but there were enough unknowns there to make him cautious, and his demeanor showed it. The Deputy Orbiter Project Manager, to whom all this was being presented, was a highly qualified and experienced engineer but wasn't someone with an acute emotional intelligence. Throughout the discussion he focused on the data, the telemetry, and the hardware history, but was oblivious to the concern that Larry was demonstrating nonverbally. After 2 hours of discussion he decided to recommend to his boss, the Orbiter Project Manager, that we fly the APU as-is, seeing no reason to pull the unit. No one disagreed, and we scheduled the topic for the full Board.

A week later the topic arrived on the Board's agenda. The Orbiter Project Manager, while an equally qualified and experienced engineer, also rated higher on the emotional intelligence scale than did his deputy. Throughout the discussion Larry again reviewed all the telemetry, qualification, and acceptance data and potential causes of the behavior and did so while displaying the same nonverbal indications of his concerns. This time, the project manager picked up on Larry's concerns based on the caution in his voice and his hesitation to offer a strong endorsement of the APU's integrity. Now, understand that the exact same data was used during these two meetings, but because the project manager could discern Larry's unvocalized hesitation, the decision was different. In the end we removed and replaced the APU and sent it back to the depot for additional testing.

Utilizing emotional intelligence is critical in decision-making. Data gives us a wonderful window into technical performance, but data doesn't incorporate experience and wisdom. People do, though—and we as leaders must pay attention to the people as strongly as we do to the data.

Sometimes emotional intelligence is not enough and it's difficult to get a sense of what another person is thinking. During the early parts of the Constellation program, I attended a 2-week Technical Interchange Meeting conducted by the program's Systems Engineering and Integration (SE&I) Office. The purpose of the meeting was to review the program and project requirements in preparation for an upcoming Systems Requirements Review. We covered the top-level requirements being flowed down from NASA HQ and the couple hundred or so program-level requirements that would be traced down to the projects. I would say there were 60 or 70 people attending the meeting.

At the time the SE&I Office was managed by a diminutive but gruff and hard-bitten manager whose pedigree derived from his former military career before coming to NASA. This person was absolutely inscrutable in facial or vocal expression—in short, a real poker player. When reviewing the program requirements or discussing areas of disagreement, it was impossible to discern how he felt given his expressions and body language. There simply was none. He would sit there, emotionless, and monitor the discussion but not contributing to it unless he had to. And yet folks around the room would frequently look to him for any indication of feedback. They wanted to know, for example, if the requirement was acceptable. Was the discussion reasonable? Did the solution conform to accepted practices or was it inappropriate? Those in attendance wanted his feedback, it was critical, but he just wouldn't deliver.

So, what did they do? In desperation, one of his staff had an idea—and I have to credit her for coming up with brilliant one. They created a series of placards out of cardstock and wooden dowels, each representing a different emotional reaction. One said "Happy," another said "Frustrated." There were placards for "Angry," "Humored," and "Satisfied," accounting for almost every possible reaction that could have arisen during the discussion. When presented with these placards, the manager viewed his new collection, decided to play along and raised the "Eye Roll" placard, which elicited a chorus of laughter from the entire room. For the rest of the long meeting he would continue his stoic body language but by using the placards we all knew where he stood on the topics being discussed.

The opposite of this are situations in which everyone knows exactly how a person feels. By January 2010, NASA had been working on the Constellation program for 5 years (some, who had been involved during the early formulation stages at HQ, had been working on the program longer than that). I was attending a leadership boot camp in Colorado Springs when the shocking news came down that the forthcoming fiscal year budget request from the White House was going to recommend cancelling the program! Many of us at this boot camp had been working tirelessly on Constellation, as had literally thousands of people across all NASA Centers as well as contractors across the country. We were devastated.

I returned to Johnson Space Center some days later and held the weekly Mission Operations Constellation Engineering and Integration panel that I co-chaired. When I sat down at the head of the table, I was presented with about two dozen very despondent faces, all concerned about the news and the implications to the work and plans we had dedicated ourselves to over the previous 5 years. It didn't take a doctorate in psychology to realize that the agenda of technical topics we had scheduled for the day was not what was on people's minds and that those in attendance wanted, or maybe needed, to talk. So instead of ignoring what I was seeing and proceeding with the planned agenda, I started off the meeting by discussing what I knew of the situation (which wasn't much at the time) and opened the table to discussion. Sure enough, it came pouring forth. Feelings of fear, frustration, anger, and concern were the predominant emotions, with the occasional bit of relief that the pressure that had driven us incessantly was now off. Underlying it all was a pervading sense of confusion, as no one, myself included, knew exactly what would now happen.

My sense walking into that meeting was that the topics we had lined up for discussion that day were irrelevant and that what we needed to do was to just talk, as a group, expressing our feelings and being heard. Had we just pressed on with the topics at hand, I was sure the conversation would be half-hearted, if even that, and while we may have made decisions, they would likely have been poor decisions at best. But more important, on this day, this group of dedicated career engineers and managers did not care about the planned topics. What they wanted to do that day was talk, and that's exactly what I let happen.

Emotional intelligence and awareness of the emotional state of those around us comes easier for some than for others. Some of our colleagues appear more attuned to the emotional state of coworkers and others less so. There's no science that I'm aware of to explain this, it just kind of is. Perhaps those who come from large families with many brothers and sisters get trained during their childhood to acknowledge and monitor their siblings' emotional states, while only children don't get as much practice? I don't know, but the level of awareness of the emotional state of those around us varies from person to person.

Where do engineers fit into this mix? Well, even before entering the profession, many engineers tend to be rational thinkers who methodically work through problems, which may be what makes us gravitate toward engineering to begin with. But once we dive in and begin our training to be engineers, our curriculum is heavy on mathematics and physics, on understanding the dynamics and interactions of the material world around us operating by Newtonian physics. It is the world of the tangible and the understandable, of the repeatable and the predictable. The end of the process delivers a potential engineer in the standard model we're all familiar with. That model has very distinct advantages in the world of engineering where college trains graduates to "think like an engineer." Don't get me wrong—engineering needs recruits like that. But to be a successful engineer, and in particular a successful Chief Engineer and leader, the human side of the equation needs to be acknowledged in our work and most college engineering educations simply don't prepare graduates for those tasks. Perhaps in the future it can become part of the education, but today it is a noted shortcoming.

So, a new engineer graduates college and gets a job at NASA. Frequently they are put to work immediately on a project or research effort, getting their hands dirty developing requirements for a system, testing a component, running analysis, determining hazards and failure modes, all the jobs of the trade. They work daily with hardware and software, in test chambers and laboratories, using computational methods and simulations and engineering development units, all the while ascending the curve of technical experience and understanding of systems. But at what point do they get exposed to and trained on the potential failure modes and idiosyncrasies of the other critical component in any successful project—the people? In short, they likely don't. Over the years NASA's engineers may pick up some of these skills through observation if they are paying attention, but there is little to no focus on this component and, as such, the engineers we create are great with understanding technical disciplines but many times not so great at understanding the people they work with.

To make matters worse, developing an ability to understand the people they work with is often consciously de-emphasized. The engineering culture we live in doesn't value emotional intelligence the same way it values technical acumen, it doesn't value understanding human nature the same way it values understanding component failure history. The uncertainties that human behavior imposes on our programs and projects is considered intangible and therefore not worth the attention of our engineers. Just get the hardware working right and your job will be accomplished. The problem here is, of course, that since the majority of the NASA workforce is composed of engineers and technical specialists, so our leaders are culled from the same pool and are developed with the same limitations. When our engineers turn into leaders, many are lacking this key skill. So, while we create world-class engineers with a full complement of technical skills to do that job, we can unconsciously lose sight of also creating world class leaders with a full complement of leadership skills to do that job.

OK, enough for the moment. I just painted a pretty bleak picture. Is it really all that bad? We all work with each other in meetings and teams and groups, interacting and discussing and arguing but also laughing and crying, sharing stories, and more or less getting along. Many of us enter the NASA workforce single and our work group becomes part of our extended family. Are NASA engineers really that ill-equipped to deal effectively with each other? No, of course not. Some teams work better with each other than others, and individual clashes do occur, but in general the NASA workforce is a socially accepting bunch who also happen to be bound together by the love of our work. All is not lost. The main shortcoming, however, occurs when we get elevated to the roles and responsibilities of leadership. As leaders, the expectations increase, and the consequences of getting things wrong commensurately increase as well. NASA's engineers can get by with poor social skills (as long as their technical capabilities are acceptable), but the same is not true for NASA's leaders. When you become a leader, your emotional intelligence suddenly becomes a critical component of your success. If our leaders are left to the same expectations as our engineers, then we introduce risk and increase the potential for failure. It's pretty much that simple.

In addition to understanding the emotional state of those around us, having emotional intelligence also means understanding your own emotional state. How good are you at recognizing what you're feeling and understanding why? Some people are reactive: when they are annoyed, irritated, frustrated, or angry, they let loose with their anger. It overwhelms their constraints and takes over their actions. And then the situation passes and they calm down, and they return to their normal demeanor. When we get angry, I would theorize that most of us can recognize the fact that we are angry and maybe even understand why. That one is pretty easy. But there are many more subtle feelings that can also affect our actions that we may have a more difficult time identifying. Jealousy and envy are good examples; they are somewhat nefarious in how they can control our actions, but we may be hesitant to identify those emotions in ourselves.

Getting to know yourself and the causes of your emotional state gives you a powerful tool. A case in point, and this is somewhat embarrassing, but here goes. I have a condition called misophonia. I've had it since I was a kid. It's a condition where a person can have a visceral reaction in the presence of a particular sound. For me and for many such afflicted that sound is the noise of loud eating, the smacking and slurping and swallowing sounds that accompany the consumption of food or drink. When I am in the presence of loud eating, I get agitated. It's hard to explain. There is even a psychophysical reaction in that my body responds with an elevated heart rate and a distinct manifestation to fight-or-flight. In the past, the only way I could mitigate these effects was to escape the area and get away from the sounds.

As I was growing up, I didn't understand why I reacted this way to these sounds. I simply knew that I did. Later, when I learned about the condition of misophonia, the reasons became clear and I could put a cause to my feelings. Today, when I am in the presence of loud eating, I cognitively understand why my heart rate is elevated and why I have an almost uncontrollable desire to run away. This knowledge allows me to deal with my physical response logically and I can control its effects on me. Or, I know that if it gets too overwhelming that I can simply leave the room and all will be well again. Having this understanding allows me to know myself and understanding what triggers my own emotional reactions is a key to emotional intelligence.

So we've established what emotional intelligence is. Now, what can we do to build emotional intelligence among our leaders? The first thing, I would suggest again, is to increase your awareness of the emotional state of those around you. I have had the opportunity to chair meetings or lead teams frequently over my career. As I'm sitting at the head of the table, listening to the information and debate, I have learned to sometimes push back a bit—not literally but in my mind—and detach from the discussion for a few minutes to start paying attention to the emotional state of the room. I watch the dynamics of the conversation and "take the temperature" of the room. Many times, doing so gives me more information to support the decision I will be required to make than just the pure technical information. That's not to de-emphasize the importance of the technical information, but to point out that decisions, as judgement calls, need to be informed by the experience of those supporting you. And those supporting you may not always vocalize all that they are feeling. Be mindful of not just what they are saying but how they are saying it. Body language speaks volumes.

Second, get out and talk with your team. If you don't do this much and rely on scheduled meetings to interact with them, do it more. As a disciplined engineer it's possible to seclude yourself in your cubicle and only come out for meetings. Much of that work can be accomplished on a solitary basis and the need to interact with others can be minimized. Not so for leaders. Spending time talking with your people will not only increase your awareness of the state of a project, but you also get practice in determining emotional states and that in turn builds emotional intelligence. Think about what they are not saying, what they may be vague on or seem hesitant to discuss. Pay attention to their eyes and where they are directed.

Third, get to know yourself and what triggers your emotional responses. This may take some deep introspection. But the benefits of knowing yourself is incalculable to understanding how and why you react to things and to controlling those reactions if they are negative. You can monitor yourself and the signs you manifest when having an emotional response in just the same ways that you can monitor others.

Look for subtle clues, physical reactions, and other ways that might indicate why you are experiencing your feelings. Pay attention to yourself and your reactions, give them consideration after the event has passed, and a deeper understanding of yourself will be illuminated.

With that deeper understanding of yourself, you'll also develop a more intuitive sense of others. As a Chief Engineer, when receiving a presentation on, say, an issue or a technical trade, you may be able to intuit biases or other predisposition that might be obscuring the true technical issue. It is not always easy to separate emotional issues from technical issues, but it can be done with practice. Evaluating the presenter is as important as the data being presented. Sometimes more so.

Emotional intelligence is an intuitive skill. There are no placards that designate a person's emotional state (except for the manager at that Constellation SE&I meeting, but that was an outlier). There may also be conflicting or vague indications, producing ambiguity and causing you uncertainty. That uncertainty is antithetical to engineers—we like certainty. Intuitive skills are wishy-washy—we want data. Well, in this case, you're very unlikely to get data and you will be left with nothing but your intuition to determine what's going on. Welcome to leadership!

But the more you practice this, the more you raise your awareness, the more intuitive you'll become. If it is hard (even seemingly impossible) at the beginning to get a sense of this, relax, that's normal. It'll become easier as time goes on and you get better at understanding other people's and your own reactions. It's work, as is developing any unfamiliar skill, but this skill is critical to leadership.

CHAPTER 2

REPRESENTING THE VOICE OF MANY

Chief Engineers are typically out in front, carrying the responsibility of Engineering Technical Authority (ETA), working with other project, program, and Center leaders, and making decisions and directing the technical team where and when necessary. When required, they chair boards, panels, and technical interchange meetings. Being out in front is indeed part of the job, and successful projects gain strength, continuity, and cohesion from a Chief Engineer leading the way. And, yes, it's fun too. However, sometimes it is necessary to lead in a different way—by flexing the authority and credibility that resides in the position through advocating on behalf of others, particularly on behalf of your team or your team members.

It's important to remember that as Chief Engineer you are first and foremost the leader of a technical team. It's not your job or responsibility to perform every task of the team, oversee every component development or operation, or make every decision to the lowest level. Even on small projects, the Chief Engineer has to delegate and flow responsibility down to other team members. While you will perform some tasks on your own, leading the technical team to success is the Chief Engineer's primary responsibility.

And a team needs a voice. As the technical team leader, you are their primary spokesperson when it comes to project management meetings, design reviews, Key Decision Points, budget discussions—all the gatherings where the engineering team is frequently represented by one individual: you. In this capacity you are not just providing your own viewpoints, opinions, perspectives, and concerns (although you obviously can), but are more generally providing the viewpoints, opinions, perspectives, and concerns of your team. You are a voice of one but represent the voices of many.

First of all, to be the voice of many you obviously have to start by understanding what those voices are saying. That necessitates remaining in close communication with your team and understanding their viewpoints, opinions, perspectives, and concerns. (In my experience, viewpoints, opinions, and perspectives are insightful, but concerns are the real windows into where your focus should be). You cannot communicate with your team effectively if you are spending the entirety of your time in the program or project office, with Center management, or with the contractor. You truly need to stay connected to your team and to remain cognizant of what their perspectives and concerns are. In other words, you can't represent the team if you don't know what the team thinks or how they feel.

Over the years I have seen leaders within NASA barricade themselves within the ivory towers of position and title, typically staying physically separated from their team by sequestering themselves with the rest of the project's leadership (i.e., closer to the boss), and infrequently if ever descending to the village at the foot of the castle to interact with their soldiers (or, in this case, their engineering team). That aloofness, while it might make you feel good from a prestige standpoint, is a disadvantage from the perspective of remaining connected to your team. To use a military analogy, in the U.S. Navy effective captains spend a portion of each day walking the ship's decks, getting to know the crew and listening to their concerns. Yes, captains are busy people, but the good ones recognize that even one hour a day interacting with their crews can reap tremendous benefits by increasing their insight into ship operations and, more importantly, by forging productive relationships with their crew.

When I was the Mission Operations representative to the Orbiter Project Office (OPO) my responsibilities included representing the entire operations community to the OPO. That community included eight technical disciplines (including power, propulsion, and life support), flight dynamics, robotics, EVA (i.e., spacewalking), mission planning—basically the whole kitchen sink. While my previous experience as a Mission Control flight controller enabled me to understand operations, I was certainly no expert on every aspect involved in Shuttle mission operations. There was just too much territory to cover.

But I did get out a lot and talk to people. Every OPO Configuration Control Board agenda had topics that ran the gamut of the technical disciplines, from conformal coating concerns inside avionics boxes to check value issues on cryogenic pressure vessels. Each of these mandated an understanding of the associated systems and their associated operations for me to provide advocacy for solutions we felt would be best for operations. Sometimes, the issue was so complex or so significant that I would be accompanied to the Board by a discipline expert, but most of the time I was on my own. Prior to each meeting I would wander over to the office suites of my colleagues in Mission Operations and ask questions about the issue at hand. Could we fly as-is, or should we recommend removing and replacing the component? Does the failure we saw represent a unique circumstance or could it be indicative of a common cause afflicting similar components? Are you uncomfortable with what is being proposed? How do you feel about all of this?

There was no way I could adequately represent their perspectives and concerns if I didn't have a bit of this one-on-one time with the folks I represented. And doing so provided mutual benefit—it served the dual role of ensuring that I understood the issue and the implications sufficiently to represent the organization, and it also provided them confidence that I would do the same. As a side benefit, trust was developed between us as my advocacy at the Board would follow their prescriptions.

Being the voice of many can take different forms. Sometimes it can mean speaking on your team's behalf, other times is can mean performing a service on their behalf, but at all times it means representing the team and not just yourself. An example of this was a task I was handed at HQ to lead a revision of one of NASA's engineering policies. The HQ Office of Chief Engineer (OCE), to which I am attached, maintains responsibility for engineering policy at the Agency-level. This is codified in the form of a document titled NASA Procedural Requirement (NPR) 7123, NASA Systems Engineering Requirements and Processes, which outlines the high-level process requirements for systems engineering across the Agency and also offers a thick appendix containing guidance, templates, and other assistive information. As with all NPRs, 7123 comes up for revision once every 5 years, and in 2017 it was time to crack the book open again and initiate a revision cycle. The responsibility to produce the revision and lead the team who would generate the content was mine.

We formed a team that consisted of systems engineering experts from across the Agency, all 10 NASA Centers, many of them having been involved in previous revisions of the NPR and some who even traced their lineage back to the very first publishing of NPR 7123 12 years previously. I also included a few non-NASA representatives to ensure we didn't get too parochial in our viewpoints, plus a handful of other subject matter experts. In totality the team consisted of about 25 people. For 6 months we discussed, debated, and decided on which content to revise, which content to remain intact, and any new content to be added as part of this revision cycle.

Right from the start I made the decision that although my office was responsible for the NPR and I was responsible for maintaining it, it was the team I would look to as the owners of the content. While HQ does have responsibility for ensuring certain expectations, it is the Centers who are responsible for implementing the NPR. They are the executors of this policy and who better to ensure that we produced a revision than the people responsible for implementing it? I decided my role was to establish the scope of the revision, develop the overall structure of the revision cycle process (schedule, budget, etc.), and oversee the development of the revision as it was occurring. But I did not see my responsibility as determining the content itself; I deferred to the team, and I became their primary advocate on behalf of the changes we recommended. When it came time to brief our results and recommendations to NASA's senior leadership, I would be the voice of many.

At about the halfway point through this process we had identified the concepts which required focus, if not the specific From/To changes themselves. While the team continued with refining these concepts, I put a package together for review at the NASA Engineering Management Board (EMB), consisting of the NASA Chief Engineer and Center Engineering Directors, providing some insight into our progress. I can tell you that there were a few of the concepts I was personally lukewarm about or had some concerns in terms of the ability to implement, but again, I was there to represent the team. I raised these concerns during our team discussions, and we had good, vigorous debate, but in the end,

I allowed the team to determine what we proposed and what we didn't. And at the EMB, it was my task to advocate for those changes, regardless of whether I thought they were good or bad. I was the voice of the team.

Now, to be fair, if there was anything that I thought was truly poor engineering policy or an idea overly parochial to one Center and not representative of policy at the Agency level, I brought that up during our team discussions. Coincident with my decision to let the team derive the content was my responsibility to also produce a set of systems engineering policies, and I constantly considered the potential for unintended consequences in enacting these changes. But once the changes passed those filters, it was my job to advocate for those changes on behalf of the team.

Sometimes when speaking for the team you might get the blame. Remember from Chapter 1 the discussion I had with the team when the Constellation program was cancelled. During that discussion, along with doing some deep listening, I also took notes of what people were saying. The program's proposed cancellation was a threat of existential proportions to the Mission Operations Directorate as, for the first time in U.S. human spaceflight history, the proposal was for U.S. industry to operate their own spacecraft and not our Mission Operations organization. MOD had been the preeminent and only operator of U.S. human spacecraft since the advent of the space age. It was the organization's bread and butter, but now other players would be vying for the same work. To survive, so the discussion went, Mission Operations would need to reinvent itself to be more competitive in a now suddenly competitive market. While folks were sharing their fears about the cancellation of Constellation, we also delved into the shortcomings of our organization constituted as a monopoly—such as a large workforce, slow pace of change—and brainstormed ideas to reconfigure the directorate to be more competitive.

Sitting in my office a week after the discussion I began to think about those observations. They were compelling, realistic, and filled with recommendations for change. They were the basis for removing, or at least ameliorating, the existential threat. So, I began crafting a white paper to tell this story, focusing on the ways the Directorate had become uncompetitive and how the organization could alter its operations to remain best in class. The paper utilized the notes I took from the meeting and represented the thoughts and perspectives of the team members in attendance, all experienced and dedicated NASA engineers. When the white paper was ready, identifying eight substantive recommendations, I forwarded it to a select few of my superiors for validation—the Chief of the Flight Director Office (my supervisor), the MOD Manager for Constellation (whom I supported), and the two Division Chiefs who would be most affected by the recommendations.

The recommendations were offered in the sincere desire to improve our condition and were derived from the expertise of some of our most senior engineers, developers, and operators. They came from the team and from their heart. They were an unvarnished look at the organization, acknowledging our faults and blemishes, but with recommendations offered in the sincere interest of improving our standing and making us more competitive. Talk about unintended consequences! When the paper was reviewed by those senior managers, the message was interpreted as an indication of my personal dissatisfaction with MOD, and the recommendations as my individual parochial viewpoint. In short, they viewed the paper as my personal opinion and overlooked the fact that they actually came from a team discussion. In distributing the paper my intent was to do so as an advocate for the team because the team members were not in a position to elevate these issues and recommendations to senior management, I did it for them. But, unfortunately, the paper was received as me stirring the pot and I got the blame. See, while it was not my message, I ended up owning it. To be honest, I didn't see that coming.

Perhaps I was naïve as to how a constructively critical message might be received. It was a difficult learning experience for me. But in looking back on it, faced with the same set of circumstances I ask myself if I would do it differently and the answer I arrive at is, largely, no. I would still have the desire to act as an advocate on behalf of the team and to represent the team in advancing constructive criticism of the organization. I've learned that I am comfortable in that role even if it results in negative perceptions of me, because the job advocating for those who cannot speak is a vitally important one. I remain proud that I advanced that message on behalf of the team and was able to be their voice.

So, I learned that speaking on behalf of the team can be empowering. It can feel good—at least it does to me when I am advocating to senior management on behalf of a team. I am representing their interests and their concerns. In the end we may not win the day and the final decision may not go our way, but in performing this service I am doing all that I can to ensure that their viewpoints are heard.

You'll note that people have differing viewpoints, and ensuring that viewpoints are heard includes allowing opportunities for minority or dissenting opinions. When the construct of Technical Authority was created in NASA in the wake of the Columbia tragedy (see Chapter 12, "Serving as a Technical Authority"), the idea of formal dissenting opinion was included in that construct. Dissenting Opinion at its essence allows for concerns with technical decisions that affect safety and/or mission success to be elevated to a higher level so that they can be reconsidered. There is some very good guidance on the dissenting opinion process out there, so I won't go into detail here, but dissenting opinion doesn't have to wait for decisions to be made and then elevated. Sometimes dissenting opinions could be included in the initial debate. In fact, they should.

We as engineers don't always agree. Our experience, backgrounds, and accumulated judgement don't always arrive at the same conclusions. Sometimes we do disagree, and that disagreement is a healthy check and balance on our discourse. Through discussion we strive for consensus, but sometimes it just doesn't happen, and we can agree to disagree. On those occasions, I have always felt that the position of disagreement is just as important as the one agreed upon. When bringing forward recommendations or establishing a position of the technical team, I have always strived to provide both; or, at a minimum, to offer an opportunity for those disagreeing with the majority position to their case.

You could say this is just good engineering, to consider all alternatives and options and rationally choose the best given the circumstance. But actually, this practice has as much to do with psychology and team-building than it has to do with good engineering. Engineers are by nature widely opinionated. That's not a bad thing, it gives us the ability to look at a situation from all angles and to consider a full spectrum of potential outcomes. But as with many things, having multiple opinions on a subject can breed substantial resentment if those opinions are not allowed to be voiced.

Have you ever been in an organization where opinion was quashed, where voices were bottled up and prevented from being expressed? I have, and the dysfunction in those organizations tends to run much deeper than stifled opinions alone. But even just focusing on the action of quashing opinions, I have witnessed the deleterious effect it has on people. In a nutshell, it breeds frustration, which can lead to resentment, neither of which are attributes of a healthy organization. When people are frustrated, they stop contributing and when people feel resentment, they no longer wish to advance the organization's mission. I have seen this on numerous occasions in a number of different organizations and feel most of these circumstances are avoidable through the practice of good leadership.

So, when you are obligated to advocate for the majority of the team, I suggest always offering any dissenters to have their say (either by including their comments in your presentation charts or, occasionally, even allowing them to vocalize their concerns themselves). Of course, you must clearly state why you consider it a minority opinion and what you've done to resolve the disagreement. But more often than not, I have found that it does little harm to include alternate perspectives. It doesn't take away from the predominating conclusions or recommendations (in fact, it may even further strengthen them), and in the vast majority of cases the board chair or decision authority receiving the message understands what I'm trying to accomplish. In my experience, when those maintaining the alternate perspective feel they have been heard, they are almost always willing to accommodate the majority position. Sometimes, just being heard is all it takes.

Another point—When you are the voice of many, it is still incumbent upon you to understand what you are stating. You don't have to be an expert on the subject, but you do have to have sufficient understanding to be an effective advocate. That may sound obvious, but it isn't always. When I first became the Chief Engineer for Aeronautics, one of my responsibilities (along with the other three Mission Directorate Chief Engineers) was to present our independent assessments to NASA senior leadership at the monthly Agency Baseline Performance Review (BPR). At this meeting the progress of nearly all the projects currently under development at NASA are reviewed with the NASA Associate Administrator as the primary audience (also in attendance are the Center Directors, the Mission Directorate Associate Administrators, and the HQ Office Chiefs or their delegates). It was up to us Chief Engineers to provide an independent assessment on the performance of all of these projects. At the time, there were two large Mission Directorates, each with a Chief Engineer, and two smaller ones that were combined for BPR reporting purposes. It fell to me to present once every 3 months.

When I started, I was the Deputy Chief Engineer for both the Aeronautics and Space Technology Mission Directorates, so my knowledge and familiarity of the projects in those two organizations was inherently high. And, due to my 21 years working human spaceflight at the Johnson Space Center, I was adequately knowledgeable about projects in that arena. But the fourth area, the Science Mission Directorate (SMD), oh man, getting my hands around that was a challenge. The Science Mission Directorate funds and manages all of NASA's science-related missions covering Earth Science, Astronomy, Heliophysics, and Planetary Exploration. At any one time they have roughly 30 to 40 spacecraft in development, each with their unique technical, schedule, or budgetary issues and all requiring monthly reporting at the BPR. In this area I was an expert on exactly none, and because of our respective workloads my window to accumulate any in-depth insight only opened once every 3 months.

Fortunately, the SMD Chief Engineer would generate the charts I would be presenting, so I only needed to become conversant in the material, and he/she would be in the room in the event there were any detailed questions I could not answer. But still, I was the one at the podium presenting to the NASA Associate Administrator and I needed to show at least a modicum of understanding of the issues (maybe a little bit more). I set a high bar for myself. I had noted some of the previous Mission Directorate Chief Engineers, when presenting, would simply read the words on the charts nearly verbatim, which the audience could have done easily enough on their own. I felt my job wasn't to just parrot the words on the charts but to explain the background and context of those words so that the room understood the issues and any position the Office of Chief Engineer was taking.

How did I prepare? Well, a few days prior to the meeting I would read through the charts provided by my counterpart in SMD, which normally consisted of about a dozen densely packed pages of technical and programmatic details. I read through the charts the first time to get a general overview and to refresh myself on issues or concerns I had presented 3 months previously. But then I went back over the charts a second time with a highlighter in my hand and highlighted the details that were relevant to our technical concerns and on which I would need to focus during the presentation. During this process I would also jot down questions on items I needed clarification: acronyms, context (what/where), and any technical tidbits I felt were germane to the audience's understanding.

When the day came to make the presentation, I always succeeded in having enough high-level understanding of the issues under discussion to present in a conversational fashion. I did not simply read the words, the audience could see them, but rather explained to the audience what the issue or concern was. I was never an expert on any of these missions nor did I have personal experience with the issues, but I could explain them sufficiently, so the audience had the same basic understanding as I did. And I was able to serve as advocate for the SMD Chief Engineer, who truly owned those issues and concerns. It worked very well.

Remember, Chief Engineers represent teams. It may be your face that's out in front, but there are many people whom your words represent. It's a serious undertaking to be the voice of many, but it's also tremendously satisfying.

CHAPTER 3

BEING THE BOX TOP

To be honest, I can't take any credit for having come up with the expression "being the box top." I first heard it from a mentor and friend, Robert Lightfoot, former Marshall Space Flight Center (MSFC) Center Director and NASA Associate Administrator.* "Being the box top" was an expression Robert used periodically to express the concept of maintaining a focus on the big picture. How did he come up with this expression? Apparently, Robert is a big fan of jigsaw puzzles, a pastime that he has always found cathartic, relaxing, and rejuvenating. The way Robert described it, when you first open the jigsaw puzzle box and liberate all the pieces from the packaging, what you have before you is a cacophony of separate, individual pieces. Looking at the mountain of cardboard bits gives you absolutely no perspective whatsoever of what the final picture will look like. It's all just a bunch of parts—haphazard, disorganized, random. But that's where the box top comes in. Printed on the top of the box is an image of what the puzzle will look like when it's all assembled. In other words, in engineering-speak, it's a system-level perspective of all the components, integrated and complete. With the box top, you know what the system (in this case a jigsaw puzzle) will look like when it's assembled. To complete the analogy with respect to NASA, Robert would say that leaders need to be the box top of their program or project.

In my mind Robert's idea is a very effective analogy and I use it all the time (with appropriate credit given, of course). I have always found it a folksy way of describing the task of being a systems-thinker and of maintaining a holistic perspective of whatever work is being accomplished. Folksy, but effective. Leaders can allow themselves to get down into the details, but there are lots of people responsible for the details. On any project the pieces can take on a life of their own, everyone seemingly having ultimate importance at any time and garnering the focus of the technical team to solve an intractable issue. But there are few if any

---

* Robert also spent almost a year-and-a-half as Acting NASA Administrator in 2017–2018—a job he did not ask for and one that I'm guessing wasn't as much fun as being Associate Administrator.

beyond the leaders responsible for the box top, for ensuring that all the pieces come together to produce the desired system, ensuring that both the system is designed right and that the team is designing the right system. The technical team's leader, the Chief Engineer, has to be able to maintain sight of the box top, focus on the big picture, at all times.

When you look at a box top what do you see? Well, I see a fully described vision. I see landscapes below and weather above as if they were parts of the whole (which they are). I see foregrounds and backgrounds, the focal points and the hidden gems that take some time to discern. I see a story to be told from beginning to end that can be communicated to others. Engineering is no different. When we develop systems, those systems encapsulate many separate parts but together they tell a much greater story. Together, all the elements function collectively to serve a role much different than the individual pieces. And that system must operate within an environment and possibly integrate with other systems that are all part of the story. That's the box top, and it should live in your mind throughout the life of your project.

As Chief Engineers, where the heck do we get this box top we are carrying around with us and referencing all the time? Well, there are a few sources we can pull from. Many projects begin development with Needs, Goals, and Objectives (NGOs). These collections of short statements provide a high-level strategic description of why the system under development is needed, what the basic goals are for the system to accomplish, and a brief list of some of the more discrete objectives, which are frequently performance-oriented. The NGOs encapsulate in just a few pages the big picture of the system under development. NGOs are frequently expanded into the form of a Concept of Operations (ConOps) from which are derived the system requirements (including the most important ones: Key Driving Requirements [KDRs]). ConOps and KDRs also are good sources for discerning the box top.

And don't overlook customer and stakeholder expectations, too. Some of these can be found within the NGOs, which serve as a great mechanism to ensure both customer and provider are on the same page in terms of expectations. At the next level of definition, customer and stakeholder expectations can be captured in Measures of Effectiveness (MOEs), which are used to validate the system at each stage of the design process. The MOEs provide insight into some of the more subjective qualities desired by the customer that aren't or can't be captured by hard requirements. Many of the "ilities" are used in MOEs where, for example, it may be very difficult to generate a "shall" statement on operability, but operability nevertheless remains an important characteristic to the customer. Finally, Measures of Performance (MOPs) are good box-top material. MOPs are normally instantiations of the most important performance requirements and are used as a metric and to track the system's ability to deliver as the design/development process proceeds.

Teams look to their leaders to be the box tops. They want to know their leaders are maintaining the big picture (partly, perhaps, so that the members can deal with the details). It's an important responsibility and, fortunately, one that the collective experience of most Chief Engineers prepares them to carry.

One of the greatest examples of being the box top was revealed to me early in my career when I was a flight controller in Houston's Mission Control Center supporting Space Shuttle flights. The flight control team for Shuttle consisted of a group of up to 17 people in the main control room, referred to as the FCR, or Flight Control Room. These were the "front room" operators, the most experienced flight controllers in each discipline, with a cadre of less experienced support personnel in various "back rooms" scattered throughout the Mission Control Center. The leader of the whole flight control team is the Flight Director, normally a former flight controller who has been elevated to the ranks of a highly disciplined group charged with, in part, to be the box top. Flight Directors carry the ultimate responsibility for overall success of the mission, second only to the commander onboard the spacecraft.

During the course of a standard daily shift during a Shuttle mission, the Flight Director could be faced with literally dozens of flight controller tasks to oversee. Some tasks are routine and occur on every mission, such as monitoring upcoming crew timeline activities on the Flight Plan, uplinking commands to the Orbiter, managing its antennas and the ground communications stations, housekeeping activities to supervise power/thermal/attitude, updating the onboard state vector or performing fuel cell purges, voice communications with the crew, and on and on. Other tasks are more specific and critical to a particular mission, such as rendezvous activities, payload deployment, onboard research, and extra vehicular activities (EVA). And of course, some tasks are off-nominal—failure of equipment and the associated safing and reconfiguration, predicted conjunctions with orbital debris, loss of communications, and a million other things that can potentially go wrong on a Shuttle mission. All of these tasks are items that the Flight Director has to be apprised and remain cognizant of and, with that information, then provide direction to the flight control team and orbiting crew. It is a juggling act extraordinaire.

Many of the nominal tasks are choreographed and specifically timelined well before the mission launches. But once in orbit, conditions frequently warrant changes and these timelined tasks need to move around a bit. Many of these tasks may now overlap or conflict with one another, and it is the Flight Director's job to ensure that their accomplishment doesn't prevent the achievement of the mission's objectives.

But through all of these myriad tasks, the Flight Director's greatest responsibility is ensuring that the mission is successful. When planning begins for a Shuttle mission, one of the first activities is to identify the mission's primary, secondary, and occasionally tertiary mission objectives. Achieving these mission objectives is what the Flight Director needs to keep in mind throughout the flurry of potentially distracting tasks. A Shuttle mission is very much a jigsaw puzzle that is fit together over the course of a week or two while in space, culminating in what is hopefully a successful mission.

As a Chief Engineer of a project under development, it will fall to you to manage and prioritize many of the various and sundry significant technical challenges that continually arise, while at the same time maintaining the big picture. Like Shuttle missions, most projects under development have primary and secondary objectives, Key Driving Requirements, and other means to establish the box top. It will be up to you, as the leader of the engineering technical team, to maintain those objectives and requirements throughout the course of all activities. That's not something you can really delegate—it's pretty much all yours and is part of the job.

You all have probably seen the much-used cartoons characterizing the importance of systems engineering. These cartoons may show, say, a satellite in four configurations: 1) As designed by a communications engineer, replete with a forest of antennas and large dishes; 2) as designed by a propulsion engineer, with a small spacecraft bus and an enormous rocket engine; 3) as designed by a robotics engineer, with a similarly small spacecraft spoked by a scary-looking robotic arm and superfluous smaller appendages; and finally 4) as designed by a systems engineer, with an optimized solution with everything within appropriate proportions. Yes, it's a humorous notion of discipline focus, but it does convey the message of what can happen if no one is looking at the box top.

Our job as Chief Engineer is to carry the box top with us wherever we go and to reference it on a daily basis. Frequently you will be asked to weigh in on design trades and to make technical decisions with multiple choices. Each trade may outline a series of pros and cons and each choice will likely include both benefits and penalties. Which one to choose? Of course, each decision is unique and has to be understood in the context of the question being asked. However, every trade and each choice are decisions made on the path to reaching the system-level solution characterized by the box top.

If you're not careful, it can be easy to lose that big picture. Take, for example, tracking Technical Performance Measures (TPMs), a common practice among the technical community used to help ensure we get to the desired performance of a subsystem or component. TPMs are used to establish the performance goals we seek and track them to tell us if we are achieving the goal or deviating from it. Mass is a common TPM, but we can also track measures like bandwidth, delta-V, flowrate, drag, or just about any technical parameter. With a TPM in hand we can track the component's analyzed or measured performance throughout the design process, assessing its ability to meet the performance objective. We can start this in conceptual design and continue the practice through preliminary and critical design and on to manufacturing, test, and verification. If performance does not meet the objectives we set, or it meets the objective but with insufficient margin, actions can be taken to remediate the situation. We can alter the design, plan for different operations, or even reduce the desired performance if the implications to meeting it turn out to be objectionable or unworkable. TPMs are useful mechanisms for maintaining focus to ensure we get what we want out of the system we're designing and building.

But, you know, TPMs can occasionally take on a life of their own and we can lose the forest for the trees. Sometimes we focus so diligently on the TPMs that it's possible to lose sight of the box top. I saw this happen recently from my perch as Chief Engineer for Aeronautics. One of the significant projects currently under development within NASA Aeronautics is the Low Boom Flight Demonstrator, better known as the X-59, a NASA experimental demonstrator "X-plane." It's charged with investigating an aircraft shape that can reduce the sonic boom noise (technically, it's the pressure wave) shed by aircraft flying at supersonic speeds, its Outer Mold Line shaped to reduce and deflect upwards the shock wave crated by the aircraft. The project has a significant development cost and complexity for NASA Aeronautics; as such they assigned a very good, experienced technical team to the effort. In 2018, as the project completed its Preliminary Design Review (PDR) and was forging ahead toward CDR, one topic of frequent discussion was how to best monitor the TPMs to provide sufficient early warning of impending problems. That is, in the standard stoplight terminology we all use in NASA, when and under what thresholds should the TPMs be declared Green, Yellow, or Red? The intent was to maintain better awareness of the state of the TPMs and to focus attention where (and when) necessary prior to a TPM becoming a significant issue.

The project was carrying something on the order of 15 TPMs on subjects such as total aircraft dry weight, afterburner thrust, "time to double" (an aircraft stability and control measure), and other attributes.

The TPMs were tracked for performance each time the aircraft's configuration was updated (roughly every 2 months or so) and the resultant margins above or below the desired performance calculated. Good stuff, good engineering! You're following this so far, right?

During a status presentation to one of the Center's monthly Engineering Reviews, the subject of stoplight thresholds came up and received a vigorous debate. Questions like "At what point does a TPM trip from Green to Yellow?" or "At what level of margin do we consider the TPM "broken" and require a redesign or reconsideration of the requirement?" were being asked. As no simple answers were available, passions were rising, voices were elevating, and at certain points things got really hot and heavy. Weight, one of the TPMs, is a constant concern in the life of an aircraft design and margins were closely managed. The aircraft's perceived noise level of the sonic boom was a vital TPM for this project, of course, and tracking it necessitated very close scrutiny of the aeroacoustics analysis each time the aircraft configuration was changed (particularly as the Outer Mold Line (OML) was tweaked and refined). Most of the TPMs were Green, a few were Yellow, and one was Red.

During the discussion I noticed a certain fixation on getting them "back in the box," leading to a forceful debate on mitigations and design trades and alternatives to get back to Green on the TPM. The perception seemed to be once we got back to Green status that victory would be declared and congratulations would commence for keeping the project successful. All that is fine and understandable, but who is looking out for the big picture? Someone out there needs to ensure that the system as a whole can still accomplish its mission, and doing so can occasionally run counter to fixing any individual TPM. See, sometimes when you fix one problem you actually create a different problem at the integrated system level. For example, ensuring the time to double for the aircraft meets requirements might necessitate a change to the aircraft's OML, which of course can affect the sonic boom noise level. Everything is interrelated and few properties, if any, can be considered in isolation.

So, I was sitting in my office at HQ and listening in to this discussion, feeling a bit uncomfortable that although we might be solving the individual technical challenges, we might also have been ignoring how the solutions all integrate. To salve my concern, I sent the project Chief Engineer, who was participating in the meeting, an email with my concern that we not get so focused on going Green on every TPM that we lose sight of the box top. Unsurprisingly, because he's an excellent Chief Engineer, he agreed and responded that he gave his team the same message just a few weeks ago. The message was received well at the time, but as engineers we simply love to focus on the minutiae and can periodically use a nudge to get us out of the weeds. The X-59 Chief Engineer did just that. He was the box top keeping his perspective at the system level. He utilized a process in which any proposed solution to fix a TPM issue was run through his internal box top, with his giving consideration to the system-level performance of the aircraft and not just the component that was tied to the TPM. Yes, you've got to fix all the small stuff to fly safely and successfully, but success for this project was tied to the system-level performance. Producing an aircraft that met all TPMs but that failed in its primary function (reduced sonic boom) would have been a defeat. He got it!

The Science Mission Directorate (SMD) at HQ provides another good practice that helps establish the box top. When missions are being proposed, they start with negotiated HQ-level project requirements that outline the mission's basic goals and capabilities. These are captured in an appendix to the Project Plan and are referred to a Program-Level Requirements Annex (PLRA). With the PLRA, there is little confusion about what SMD wants from the mission. While PLRAs can range up to a dozen pages or more and cover a variety of key details, expectations, and constraints, the key elements are the requirements themselves, which normally fill just a page or two.

Speaking of constraints, note that all we have discussed so far refers to what a system does, but it's also important to understand what the system and the project organization won't do. That is, the Chief Engineer needs to be aware of constraints and limitations. In this regard I'm not referring to the standard operational constraints and limitations (such as red lines, launch windows, and certification thresholds). At the box top level, I'm referring to considerations such as project budget ceilings, international and International Traffic in Arms Regulations (ITAR) restrictions, workforce prescriptions, NASA Procedural Requirements (NPRs), and other items that may provide limits to the envelope within which you will have to work. It is equally important to keep in mind these limits as they can define the scope, size, and complexity of your project's box top.

So, NGOs, ConOps, KDRs, MOEs and MOPs, PLRAs, constraints, and limitations all can be useful to a Chief Engineer in crafting a box top. But wait, there's more! Those items are predominantly paper products, deliverables, documents, and things of that nature. In addition to those, the box top can also be forged through discussions with the project manager and Decision Authority, meetings with the customer and stakeholders, and even at initial life-cycle reviews like the MCR (Mission Concept Review). While every detail of these conversations may not be documented, a Chief Engineer can still use the information that is conveyed to form the picture in his or her mind of what the box top looks like. That's qualitative, yes, but qualitative is OK in this context since what you're gathering here are customer expectations, which are qualitative by their nature and not hard requirements.

To summarize, the box top provides a systemic-level (even enterprise-level) perspective of a development effort and informs both the objective specific requirements and the more subjective things that will satisfy the customer, all at the big-picture level. Now expand that temporally and give consideration for how time affects the box top. Many systems at NASA are developed for a specific mission, perform that mission, and are then retired or disposed of. But occasionally we will develop a capability that's intended to be evolvable (such as through block upgrades like the Orion spacecraft or the Hubble Space Telescope), or expandable (like the International Space Station). The box top for these sorts of projects will change depending on the time at which you snap the chalk line. An early configuration may look and perform differently than latter configurations. Each phase has a box top, and for these development efforts the program may contain a series of box tops over the life of the system. The Chief Engineer needs to be aware of which box top is being discussed at any time and how each box top differs from others. Confusing? Actually, it's not that confusing because the overall system, even an evolvable one, remains familiar to those who work on it day in and day out. There is potential for confusion, especially to those who are not working the development on a day-to-day basis, but that potential can be easily mitigated with just a modicum of awareness.

And finally, as noted to me by David Mobley, former NASA HQ Chief Engineer (who peer-reviewed this book), "The NASA integrated life cycle (NPR 7123) is an excellent way to implement and assess against the 'box top.' It provides a systematic, disciplined approach to develop the system and I would strongly suggest that each design review be used to technically sync all disciplines input data at each review. This saves a lot of integration after each review and if not synched for a few reviews it is nearly impossible to achieve synch again without delays and lack of knowledge of the box top vs. the current program. 'Box top' is a good term!"*

If we don't know what the box top looks like we won't know how the puzzle comes together, and guess whose primary job is putting the puzzle together? Yours, the Chief Engineer! So, the box top is critical to your activities. As a leader, you'll be responsible for keeping the box top in mind throughout the life of your project. Can you do it? Of course you can!

---

* David Mobley. Peer-review correspondence with the author.

CHAPTER 4

GETTING A MENTOR/ BEING A MENTOR

Mentorship is one the very best ways that we as an Agency can educate ourselves and transition hard-earned experience to future generations. Societies throughout human history have depended on oral communication, not just for storytelling and recounting histories but for teaching and transitioning knowledge from generation to generation. NASA is no different. Well, OK, we're a little different, evidenced by the many tools available to us for transitioning knowledge, such as handbooks, lessons-learned databases, and the like. But few tools are as effective as the person-to-person interaction you get through mentorship.

Over my career, I've participated in dozens of training classes, so many that I've lost count. Most of these classes provide the student with a snapshot of the topic being discussed, maybe an exercise or simulation to give a taste of the experience, and perhaps a set of charts to reference in the future. Many training classes tend to be pretty academic—or at least that's how I view them when I'm taking one, imagining myself back in college—and they are over fairly quickly—in a day or three and then back to the job. On the other hand, having a mentor can endure for an entire career and the knowledge gained is rarely academic but instead eminently practical. Mentorships focus on the experience and wisdom gained over many years or decades of performing our jobs, intimate knowledge of what works and what doesn't, stories and tall tales that recount how the mentor got their scars, scars that they have earned the right to display as badges of honor. A mentor can be a friend, an advisor, a sanity checker—all of these things—but fundamentally a mentor can be a window on the future, helping you envisage where and what you might be after you've accumulated years of experience.

NASA, as with most organizations, tends to reinvent the wheel on a generational basis. We make mistakes, learn lessons (some of them painfully), improve our processes and practices, and press on. Eventually, each of us moves along or retires, and as we walk out the door, we might take all that experience, knowledge, and wisdom with us instead of leaving it behind. The next generation of engineers and leaders that comes in to replace us must then go through the same learning process again. The lessons we learn live with us through the experience we carry (as in "I got hurt before and I'll be damned if I'm going to get hurt again!"), but we find again and again that those same lessons have to be learned all over again by the next generation—those who haven't yet been burned. Wouldn't it be great if we could shift our behavior toward mitigations before we got into trouble? If you're smart, and I know you are, you've already figured out the answer to that question: Yep. How? Well, in part, through mentorship.

Learning from the past is important. Failing to learn from the past is regrettable, maybe even inexcusable. The most obvious example from NASA's history of failing to learn from the past are the Apollo 1, Challenger, and Columbia accidents. All three events resulted in the deaths of amazingly brave crews, a loss of 17 American heroes, and while they were caused by seemingly isolated situations, the causes were in fact related and possibly predictable if new generations were sensitized to past experience. In studying these tragedies, it would appear that the events were precipitated by separate and unique hardware failures: an electrical spark in a high-pressure 100 percent oxygen environment (Apollo 1); insufficient pressure seal at a solid rocket motor segment interface due to cold temperatures (Challenger); and insulation foam shedding from the Shuttle's External Tank, which struck and damaged a wing's leading edge, allowing hot gases to enter vehicle structure on reentry (Columbia). Not a lot of similarity there, right? And yet, all three events can be traced back to the same root cause—the human belief in infallibility causing reduced vigilance in system-wide safety.

It's not a coincidence to me that each of these tragedies occurred in separate generations of our NASA workforce. Those who were in the workforce at the time of each accident were stung by tragic events, and that sting will be carried by them for the rest of their lives. But time passed, and they left NASA, and new generation of engineers, managers, and leaders came in behind them, and that new generation operates without the sting of loss. Until, of course, it happened again. Have we learned from this cycle? In one aspect, I think we have, in that we're educating new generations of NASA engineers about these tragic events. In today's NASA there are efforts to keep the lessons of Apollo 1, Challenger, and Columbia alive within the workforce, and those are extremely worthwhile and positive things to do.

In the same way that those who experience tragedy carry those lessons with them, having a mentor who can recount his or her career stings can be a critical inhibition on a belief of infallibility. Those personal and real-life ways go to the heart of what it actually feels like to live through a bad day. A mentor can make the experience personal and real in ways a classroom never can.

As fortune would have it, I was given a mentor on my very first day at NASA. In January 1990, fresh with a graduate degree in aerospace engineering, I arrived on the doorstep of Houston's Johnson Space Center where I had been hired as a Mission Control flight controller. Mission Control and the flight control community at that time were still alive with veterans of the Apollo program. I was assigned an office along the west wall of Building 4, which I was to share with three other people: An Air Force officer assigned as a flight controller for classified missions, another new hire who was only a year out of college, and a stately gentleman who went by the name of Dick Brown.

If you don't know the name Dick Brown, you should; he took part in history. Dick, who preferred the nickname "Brownie," had been a flight controller since the advent of NASA's human spaceflight efforts and was a master of the art. Brownie worked as a contractor providing technical expertise on fuel cells, batteries, and electrical systems to the NASA civil servants who staffed the main operations room, the Mission Operation Control Room (MOCR). He supported NASA human spaceflight during the Mercury and Gemini programs, diligently working behind the scenes in the "back rooms" but creating an undeniable reputation for being one heck of a flight controller. A few years later, during the Apollo program, Brownie was the go-to person for back room support. He was in John Aaron's back room during the Apollo 11 lunar landing and a member of Gene Kranz's history-making White Team (if you search for pictures of Kranz's first lunar landing team, there's Brownie). And if that wasn't enough, Brownie was in Sy Liebergot's back room at the time of the Apollo 13 oxygen-tank rupture that made that famous mission somewhat infamous. He was the electrical systems specialist on console at the time all chaos broke out—a fortunate happenstance for the crew hurtling towards the Moon. Sy Liebergot's autobiography contains a CD on which is recorded much of the Mission Control voice loops at the time of the accident, the recording continuing for some hours after as they fought to figure out just what happened. When Sy calls out to his back room support, that's Brownie responding. And now I was sharing an office with him. Imagine!

When I started at JSC, Brownie was rapidly approaching retirement and would in fact retire only a few months after I came onboard. But what a ride those few months were! The three of us who shared an office with him would sit almost enraptured as he recounted many of his career stories. Surprisingly, having been in the room for the Apollo 11 landing and the Apollo 13 mishap, Brownie tended to focus on the other life lessons that his flight control career taught him and not those two major events. He would recount the endless tedium on console when testing the Apollo spacecraft, watching streams of telemetry on console monitors with a cold sandwich in one hand and a cup of stale coffee in the other. Supporting the Shuttle program now, we would discuss the details of the Shuttle electrical systems—the fuel cells, the electrical distribution buses and circuit breakers, and the cryogenic fluids that supply the fuel cells, and he would reward us with his experiences on the vagaries of their operations. He'd recount the gray areas of these devices and what to do when faced with circumstances that would occasionally fall outside the boundaries of procedures and flight rules. And in team meetings Brownie would hold charge, the gray beard in the room, and we'd listen and learn.

Brownie was also a gentle personality who cared about the people he worked with. For those few months we shared an office, Brownie took me and the other new hire under his wing, walking us through the system details and operational complexities with patience and care and an eye for learning. He was a great mentor and became a friend to boot.

I think there was some acknowledgment on his part that, as he approached the end of his NASA career, that it was incumbent on and important for him to pass along his knowledge to us young kids. There may have been a legacy aspect to his desires, I don't know, but ultimately, he wanted to help raise the next generation of flight controllers and mentoring was, to him, probably the most productive thing he could contribute at that late stage of his career.

Sometimes we get to choose our mentor and sometimes our mentor chooses us. For the first situation, how do we go about choosing a mentor? Well, to me, it's kind of the same as choosing a doctor. There are thousands, maybe hundreds of thousands, of physicians out there, all educated and certified and ready to treat our maladies. The choice of whom we should choose as our doctor is almost limitless. In narrowing that choice down to the point of selection, a gut-feel for the person can be a strong indicator. Sure, when choosing a new doctor, I consider education and background, experience, and locality (as in the doctor's office's proximity to me). But ultimately, for me, it comes down whether I feel that this would be a person whom I could trust with my medical care. That tends to be more of a subjective decision than a purely objective one. I can give wide latitude to where a doctor got his or her education, I'm willing to travel longer distances if it's the right doctor, but I won't go to a doctor I don't trust. Finding a mentor is very similar.

As NASA engineers, we get the opportunity to interact with a vast number of people. As Chief Engineers, we frequently get the additional opportunity to interact with many of the most senior and experienced technical leaders and managers in the Agency and across Government. You've probably had the chance to work with emeriti through Standing Review Boards and other groups performing our formal design reviews, some of whom have been part of the technical community for decades. These people may be wonderful candidates as mentors, at least from a technical and experiential standpoint. Not everyone will resonate with you, and not everyone will be a good mentor for you. But still, some may be perfect.

Also, realize that even if you do find someone who you feel would be a good mentor, not everyone knows how to do the job. This isn't necessarily a fault on their part, they may simply not know what it means to be an effective mentor. When I was the Technical Assistant for Shuttle in the MOD Systems Division, I asked my immediate boss (the Division Chief) if he'd be willing to mentor me. I had observed his management and leadership style and came to appreciate it as a style I'd like to emulate. I had regarded him favorably, felt he conducted himself with integrity (which is important to me), and thought I could learn a thing or two from him. He replied immediately, saying of course he'd mentor me, and we set up our first session for a few weeks in the future.

After that few weeks passed, we got back together in his office, closed the door and began the session. He sat there quietly for almost a full minute, staring at me as if wanting me to begin, and then finally said "Ummm, do you know what we're supposed to do?" I nearly burst out laughing. How ridiculous, I thought! My boss was an experienced manager and a Senior Executive Service to boot, and he had no idea how to mentor! I didn't laugh, of course, and proceeded to discuss my expectations of a mentoring session. I wanted to learn, to understand from him what worked and what didn't work, to use his experience to help me prevent making similar mistakes, and to increase my level of wisdom in how the MOD (or NASA writ large) job is done. He seemed to struggle somewhat, finally offering a few items of information and asked if those were hitting the mark. "A start," I replied with a comforting smile. And then it was over and we went back to our jobs. I have no doubt that he was happy when the session ended.

Was that a disappointment? Yes, but I also learned that even experienced managers may not be good mentors.

You may also find it useful to employ mentorship without the mentor even being aware of it. As the MOD rep to the Orbiter project, I would attend their weekly project configuration control board. One of the members of the board was an engineer whose career spanned more than 40 years. This gentleman had been through it all and his advice to the board chair was typically sage. When he talked, I tended to listen just a little bit harder, as his explanations of the positions he took on the day's topics and counsel to the chair was laced with wisdom. He would discuss the day's technical questions in terms of similar circumstances from earlier in his career, and those recollections included important lessons. Each time he spoke, I felt like I was getting a free course in practical engineering. Not only were his explanations insightful, but I found him a man of character and integrity, which accentuated the import of his words. Although he and I never discussed mentoring, I nonetheless looked to him as one.

In similar manner, when I first came onboard to the HQ Office of Chief Engineer, I was deputy to the Chief Engineer for Aeronautics, a gentleman named Rob Anderson. About half of my time was spent in Rob's office just talking shop. We would discuss technical topics pertaining to aeronautics, but we'd also hit on areas of program and project management, for which Rob had a particular fondness. We'd bandy back and forth on any given subject, sometimes in active debate, but I always came out of those discussions feeling like I learned something. Rob and I got along famously, which may have been why he offered me the position as his deputy to begin with. But in Rob all the elements of a good mentor were present—I respected him as an engineer and as a person, I regarded his experience highly, I found him as someone from whom I could learn, and he interacted with me with similar levels of respect. We laughed often and found we could get off subject (occasionally way off subject), but always eventually got back to the job of being the Chief Engineer for Aeronautics.

Too soon, Rob departed for an extended medical leave to battle cancer, a battle he tragically lost less than a year later. I was heartbroken, of course. A few weeks after Rob's passing, I was standing again before Agency senior management at the BPR and at the opening of the meeting the chair, the NASA Associate Administrator, mentioned Rob and his long career. With my emotions barely in check, I told the room something that I have believed strongly for many years and still believe strongly today: The greatest compliment I can give to a person is that I learned from them. In truth, I learned a lot from Rob, about aeronautics, about program/project management, about being a Chief Engineer, and about life. He was a good friend.

So we've discussed getting a mentor, now we'll turn to being a mentor. Just as it has been vital to your career growth to have a mentor, you can be just as vital to others who are at an earlier stage of their career and who can benefit from your experience and guidance. In some ways being a mentor is both easier and more difficult than having a mentor. It's easier, in that all you need to do is to recount your experiences. Talk about yourself—and that's something that comes easily for many. It's harder, though, because you are responsible for the advice you give, and advice offered carelessly can have serious implications on a person's career. Mentoring is work but it's fun and is generally a rewarding way to spend your time. And most importantly, in passing along your experience, it furthers the maintenance of NASA as the preeminent space and aeronautics agency on Earth (or off of it).

Sound good? So how do you become a mentor? NASA has many formal mentoring programs at each of our Centers which can bring together mentor and mentee. These programs can be potluck, you may or may not immediately find someone you synch with, but they're a great way to throw your hat into the ring and gain some experience in being a mentor. Alternatively, you can seek out mentees on your own. Look for early- to mid-career colleagues who: 1) impress you with their technical knowledge or emerging leadership skills, 2) have a strong desire to advance their career, and 3) you feel you can develop a relationship with. Note in particular people who you view as having the potential for growth and the rough abilities that could benefit from some molding and shaping.

Back to Rob Anderson. Before becoming Rob's deputy, I was an integration manager supporting one of NASA Aeronautics' research programs. The program invested in mid-Technology Readiness Level (TRL) aeronautics demonstrations of integrated systems in relevant environments. As Chief Engineer, Rob maintained a significant amount of insight into the program and both of their projects, particularly as they approached Key Decision Points, and it was through that work in which Rob and I became acquainted.

As we crossed paths and interacted, I don't know what it was that Rob saw in me exactly, but it was clear he saw something that he liked. I was technically competent, self-motivated, and had the ability to think strategically, all of which appealed to Rob. And also, I could listen. While Rob's medical conditions had not advanced to the point of incapacitation yet, he knew he was sick, and in retrospect I surmise he knew he would have to eventually bow out and was actively looking for a replacement. Some of the reason Rob gravitated to me may be simple luck, or that I was at the right place at the right time. But I've always believed there was a deeper sense in Rob that we both thought similarly and that he saw an appealing amount of potential in me. As we began to work closer and more frequently together, attending many of the same meetings, the relationship grew more firm. After 6 months of these interactions and a blossoming friendship, Rob came to my office and asked if I've ever considered doing a detail with another organization? I had considered it but had never pursued it to any extent. He encouraged me and requested that if I did apply that I consider doing a detail in the Office of the Chief Engineer, his organization. He approached my recruitment in a coy manner, but maybe it was actually strategic? Either way, it worked, as I did end up applying to the HQ detail program and indicated interest in the Office of Chief Engineer. Guess what? They accepted, and within a month I was officially on detail to the office as Rob's deputy.

The point here is that Rob was the active participant in this dance. He actively pursued me—nicely and with grace—but he selected me as his target and gently made it happen. Once I was on board our relationship grew quickly and we spent many hours talking and debating, mentor and mentee. The moral here is that it is possible to find someone whom you would enjoy mentoring.

Now, to a bit of mechanics. How does being a mentor work? Well, let's start with the scenario where, say, you're paired up with an early- or mid-career employee who you do not know. The first meeting will obviously include initial pleasantries and introductions, spending much of the time just getting to know each other and developing the relationship from scratch. You can ask about them and they will likely ask about you. Some good items to initially explore with your mentee are his/her career goals and their development plan. This is always a good place to start, because if their goals and plans are anything like mine were at that stage of my career, you'll likely find them to be boilerplate and not very well thought through. I would suggest, however, avoiding giving a lot of specific feedback during this first meeting. Should you discuss their mid- and long-term career goals and development plan (if they have one) and then jump immediately into suggested solutions to achieving their goals, they will likely think that they've accomplished their mentoring objectives and may never come back to see you again. Mission accomplished, they may think! But, of course, mentorship is about much more than just filling out an Individual Development Plan (IDP), it's about the construction and maintenance of a relationship. Don't try to achieve everything on the first visit.

I tend to look upon mentorship as I do with counselling. Now, I have been cautioned by experts in the field not to conflate the two—mentoring is not counseling—and mentors are not intended to help others work through their life's personal challenges. Counsellors are available for that. Fair enough. But the connection to me between mentoring and counseling is that both aren't responsible for providing answers, but instead for assisting recipients in finding their own answers. Your mentee must own their solution and feel in their heart that the solution is the right path for them. They need to discover it themselves. But you, as their mentor, can help them find it.

Some mentees may have very specific, already defined ideas of their career goals and are just looking for a bit of sanity-checking of the path to achieving them. Alternatively, many people have a general idea of where they want to go in their career but really no idea how to get there. And others may be totally lost, working diligently in their present field but with absolutely no clear idea what they want to do or where they want to go, even in the short-term. A mentor can help with all of these situations.

One final word on mentoring. It's a bit ancillary, but it's still relevant. Should you find a good mentor, someone you regard and respect, it's highly likely that they will also serve as a role model for you. They may reveal behaviors you might wish to emulate, setting an example for excellence and a high bar for performance. Even if you don't find a mentor, I cannot recommend more strongly finding a role model for yourself. This can be a person, an organization, or even a concept that represents who you want to be and helps guide you in terms of how you want to act. Having a role model sets a bar against which you can continuously compare yourself and see if you're measuring up.

What's my role model as Chief Engineer? I'll tell you, but you got to promise not to laugh. See, it's Star Fleet, the fictional exploration/quasi-military organization envisioned in the television show *Star Trek*. Or maybe more accurately it's the starship captains who embody the virtues of Star Fleet. While there are some famous figures who are synonymous with *Star Trek* itself—Kirk and Picard and Archer—it's not a specific character that I use as a role model but rather just the general notion of a Star Fleet captain, one who represents the character, capabilities, integrity, and leadership that I strive for. This ideal, this concept, provides me with something I can compare against my own actions and see if they measure up. It's not a perfect analogy as there certainly were *Star Trek* captains who didn't fulfill the ideals of Star Fleet. And yes, if you don't like *Star Trek*, then comparing yourself to a Star Fleet captain can be a bit silly. But it works for me. To this day I still find it provides me with a role model which attains high standards of character. It's not Star Fleet I want to sell you on here, but the idea of finding a role model that can help you achieve the best you can be.

CHAPTER 5

DEMONSTRATING KNOWLEDGE OF SYSTEMS ENGINEERING

Systems engineering is the foundation of just about all technical development in NASA (and outside of it too). It forms the basis and structure by which we develop complex systems, from concept development to requirements and design, risk and configuration management, life cycle reviews, verification and validation and all the vital activities leading to an operational capability. Systems engineering walks us through the life cycle of the development process and ensures that the solution is an integrated one commensurate with the needs of the system and the stakeholders. It is more than just a process but rather a mind set and a commitment to excellence. As a NASA Chief Engineer, you'll need to understand the systems engineering process, speak the language, and be the hand on the technical tiller as the project navigates through its development life cycle.

Systems engineering within NASA is codified in NPR 7123.1B, NASA Systems Engineering Processes and Requirements. Although it's not necessary for a Chief Engineer to completely memorize that tome, all NASA Chief Engineers should at least have a working knowledge of the document. What is necessary, though, is for Chief Engineers to have an intimate knowledge of the NASA systems engineering life cycle, products, deliverables, and associated levels of maturity at each stage. They should be very familiar with the expectations of entrance and success criteria for the life-cycle milestones and how to navigate the technical team through the process. Anyone can simply reference NPR 7123 for the specific entrance criteria elements at a design review, but a Chief Engineer should be able to understand intuitively when to declare the design sufficiently mature to enter the milestone, which is a judgement call. Referencing information is easy for any engineer, but only experience and acquired wisdom will provide a Chief Engineer with the confidence to declare that the design is appropriately maturing.

A Chief Engineer needs to know some basic systems engineering facts of life, such as that a configuration-controlled requirement set with traceability is a key to project success; but burrowing down one level further, a Chief Engineer also needs to have a feel for what makes a good requirement and to be able to differentiate between a good requirement and a poor one. Or a Chief Engineer needs to understand the basic difference between verification (Did I get the system right?) and validation (Did I get the right system?). But burrowing down one level further, a Chief Engineer also needs to be able to ask the right questions, particularly during the validation process of ensuring the customer is satisfied with the delivered system and be able to work with the qualitative side of the equation that typically embodies validation. Again, a Chief Engineer needs to be able to understand the importance of Entrance and Success Criteria at design milestone; but burrowing down one level further, a Chief Engineer also needs to be able to discern which products are truly required and which are simply nice to have or even superfluous and just extra work for the project. In each of these examples, the first can be obtained by reading NASA policy, but the latter is only the result of years of experience.

The point here is that a Chief Engineer needs to understand the NASA systems engineering process, oversee the process, and be an advocate for its value to the project. The Chief Engineer must also be able to use their experience and judgement to implement it appropriately for their project. Understanding the process alone is insufficient—almost anyone can follow a checklist—but adding on to that the wisdom to guide a team through the process in ways that accommodate your project is the quality that a Chief Engineer brings to the table.

At the beginning of a project, the Chief Engineer is critical in helping the technical team assess NPR 7123 for applicability and to right-size its implementation. In a word, the Chief Engineer should tailor the approach so that it is appropriate given the project's cost, complexity, and risk. How do they do that? Well, there is no checklist, so don't go looking for one. There are some useful tools out there produced by a few NASA Centers designed to help Chief Engineers and project managers narrow the trade space on systems engineering implementation and these tools can offer approximate solutions, but only that—approximate solutions. Any output of these tools should never be interpreted as the final answer. You can't just turn the crank and have the tool spit out your answer. Instead this is one of those enviable moments when you'll appreciate all those years of experience, because it is *that* experience and that alone that will provide you with the right answer. Tailoring or right-sizing NPR 7123 is a judgement call based on your experience and assessment of how much rigor is necessary for the project to be successful, and no calculator can give you the right answer. Although we rarely rely on judgement and feelings in the course of our engineering work, this is one circumstance in which it is appropriate. And don't assume that you have to do this tailoring alone, because you don't; ask for advice from colleagues, peers, and supervisors. Utilize other people's experience as much as rely on your own. Remember, while systems engineering is a critical key to success in NASA, finding the right level of implementation for your project is a balance between technical/process rigor and cost/schedule. Too much systems engineering can be as damaging to a project's success as too little (although, admittedly, we see too little more far more often then we see too much).

As Chief Engineer for Aeronautics I am attached to a research organization, and implementation of systems engineering doesn't come up in conversation as often as does the more research-related concepts like the scientific method (observe, hypothesize, and test). However, occasionally, the subject is discussed. If you recall back in Chapter 3, "Being the Box Top," I mentioned the X-59 supersonic flight demonstrator. When the project was initiated in 2016, it had been more than 2 decades since NASA had developed a piloted X-plane, and much of the requisite system-level aircraft development experience had to be recreated. While this project would be costly (in the hundreds of millions of dollars) and complex (a system-level vehicle developed from scratch), in essence it remained a research project and, as such, wouldn't have to undergo the same development rigor as would an operational certified capability. A good percentage of the systems engineering on this project would be familiar to those used developing large NASA projects, but because it was a research project, some aspects would be peculiar. As an example, the verification on this project would end up taking a slightly different path from the usual.

Let me explain; typically, when NASA procures a system through a prime contractor, it gets built on the factory floor. When the build is complete, the contractor ensures that all requirements have been met (e.g., verified) and then hands the system over to us. Should we accept the system, the contractor is pretty much done—we take ownership, integrate it with its launch vehicle, launch it into space, and they take their award fee and return it to their shareholders. However, for this aeronautics supersonic demonstrator, the contractor isn't finished once the aircraft leaves the factory floor and there is no immediate hand-off. Instead, a rigorous process of airworthiness certification and flight envelope expansion occurs with the contractor flying the aircraft. Some may consider this an operational capability at this stage, but in this case the aircraft isn't handed over to NASA until the contractor ensures it is airworthy and can demonstrate in flight that the design meets its performance requirements. That is, not all requirements can be verified until they actually fly the aircraft and it is certified as airworthy. Once that is completed, then the hand-off will occur and the aircraft's true operational mission begins. This is a subtlety of aircraft development that differs from spacecraft development, and the systems engineering process needs to account for these differences from the NASA norm.

This brings me to an interesting and yet perpetual question—What's the difference between a Chief Engineer and a Lead Systems Engineer? As I mentioned in my note at the beginning, in some organizations and at some NASA Centers, there's no real difference at all. It is a question of semantics and the titles they prefer, but the roles and responsibilities are effectively the same. In some projects, though, the difference can be substantive and both a Chief Engineer and a Lead Systems Engineer are assigned. In those cases, there are obviously differences.

I've searched for some of these differences and eventually found a set that makes sense to me, drafted by the Glenn Research Center (GRC). With the advent of the Constellation program in the mid-2000s, the Glenn Engineering Directorate developed a common approach for providing engineering support for all its development projects. This approach is often referred to as their "Engineering Model" and has been successfully applied to both spaceflight and research projects. In the GRC Engineering Model, their Chief Engineers are responsible for technical integration during the design and development of the project in concert with the project manager, providing leadership to the broader engineering team and serving as the project's engineering technical authority. Alternatively, the Lead Systems Engineer (LSE) is responsible for requirements definition and verification, hardware assembly, integration and test and leads those personnel comprising the systems engineering team. The LSE manages the systems engineering processes while the Chief Engineer maintains broad oversight of all things technical. Inherent in both positions are the responsibilities of leadership and leading teams, with perhaps the scope and composition of those teams being a discriminator. The LSE knows what the next step is and can help navigate the technical team through the systems engineering process, while the Chief Engineer maintains the authority for technical decisions, owns the technical baseline, provides oversight of the entire system development, and is the primary technical interface with the project management team. While these descriptions are somewhat simplistic, they work well for GRC and you know what, they seem pretty reasonable to me! Is the conflated usage of Chief Engineer and Lead Systems Engineer a large problem in NASA? No, but it has been the cause of some confusion.

At the time systems engineering was first characterized as a discipline within NASA, in 2005, with the initial publication of NPR 7123, NASA Systems Engineering Processes and Requirements, systems engineering as a specific discipline of practice was fairly new. NASA has used structured development philosophy going back to the Apollo program in the 1960s that emulated or approximated systems engineering, borrowing liberally from the military services and their experience developing of our Nation's early ballistic missiles. But it is only since 2005 that systems engineering, per se, has been a documented, methodical set of processes and procedures governed by Agency-level policy. Over that time, NASA's cadre of systems engineers have become intimately connected to those SE processes and policies, which has led to some unfortunate misunderstandings.

See, one of the issues facing NASA systems engineering today is the perception by some outside of engineering that systems engineering is simply processes and policies, and complying with it requires no more work than following a checklist. In the engineering world that's never been true—systems engineers are not just process custodians but also technical leaders. And those responsible for ensuring effective systems engineering in our projects, our Chief Engineers and Lead Systems Engineers, are also the projects' technical leaders. They are team builders, negotiators, decision makers, and this necessitate all the same leadership skills as our project managers. Leadership is as much an attribute of systems engineers as is their understanding of requirements and verification. And what's more, as former NASA Chief Engineer David Mobley put it to me, "I had written on my white board in my office the principle of 'P to the 5th power': Poor Planning Perpetuates Poor Performance."*

Let me share another example. The Stratospheric Observatory for Infrared Astronomy (SOFIA) is the largest portable telescope in the world. It is a 2.5-meter (100-inch) infrared instrument mounted inside a Boeing 747-SP and is flown around the world conducting astronomical observations. Modifying a commercial 747 to accommodate a large telescope was a complex venture, but one the Agency considered significantly less costly than developing and launching a similar space-based orbiting observatory. SOFIA was proposed in 1996 as a joint venture with NASA and the German Aerospace Center, known as DLR, with NASA providing the aircraft and DLR providing the telescope. Development and integration of the telescope was led by the DLR Principal Investigator (PI) with a modicum of NASA oversight. Almost 10 years later—after a series of schedule slips, cost overruns, contract issues, and even some mishaps—progress had stalled, forcing NASA to threaten to withhold funding and possibly even cancel the program outright. Through the influence of Congress, the German government, and the science community, NASA relented on the threatened cancellation

---

* David Mobley. Peer-review correspondence with the author.

but commissioned an independent review team to provide recommendations to see the development successfully through completion.

The independent review team's findings were glaring. It declared that the SOFIA program's system requirements were lacking and disjointed. Only a small percentage of the specifications had been baselined. Interface Control Documents, the lifeblood of how elements fit together, were not centrally managed, and it was unclear who owned them. Configuration Management processes were dysfunctional, leading to hardware configurations being approved without any supporting documentation. Risk was being assessed and managed only informally. More than 50,000 telescope assembly documents existed only in hard copy, with many documents owned and managed by different subcontractors, each using a variety of document control processes. In a word, SOFIA was a mess.

The review board clearly saw the project's deficiencies and were not bashful in pointing them out in their report. They identified the root cause as the lack of systems engineering and recommended fixing these issues through a variety of activities. They suggested establishing an organized and established systems engineering lead with support teams for key systems engineering tasks, pointing specifically to an established and dedicated requirements manager as a top priority. They suggested revising the program systems engineering documents and processes and developing a new Systems Engineering Management Plan (SEMP) to define technical processes and requirements that complied with NPR 7123. They recommended establishing Program Management Control Boards for both programmatic control and observatory control and establishing a SOFIA Observatory-level Integrated Product Team to address Observatory and "cross project" technical issues. And they recommended establishing a process to manage and track the status of critical program and technical documents and risks.

As you read through the review team's recommendations, I hope that many of them seem a bit obvious to you. But in the early 2000s, systems engineering as a methodical, defined discipline was just becoming established within NASA and hadn't yet been baked into our culture. A

Systems Engineering and Integration Manager position was created to oversee many of SE these processes, with the Chief Engineer still maintaining system-level authority over the requirements, design solution, and verification and validation. This SE&I Manager turned the lack of requirements definition into a programmatic risk, elevating the issue to the highest levels of the program and effectively ensuring it received the attention it needed (upon which the program made a highly visible long-term commitment to correcting this problem). A realistic plan to phase in development was created, embracing more of a spiral development cycle, which allowed time to refine the product tree and systematically review the requirements. They realized that having a comprehensive specification/product tree is critical to system integration. After making these (and other) changes and implementing more rigorous systems engineering, SOFIA eventually gained the success it was looking for. Today, the SOFIA airborne observatory is a success story, not only from the astronomical and science perspective but when viewed in light of systems engineering as well.

I have found that one of the greatest values of systems engineering, a value often overlooked, is that it is an enormous contributor of risk mitigation to a project. The proper and appropriate application of systems engineering is, to me, a major factor in a project's success and is the largest mitigator of the conditions that lead projects to fail. While the value is evident in my mind, it is difficult to show the value of risk mitigation in tangible terms (such as money saved) because many managers and decision-makers *expect* their project to be successful. But systems engineering is problem avoidance, and how do you show the value of avoiding something that never happened? When things go bad it is easy to show the cost, but when everything works right it is difficult to show the value of the systems engineering investment because managers are expecting everything to go right. That is a conundrum for systems engineering as a discipline. In the case of SOFIA, the value of adding systems engineering was evident through the eventual success of the project. But in many cases, that value is hidden because its success means problems never occurred.

Because of this, a Chief Engineer needs to be a constant and tireless advocate for the application of systems engineering in a project. Some project managers are renowned for viewing systems engineering as burdensome overhead, believing they drive additional cost and even add risk to a project. A Chief Engineer knows better and understands that systems engineering is a contributor to cost avoidance and a mitigation of risk to projects. While the PM might hear those words from their engineering staff, it is the Chief Engineer who must really make the case and ensure that the manager truly understands the benefit of good systems engineering and the risks of poor systems engineering.

Try as we might, this may continue to be a constant debate between Chief Engineers and project managers. Future project managers are unlikely to relent in their drive for delivering systems on cost and on schedule and may not tire of trying to reduce the systems engineering implementation. On the other hand, Chief Engineers need to act as the fortification that prevents its elimination. Are Chief Engineers smarter? Well, in this case, probably yes, they are! Or at least they understand more the needs of technical development that systems engineering provides.

CHAPTER 6

BEING THE ADULT IN THE ROOM

This chapter is likely to get me in trouble if I'm not careful, because I can give you lots of examples of childish behavior that I've witnessed, but I assure you no names will be used in the course of this chapter. Relax, I'm trying to be humorous, but there are some behavioral skills that separate poor or just barely adequate leaders from the truly exceptional ones. Technical acumen, while vastly important in a technical organization such as NASA, will only get you so far as a leader. You may know the difference between mechanical *stress* and *strain*, see potential shortcomings in a test configuration just by looking at it, or have the ability to discern when zero fault tolerance is sufficient—all, certainly, excellent traits for a Chief Engineer. But as leaders, particularly as effective leaders, your reputation and the way your team perceives you will be equal parts technical acumen and how well you deal with the people on your team. This chapter is all about the latter.

This is a touchy subject, because who doesn't want to be thought of as an adult (or worse, who wants to be thought of as a child)? No one I know! But the reality is that many of us are elevated into the position of Chief Engineer based on our technical understanding and not our people skills. That's a shortcoming in our promotion process and how we select individuals for leadership positions. And so, some Chief Engineers, while exemplary at the technical side of the equation, lack the requisite people skills to be truly exemplary leaders. That's a shame, but that's the nature of our business. This chapter will focus on just one aspect of those people skills, but those skills are probably the most critical factor in my mind from the standpoint of earning people's respect as a leader. Have I gotten into trouble yet? Hope not.

Being the adult in the room means many things, but in a nutshell, it means a combination of taking the high road, controlling your emotional outbursts, treating people respectfully, making decisions based on the good of the whole and not of an individual, an individual side, or yourself. In a word, it's about maturity. It's about being emotionally stable and conducting yourself with a firm grip on that maturity. It's being the person to whom people look to be the adult in the room, and who people choose to go to when they need a considered, mature decision. Being the adult in the room is about exhibiting all the better qualities that are incumbent in effective leaders. Through this conduct, while your decisions may not make everyone happy, you are likely to gain at least everyone's respect, even from those for whom the decision did not go their way.

Chief Engineers are expected to be mature individuals, to be able to appropriately keep their emotions in check, avoid berating members of their team when they disagree, and hold their tongue when not doing so would be inappropriate. Chief Engineers represent in many people's minds the better reflection of themselves, the manifestation of who they'd like to be, and their own better instincts rolled into one. Is that a hard standard to uphold? Sure, but no one said this job was going to be a cakewalk. Rather, being a Chief Engineer holds you to a higher standard, and it's up to each of us individually to make sure we attain those expectations. If we don't … well, read on.

Unfortunately, as I think over the course of my career, I can recall more examples of these expected behaviors being demonstrated poorly than effectively. Maybe that's because those negative events stand out more clearly in my mind than the others. Regardless, I'll recount a few experiences where the leader in a meeting was not acting as the adult in the room. These may induce some uncomfortable squirming and be somewhat difficult to read, but they still are insightful as characterizations of not being the adult in the room. As I often say, everyone I deal with is, to me, a teacher. Some teach me behaviors to emulate and others teach me behaviors to avoid! So, I'll start with some egregious examples of behaviors to avoid.

In the early 2000s, after I transitioned from serving as an active Space Shuttle flight controller and representing the flight control community, I was brought up to the Flight Director Office to technically integrate much of the Mission Operations capabilities being developed for the Constellation program. They gave me the title of the organization's Lead Engineer for Constellation. As an integrator of our technical development and with the charge of getting everyone on the same page, one of my first actions was to stand up a forum, an engineering integration panel whose responsibility was to ensure that all aspects of what we were building was in lockstep with ourselves and with the Constellation program. At the time I was socializing the idea for this integration panel, I became aware of a similar idea being floated by a former Flight Director. Both of us needed formal approval to start our panel's activities, and while the concepts were not precisely the same, we decided to combine forces and create a joint panel on which we'd serve as co-chairs. This became the Mission Operations Engineering and Integration Control Panel, or MEICP (admittedly not a great acronym, but the name itself was self-explanatory).

My partner in the MEICP started his career as a flight controller during the Apollo program, transitioned to Shuttle, and after a few years was elevated to Flight Director. For many years, this gentleman was really the cream of the crop of Flight Directors, possessing a deep understanding of the Shuttle systems and how they operated. Flight controllers really wanted to get on his teams, as his technical knowledge of the Shuttle systems was second to none. They didn't need to explain some complex idea twice—he got it on the first explanation. His leadership and team skills were rated as acceptable, but his knowledge of the details of Shuttle design and operations was exemplary. When, as a flight controller, you made a call for the crew to take action, you knew that he intimately understood what was going on and why you were requesting the action. There was little need to explain the circumstance in detail (as some other flight directors required)—this guy just intuitively understood and could glean that understanding with a minimal amount of details. Flight controllers loved it. I even had a chance to work with him on a number of occasions, he as flight director and I as flight controller.

But as the years went on, this favorite of flight controllers developed a medical condition that removed him from console. You see, flight controllers and flight directors both need to pass an Air Force Class III physical to serve on console, and if you cannot pass the physical you are restricted from working on console. This stringent rule is put in place to ensure the safety of the astronaut crew and the success of the ongoing mission. It would be bad if, say, a flight controller were to pass out due to a medical condition right at the moment of some critical activity or at the exact time they need to make a life-saving, safety-of-flight call. The medical folks who set these standards are very strict with the physicals' relationship to flight-controller certification, and few exceptions are made. In this gentleman's case, there was no exception. After years of service, he was off console.

As you can imagine, this was an enormous blow to him since he loved being "on console" and directing his flight control teams. It satisfied his professional needs and, as I was to learn later, his desire to be perceived as a decision-maker. Suddenly, he lost the thing he most valued, and with that loss went his purpose and his standing within Mission Operations. Having lost his grounding, he bounced around the Flight Director's Office for a few years, gaining token tasks but never really being responsible for anything significant. Eventually, he left the office for another organization within the Directorate. That's when we formed the MEICP.

It was a disaster. For 2 years I was forced to deal with another person's petulant behavior. He was acerbic, argumentative, even insulting. He would interrupt me and commandeer the conversation, moving it in a different direction from the line of questions I was asking. He would consciously undermine my position as co-chair, and rarely if ever cooperate as partners in leading this forum. He even threatened me once with physical violence in a meeting, offering to "take me to the mat" when I countered one of his opinions. Week after week, it was a constant battle to move the panel forward and advance the good work that most of the attendees were interested in.

In the end I was not angry, but rather remorseful. I pitied him and what he had become. He had regressed from a respected leader with almost unimaginable responsibilities as a Flight Director to a shell of his former self, relegated to a much smaller piece of the pie, and he resented his situation. But he also lacked the emotional maturity to deal with his situation in a constructive manner and opted to be disruptive. His motto might have been "If I'm miserable, then I'm going to make damn sure everyone around me is miserable, too." He had lost the ability to be the adult in the room.

Another example that comes to mind was the case of an individual who had ascended to one of the most senior positions within NASA—a Center Director. (Sorry, no names!) NASA's Center Directors manage, lead, and have overall responsibility for the 10 NASA field Centers. Some Centers are small, consisting of maybe a few hundred people, while others are much larger and can account for a workforce of thousands. Center Director is the highest position a NASA employee can attain outside of HQ and it carries enormous responsibility and prestige. It also carries enormous authority, and that authority can sometimes be abused.

One day we were having a meeting at NASA HQ with the NASA Aeronautics leadership discussing a topic that affected the four NASA research Centers that deal with aeronautics—Armstrong Flight Research Center near Edwards Air Force Base in California, Ames Research Center in Silicon Valley, Glenn Research Center outside Cleveland, and Langley Research Center in Virginia. Along with me in the room at NASA HQ was most of the Aeronautics leadership plus a number of representatives from the Centers. On telecon were the four Center Directors. Or at least that was the plan. When the meeting began only three of the four Center Directors were online; the fourth was AWOL.

At the allotted time for the meeting to start the Associate Administrator for Aeronautics welcomed everyone and we got down to business. After about 10 minutes with the presenter at the front of the room walking the audience through his charts and building his cadence, a bark erupted from the telephone. Literally, a bark like a dog might do when the mailman appears at the front door. It was the fourth Center Director, and he was livid. Apparently, the meeting wasn't on his calendar and he didn't get notified of it until just a minute before. OK, that's a fair excuse and no one was going to question his tardiness. But instead of diplomatically apologizing for being late and allowing the presenter to continue, he entered into a tirade about how the process of meeting notification is broken and how heads need to roll! He went on and on about this for many minutes in a loud voice, berating the Aeronautics staff for their incompetence and his own staff as well. In short, he completely commandeered this important meeting, disregarding the fact that the room was filled with other Agency leadership who were committing their time to have this discussion. Quickly, it became "his" meeting. I remember gazing over at the AA for Aeronautics sitting at the head of the table and seeing him cradling his head in his hands. Believe me, he was not laughing. This Center Director was not being the adult in the room.

Being the adult in the room is how the majority of us behave most of the time and how we expect others to behave all the time. It is a calm demeanor and the ability to navigate the ship through stormy waters and high winds with both competence and emotional stability. That emotional stability is very important. It provides a measure of calmness and grounding to a meeting when difficult issues could incite passions. It is a shock absorber to what can be highly opinionated and passionate engineering discussions (as I'm sure you know already, many of our NASA technical discussions can get quite passionate). Almost anyone in the room can provide that stability, but it is the leader who is "expected" to provide it. When it's not there, it's glaringly obvious, and the fault commonly goes to the leader.

Don't get me wrong, passion in your job can be a wonderful thing (I will touch on this later in the book) and I have worked with many passionate engineers. But it can be misplaced. One who crossed my path with extraordinary passion was the Deputy Chief Engineer for the Space Shuttle Orbiter (eventually the Chief Engineer), a gentlewoman and a friend. This person was one of the most competent engineers I have ever met, someone who had come up through the ranks of the engineering community through positions of increasing responsibility and who intimately understood the expectations and demands of good engineering. You could say she was good engineering incarnate. She could just sense when three-sigma dispersions weren't accounted for correctly, or when scatter factors were misapplied, or when requirements for qualification or acceptance were taking a shortcut. Not a lot got past this fine engineer and she frequently became the conscience of the Orbiter engineering community as she set and maintained a high bar on competence and engineering rigor. She did a lot to ensure vigilance and helped us keep our eye on the ball on safety and mission success. She was a fine engineer and also a nice person to work with. But—yes, there's always a but—her passion could occasionally get the better of her.

We both supported the Orbiter Project Configuration Control Board, I for Mission Operations and she for Orbiter Engineering. The Board met weekly in JSC Building 1, discussing all varieties of issues pertaining to maintaining the Orbiter fleet and keeping them flying. We discussed hardware issues, certification tests, modifications, pondered over analyses that indicated insufficient margins, debated subsystem operations that were off-nominal, agonized over contractor and vendor issues—and all this being conducted in the language of engineering and human spaceflight. A normal day's agenda would typically cover four to six issues, with each discussion typically lasting about an hour. At these meetings the Space Shuttle Orbiter Chief Engineer occupied a prominent place at the table and their word, opinions, and counsel was always highly regarded by the Orbiter project management.

Not everything can be exciting, and the discussion topics could also focus on generally mundane technical concerns, too; but even when that occurred, the Orbiter Chief Engineer brought an abundance of passion. I think this was due to two facts—one was that she loved her job and loved being around these fantastic engineers, but also that she took her responsibilities very seriously. She recognized and embodied the idea that the business at hand protected not just a very expensive national asset—the fleet of Space Shuttle Orbiters—but more importantly the lives of a half dozen or so people carried within it every time it flew. She took that fact very seriously.

That seriousness drove a persistence that was equaled and occasionally accentuated by her passion. But, imbued with that passion, she would occasionally brandish it inappropriately. She was prone to raising her voice, gesticulating wildly, pounding the table, all to emphasize whatever technical point she was making. Normally this passion was interpreted as exuberance and dedication to her work, but every once in a while, it exceeded the limits of acceptable behavior. On those occasions, when her passion got out of control, it devolved into name calling, throwing papers, and other demonstrations that were both unbecoming and disruptive. The chair of the meeting, the manager of the Orbiter project, was well aware of this Chief Engineer's proclivity for passionate displays and would allow her a lot of latitude. He recognized that, almost always, the Chief Engineer had a valid point. But sometimes, when required, he would be forced to dial her back. The situation required him to interject himself, be the diplomat, mandate that she cool off, and through his authority as chair to lower the passions in the room. I never saw the chair lose his temper or patience or contribute to the passion of the moment. He was always a calming influence, and that calm got us through the discussion and to a decision. He, in fact, was always the adult in the room.

Does being the adult in the room mean that you have to leave your passion at the door? Not at all! Passion, when applied constructively, is assuredly a tool in the leader's toolbox. A leader who never shows passion is one whose team will be apt not to follow. But passion applied inappropriately, when influenced by personality shortcomings or insecurities, can be a destructive influence. It is incumbent on leaders, including Chief Engineers, to modulate that passion, temper it, and regulate it so that it can be used to positively affect a discussion. An effective Chief Engineer will control their passion's influence so that it doesn't control them.

Consider now a theoretical situation in which you are chairing a design review and leading a discussion on a technical change to your system's configuration. Let's say the component in question has inadequate margins of performance and while it meets the system requirements, the team feels it can do better. Alternatives are proposed that can increase the performance margin to acceptable levels, thereby reducing the risk to the system but at the price of increasing weight, or power, or cooling, or some other tradeoff. Margin is a critical factor in the safety and reliability of a system and provides important confidence that the system will indeed meet its operational needs and objectives. Margin makes us all feel comfortable and holding it allows us to focus on other more critical concerns. It's good to have, we want it, and many engineers vigorously protect it, particularly when it is applied to safety. But as mentioned, margin almost always doesn't come for free and the price we pay are penalties in other areas. These are the sorts of trades that face the Chief Engineer on a daily basis, and these discussions are likely to be coupled with passion by strong advocates on both sides of a debate.

In this example, those recommending an increase in margin might anchor their argument in probabilities of catastrophic loss, engineering design standards for factors of safety, and other very legitimate concerns. Those recommending against it may be the engineers who are managing mass/weight or power allocation and may already be tight on their budgets with little ability to accommodate any growth. The former may argue loudly that safety is at stake and the latter may argue just as loudly that the system may never even get off the ground if we keep adding new liens. Both are valid, both are concerned with the overall success of the project, and both may be passionate about their advocacy. As such, both may lose their temper, they may become uncivil, and may drive the discussion to resolution by schoolyard brawl. I've seen it happen.

As the adult in the room, it's the Chief Engineer's responsibility to ensure the audience never empties for the schoolyard. It's likely that your team will look to you to control these situations. A calm demeanor is your best defense: a willingness to hear both sides of the equation with equanimity, an openness to both arguments, and interjecting a pacifying tone when the discussion gets heated. Never antagonize, insult, demean, or otherwise inflame the participants with exaggeration or innuendo. While it is your job to ultimately get to a decision, it also is your job to ensure the discussion proceeds civilly and progress is made toward reaching a decision.

I can tell you from experience that it's not always easy being the adult in the room. There are times when I would like to give in to my inner urges to be argumentative or flippant. Or sometimes I tend to inject a joke with a desire to lighten the mood of the room, but recognize that if not carefully considered, inappropriate or poorly targeted humor can actually inflame a situation. I have to consciously think about what I say before I say it.

Furthermore, during meetings I also have to actively monitor the room for escaping passion and note it before it gets out of hand. Controlling the temperature of the room is a necessary skill. Being able to recognize that intervention is necessary to prevent spirits from boiling over is normally the function of the person sitting at the head of the table. (Write this down—that's you!)

When passion does boil over, what do you do? Some would prefer to run away and get out of the line of fire. Believe me, I definitely understand the desire. But, as Chief Engineer, you really can't do that. Rather, you have to get folks to sit down, stop shouting, pocket their daggers, and get back to the work and solve the problem at hand. It's a tactful skill to get people to stop throttling each other and one that requires practice. It necessitates empathy, understanding, and competence in human psychology, something that doesn't come intuitively to many of us engineers. But focusing on the importance of the work at hand and the need of the team to forge solutions is something that does resonate with many engineers.

Being the adult in the room is about being a peacemaker, a negotiator, a decision maker and a diplomat. It's about being a technical expert, a responsible system owner, a risk manager, and a design thinker. It's about being a bartender, a psychologist, a sociologist, and a human behaviorist. But ultimately, it is about being an example for the entire team of maturity and teamwork.

CHAPTER 7

ACTING AS THE LEAD TECHNICAL INTEGRATOR

Any complex system is made up of thousands of parts. Millions! Tens of millions! I don't know—a lot. The system is composed of subsystems, which are congregations of assemblies. The assemblies are collections of components, which can be broken down into piece parts. The piece parts can be resistors and capacitors, springs and gears. The components assembled from those piece parts can form values and regulators, circuit boards and igniters. Put the components together and you get assemblies—actuators and reaction control jets, power buses and distribution units. And what do you do with assemblies? Why of course you integrate them to construct the subsystems that become the familiar territories to many discipline engineers—power, propulsion, communications, avionics, and so forth. Lots of parts.

Each of these parts needs to operate in seamless cooperation in order for the system to function as a whole and perform its mission. They need to interact with each other, interface at designed connections, each performing a small part of the collective entity. Each is procured according to design standards and specifications, sometimes wildly different, and supplied by any number of separate vendors. If one part fails, its effects on the whole must be understood and, if necessary, controlled. A system is much like a society or city with thousands of individuals, each performing requisite functions for the community to function. It's a complex, interactive, and intertwined collective that only works when all the individual parts are doing their jobs. The complexity can sometimes be mind boggling in scope and difficult to comprehend. And guess who has to integrate it all? Yup, you!

The Chief Engineer is the master integrator. It falls to the you to ensure that the overall system performs as required, as designed and as built, and that the system design adequately integrates all of these innumerable parts for optimized effect. This sometimes requires decisions on trades that can result in some winners and some losers (so to speak) across the parts. But it is the integrated system's performance that is ultimately important, not the individual parts. Getting to that integrated optimized system can sometimes necessitate some pretty intense negotiations (see Chapter 8) with a multitude of advocates each pushing for their desired solution. The integration of a system is a complex dance with a host of players, a deck of cards lying face down on the table and all mixed up but with a mandate of being identified and put into sequential order.

It is not magic that ensures good integration but, instead, a few key factors. I outline four of them here.

1. **A clear vision of the system as a whole.** You can't fit the pieces together if you don't know what the final product is to look like. It's what we talked about back in Chapter 3, "Being the Box Top," but worth repeating in the context of integration; the Chief Engineer has to navigate through the design process with a final, intact vision of the system. This vision is not necessarily a pretty graphic of what the physical system looks like in its operating environment (although as a visualization tool something like that can be helpful), but rather an intimate knowledge of the key goals, objectives, and driving requirements defining the system. A vision necessitates a keen understanding of the stakeholder expectations, a physics-based familiarity with the operating environment, and constant acknowledgment of the constraints and limitations placed upon the system. The box top is the destination, where you want to end up, and exists as a fundamental guide while everyone struggles to get there. Holding to the system vision is mandatory to acting as an integrator.

2. **An understanding of how parts fit together.** Everything, or at least 99-point-something percent of the parts that compose the system, will need to interface with other parts in some way. They need to connect, to talk with, to transfer commodities, and interact in any number of other ways. Not everything will connect easily. Some things will refuse to talk with other parts. Some commodities won't easily transfer. And you can pretty much expect that some parts interface in ways that weren't intended and wasn't even imagined when they were designed. Fitting Part A into Piece B is not an easy task as it requires consideration of a complicated number of variables, some of which include dimensional tolerances

and geographic locations, data processing standards, environmental and physical compatibilities, consideration for loads and forces, and other aspects that may prevent the efficient union of the two parts. Interfaces may contain one or simultaneously many of these considerations. Understanding the requirements of interfaces, and their limits, is mandatory to acting as an integrator.

3. **The ability to make concessions while holding on to the above vision.** If everyone had their own way, then everyone would have their own way. I bet Yogi Berra said that (or should have). The point is that design responsibilities are normally distributed by discipline, and each discipline owner or expert can be expected to prioritize their area of concern. The Chief Engineer can't afford to do that for everything, and, as a result, choices need to be made. These choices are not always easy as both sides of a debate may have very valid rationale for their solution. Or, sometimes there is simply no good solution, but nonetheless a solution is still needed. These choices, or trades, will confront the Chief Engineer on a weekly basis, and they will be expected to make decisions. With the overall objective being staying true to the system vision, some of these decisions may necessitate making concessions in particular areas. Few of those concessions will be easy to make or be considered no-brainers and might necessitate the occasional decreased performance in some areas. Being able to make these concessions while holding true to the system vision is mandatory to acting as an integrator.

4. **Communication, communication, communication.** You'll hear this elsewhere in this book, but the concept holds true when discussing Integration. To integrate, much of your time will be spent talking with people—with engineers and discipline subject matter experts (SMEs), with stakeholders and customers, with flight and ground operators, with hardware suppliers and vendors—so that you can stay abreast of the multitude of hardware requirements and idiosyncrasies that may prevent integration. It is doubtful that you'll be able to get all of the information you need from design

specifications or vendor fact sheets. No, you're going to have to talk with people. And the discussion will need to go in both direction as they will need to understand the system constraints as well as their own more parochial concerns. There is really no other way around this—broad communication is mandatory to acting as an integrator.

Here's a case in point. It may not be obvious, but the job of a Mission Control flight controller entails a dizzying amount of integration. Each console position is handed a set of responsibilities. Some responsibilities concern systems, while others demand oversight of the vehicle's trajectory or the activities of the crew. At the console position I supported, the Electrical Generation and ILlumination (EGIL) console, those responsibilities included monitoring and operations of the Shuttle Orbiter's electrical systems. The choreography of producing and distributing electricity in the Orbiter was a complex dance of elegantly interrelated components. That dance started with the Fuel Cells subsystem, three suitcase-sized units located under the blanket-like payload bay liner (so hidden from view), which through a four-step electrochemical reaction produced a current of electricity. The fuel cells are the first component in this waltz, but fuel cells alone can't generate electricity without the food that feeds them, and their diet consisted of cryogenically stored oxygen and hydrogen, encapsulated in the Power Reactant Storage and Distribution (PRSD) subsystem. Here, tanks of liquid oxygen and hydrogen are stored separately and maintained at extremely low temperatures (under -200 °F for oxygen and well under -400 °F for hydrogen). The PRSD is manifested as a series of tubing, valves, tanks, regulators, and heaters that maintain the cryogen at required pressures and temperatures to supply the demand required by the fuel cells.

On the output side is the Electrical Power Distribution and Control (EPD&C) subsystem, the network of electrical buses, sub-buses and circuit protection devices that receive the current of electricity from the fuel cells and feeds it to the power demanders (i.e., anything on the Orbiter that requires electricity to run). There is a main bus for each fuel cell (FC), which partitions the current to a hierarchy of downstream sub-buses in the forward, mid and aft portions of the vehicle, and also specialty buses (called Essential and Control buses) which power switches and other critical functions. Taken collectively, FC + PRSD + EPD&C has to operate as in integrated unison for the Orbiter to perform its functions as an operable spacecraft, crew transport, and platform in low-Earth orbit.

And then, there's more. The fuel cells produce electricity, but they also produce wastes as by-products of the electrochemical reaction that creates the current. One of the waste by-products produced by the fuel cells is to the purest water you can possibly imagine, created through combining the cryogenic oxygen and hydrogen. But if that water is not removed the fuel cell would flood, and all chemical and electrical reaction would cease (which would be a bad thing). To prevent this the water is extracted through a centrifugal pump and sent on its liquidly way to the Environmental Control and Life Support System, (another interface) where it is stored in tanks for use as drinking water by the crew and cooling water for the vehicle. If excess water is produced it is dumped overboard (another interface). Besides water, the fuel cells also produce heat that must be removed or the unit overheats, comes apart, and leaks reactants (another bad thing). Each fuel cell contains a small internal coolant loop that dumps that heat into a dedicated heat exchanger, part of the Orbiter's Active Thermal Control System (ATCS)—yet more interfaces. The ATCS transports that heat from the fuel cell heat exchanger to the Orbiter's main Freon Loop coolant system, which collects excess heat produced by all the vehicle's electronic equipment and directs it to a network of tubing within the inner surface of the payload bay doors (interface), which are lined with radiators for rejecting the heat to the deep cold of space.

The fuel cells, PRSD, EPD&C, ECLSS, and ATCS are interrelated, interconnected, interdependent and, like the organs in a human body, each providing separate functions but supporting the body as a whole. The Orbiter as a system functions only if it all works together in unison and cooperatively. No single subsystem is responsible for making the Orbiter work, they do it all together, and ensuring their proper integration is a constant responsibility of the flight control team.

So integration is critical, but integration can alternatively act as a barrier if it's not handled well. An example of this can be taken from the Constellation program. As programs go, Constellation was a large one, composed of many smaller projects and of thousands of individuals. The flight architecture was composed of a number of different flight and ground elements, each managed by a separate project office, which all needed to work together to successfully perform the program's mission. This consisted of the crew-carrying spacecraft (Orion), the launch vehicle (Ares), the launch facilities (Ground Ops), the mission control facilities (Mission Ops) and the spacewalking apparatus should the crew needs to exit the vehicle while in the vacuum of space. All five of these architectural elements would have to communicate with each other through commands received and telemetry transmitted, the management of which was referred to as Command, Control and Communications Interoperability (C3I). The vision for C3I in Constellation was that each project element would utilize a common and consistent methodology in terms of the way command and telemetry data was formatted and structured. It was desired to utilize this common framework to reduce the overall complexity of the system and to help ensure that the interrelated communications among all the elements was successful. Furthermore, it was felt that having a common framework would make it easier (and cheaper) to invoke changes in the future. A great vision, and sensible too. Unfortunately, it never worked!

The major hurdle in implementing C3I was not the complexity of a common framework nor the system that was to manage it. No, it was institutional practice. See, since the advent of the space program, each of these five elements performed the task of command and telemetry a little bit differently from each other. Human spacecraft are designed and managed by Johnson Space Center in Houston, TX, which has one way of doing this job. The launch vehicles are designed and managed by Marshall Space Flight Center in Huntsville, AL, which uses another. Launch facilities, at Florida's Kennedy Space Center, resolved to use a third. And so on. Each of these local practices had become so imbedded in the culture of those Centers that it turned out to be impossible to break those institutional practices and forge a common framework. It's silly, but that's what happened. The integration of the Constellation architecture's elements couldn't be enabled, and if these cultural impediments continued, the result would inevitably be an inoperable system of systems. Eventually, I think we would have figured it out, but the Constellation program was cancelled before we got past PDR, yet it remains a good example of the inability to integrate having substantial impacts on a program.

So how does a Chief Engineer ensure good integration? Well, for starters, you can't have good integration without sufficient communication. You can't put the pieces of the puzzle together so that they operate effectively as a whole without knowing what's going on technically inside the projects at all stages of the life cycle. Most Chief Engineers get together with their technical staff on a weekly basis, whether that be a Chief Engineers' tag up, a more formal Engineering Review Board, or other meetings depending on the size and complexity of the project. It doesn't matter very much what forum you select or even if you do this outside of a forum, but what does matter is that you stay connected with your team and understand the needs of the individual disciplines and the challenges and hurdles they are facing.

Your discipline engineers are concerned about how the system integrates, but in the end their primary responsibility is to ensure their specific discipline performs adequately. They can rely on Interface Control Requirements and Interface Control Documents to ensure the adequate integration of their subsystem with others, but generally their responsibility lies with their own subsystem. The Chief Engineer, on the other hand, has to ensure it all integrates and the system as a whole performs adequately. Your discipline engineers are likely to be competent and dedicated, but It may not be possible to completely rely on them to ensure integration—you have to ensure it yourself.

But you can get your discipline engineers together on a regular basis and talk through the integration as a team. These meetings can be invaluable in terms of understanding the integrated performance of the system and getting your hands around the impediments that may prevent it. I have seen in the course of discussion among technical teams where a subject is brought up and the owner of a discipline not under discussion raises their hand and states "Wait, that won't work, my system can't operate that way!" These revelations aren't always identified through requirements or design documents; sometimes, they need to be acknowledged through the experience and knowledge of the discipline experts, and sufficient communication is the best way to extract that. Once acknowledged, then you have something tangible to go figure out how to fix.

Another example, we trained a lot as flight controllers through activities called "simulations" with our team in the control center and an astronaut team in the vehicle simulator in a separate building. On one occurrence, the sim team failed a component in the Orbiter's supply water system that feeds the crew their drinking water and supplies the Flash Evaporator System (FES) that helps with cooling the vehicle (particularly when the payload bay doors are closed and the radiators cannot be exposed to the cold of space). Suddenly, there was insufficient water getting to the crew and the FES and we needed to do something quickly. Well, the supply water system obtains water from the fuel cells (a by-product of the fuel cell reaction) so what do you do to get the fuel cells to produce more water? You increase their power output by turning things on—more power equals more water produced. We needed a lot of water quickly, so we concentrated on the equipment that required a large amount of power. The Shuttle's computers are large power users and normally only two of the five are operating while on orbit. So, let's turn on the other three computers. OK, that was a start, but we needed more.

Interestingly, one of the ways you can power things quickly is by having the crew turn on all the lights inside the flight deck and the mid-deck. So, we had them do that. Getting there, but not enough yet, and the big-ticket item was still out there—the Circ Pumps that circulate hydraulic fluid to the vehicle's aero surfaces and main engine gimbals. Normally, while in space, there's no need to move these surfaces, so the fluids within the hydraulic lines remain static. To prevent the fluids from freezing, the Circ Pumps would periodically turn on and regulate the temperature of the hydraulic fluid to prevent out-of-limit conditions. Well, these are the largest pumps on board the Orbiter, each pulling about 2 kilowatts of power, which is a lot of power. So, if we need to power up quickly and produce water, let's turn on all three Circ Pumps. Nothing better to increase power quickly! I checked with the console operator responsible for the pumps, the Mechanical, Maintenance, and Crew Systems (MMACS) console, who said sure, we could do that, no problem. As we were discussing our plan with the Flight Director suddenly the Environmental, Emergency, and Consumables Management (EECOM) console operator, who is responsible for environmental control, interrupted the discussion and said we can't do that! The hydraulic fluid interfaces with the Orbiter's Freon Loop at a heat exchanger. Normally, when a circ pump is turned on it sends a slug of cold hydraulic fluid past that heat exchanger, but the Freon Loop system can handle that slug. But if all three pumps are turned on at the same time, the Freon Loop can't handle that amount of cold hydraulic fluid and we could damage the heat exchanger, possibly rupturing it (which is a very bad thing indeed.) If all the Freon were to leak out it likely would be an unsurvivable event for the crew. With that information, we quickly resolved to come up with a different plan. Integration at its best!

When we discuss integration we normally think about design. Hardware parts have to fit into other hardware parts. The interior layouts of aircraft and spacecraft are complex mazes of interweaving lines, cables, equipment, and structures that fit within ergonomic packages that optimize volume, environment, and center of gravity. Fair enough. But we should note that integration extends beyond just parts fitting into other parts. A NASA Chief Engineer has to ensure integration of requirements, for example. A system's requirements set can run into the multiple hundreds of individual requirements and it's very likely that there will be some incompatibilities among them that need to be resolved. Yes, the project may have a dedicated requirements manager, but that manager may not have the experience or technical acumen to identify these incompatibilities, so ensuring an integrated requirements set can fall to the Chief Engineer. At the end of the development process, after the system has been manufactured and verification of the requirements begins, there will likely be hundreds of separate activities that will need to be integrated, starting at component-level verification and working to the integrated system level. This often is represented using a fishbone diagram. Yes, a large project also may have a dedicated verification manager who can construct a fishbone and check off the tests as they are completed, but ensuring an integrated series of verification tests falls to the Chief Engineer.

And as I mentioned, just getting people to talk together and share information is an integration task in which the Chief Engineer plays an enormous role. Over the course of the standard day, a Chief Engineer can receive a tremendous amount of information covering a wide variety of technical subjects. It is up to the Chief Engineer to distill all that information, maintain what's important, file away the rest, and communicate the most important information effectively to the rest of the team. In this context, effective integration is not just the dissemination of communication, but also the confirmation that the information is understood contextually. In this light, consider the feedback you receive as an important part of integration. If information is simply flowed down the chain but not well understood, it would be hard to say that effective integration is occurring. Making sure that heads are all nodding in the same direction and that technical concepts and ideas are understood is also an integration role of the Chief Engineer.

CHAPTER 8

NEGOTIATING SOLUTIONS

I've been told that NASA engineers and managers are neither opinionated nor passionate people. Well, actually, that's a lie; I've never been told that, and even if I had I would know it to be untrue. NASA engineers and managers have a broad diversity of opinions, and there is little we are more passionate about than helping NASA succeed in our missions of exploration and research. That diversity of opinions stems from a wide field of experiences, derived from both life and our professions. We have worked on projects covering any number of domains from launching and flying humans in space to touching the distant reaches of the solar system, galaxy, and universe. We work in space and in Earth's atmosphere, and sometimes other environments, and many of us get to cross over those professional domains many times over the course of a career. And passion—nobody beats NASA engineers and managers for the passion they bring to their work. That is one of the reasons why NASA routinely ranks as one of the best places to work in the Federal Government: we love what we do and happily dedicate our professional lives to its pursuit. And we get paid for it, too. Sweet!

It's true that having all these opinions means we won't always align, and having all that passion can sometimes produce conflict. Overall, I'd say we generally do a good job working through these issues because every one of us is dedicated to the Agency's mission and sincerely wants NASA to succeed. We find common ground, we listen to each other's viewpoints, and when someone finally makes a decision we salute and move on. That occurs on a daily basis across the Agency and through that collaboration we make progress. But sometimes, through our understanding of the consequences of getting a disagreement wrong, the pressure can become too great or the passion invested in a position can become elevated. We disagree, our position becomes firm, and progress halts. When it comes to technical disagreements, call in the Chief Engineer to negotiate!

As a negotiator you may find yourself in the middle of disagreements that involve... well, just about every aspect of the development process. Disagreements can start at the very beginning of a project when meetings are held with the customer on stakeholder expectations. Customers want a lot from their investment, sometimes reaching for the "unobtainium," and understanding what's deliverable and what isn't, and the Chief Engineer might disagree. During requirements identification you will likely find countering parties, one side demanding the absolute necessity of a certain requirement and the other side arguing against it. Design trades are rich with differing points of view as the increase in one capability can many times result in the decrease in another (therefore the "trade"). Some will argue for redundancy, others will argue against it. Person A might push for additional margins, while Person B might declare them unnecessary. One may feel passionate about the application or waiving of standards, another more blasé. When the system is finally built and we verify against requirements, it's not infrequent for one engineer to insist that a requirement has been successfully met and a second to demand forcefully that it hasn't. At every stage disagreements can arise, and the only way through is to facilitate negotiation.

Many of these arguments and demands will have very strong defenders who believe adamantly in their particular position. Remember, these folks are not being disruptive because they enjoy conflict but are just as dedicated as you are to the success of the project. It's just that they may have a particular vision or past experience that points them in one direction. They may have seen a similar issue arise in a previous project and learned the hard way that their solution works well. Their opinion may be driven through falling back on education or advice from a mentor. All sorts of reasons! But, ultimately, they want the project to succeed just as much as any other dedicated engineer, manager, or scientist on staff and are doing what they perceive to be helpful in moving toward that success. Good intentions, I have found, are almost always true. As you negotiate, try to avoid doubting people's intentions, it's normally not very productive.

You'll be faced with positions that may be strongly defended, like a fortress under siege. Dealing with this isn't a particularly easy part of the Chief Engineer's job because few of us enjoy conflict and being placed between two hard points of view can be uncomfortable. I, for one, absolutely hate being in the middle of an argument. But it remains necessary to resolve differences, come to consensus or decision, and allow the project to move forward. In accepting the responsibilities of a Chief Engineer, you accepted the role of tie-breaker, resolver, and negotiator, and while admittedly difficult these responsibilities are incumbent in the position you hold. What's more, your team will be looking to you to perform these duties. If required to make tie-breaking decisions on technical matters, you most likely have the authority.

Realize that you may ruffle some feathers in the process. Not intentionally or with antagonism toward any of the parties, but it's unavoidable that your decision has the potential to breed dissatisfaction. Not everyone will see the big picture you see or happily relent when a decision goes against their desires. Feelings can be hurt, no question about it. The mitigation of this, of course, is to ensure that everyone knows any decision is being made for the good of the project and that none of the discussion is personal or based on personal animus. Many will accept this, some will not. Can you live with the knowledge that some may not accept your decision and incorrectly feel that you are holding a grudge? Well, you'd better, Chief Engineer, because it happens. But there are ways to handle this constructively, too.

In the big picture, handling these situations constructively is as much about dealing with people as it is about decision-making or the technical rationale. It is about understanding how people on your team deal with disappointment. Use that emotional intelligence we spoke about in Chapter 1 to recognize that there may be disappointment. It's a human reaction, it's natural, allow for it, and acknowledge it. Tell your team you understand there may be disappointment with the decision and that you are sensitive to it. The worst thing you can do is to admonish your team for their disappointment. Their disappointment may well frustrate you but try not to show it. You don't have to assuage their disappointment by rewarding them with something else, but the simple action of acknowledging their feeling can go a long way towards salving their wounds. Remember, the most brilliant Chief Engineer who can almost magically intuit the right technical path for any given issue can only be successful if he or she also masters the ability to effectively manage their team.

But back to negotiating. What are some best practices for a Chief Engineer to negotiate a technical solution on a NASA project? Let's say, for example, the discussion surrounds the application of margin being applied to the performance of an attitude control thruster for an Earth-observing satellite. The thruster will be designed to meet a defined performance specification, but given the past history and reliability of the selected thruster the design team feels it's necessary to certify the thruster to margins above the spec. One camp on the team feels that 5 percent margin above spec will be sufficient. Another camp believes 5 percent is insufficient given the importance of the thruster to the spacecraft's mission and is strongly advocating for additional margin, say 10 percent above spec. And lastly, the test team will have to make modifications to their test fixture to test at any level above the spec at all and is against adding any additional margin at all. What follows is a look at how the process breaks down.

The Technical Issue: First, understand the problem as much as you can using all the data you have available. No technical decision can be made without a thorough understanding of the situation. Have as much information as you can gather on the thruster, its design, its pedigree and history and its past performance. Have a thorough understanding of the criticality of this thruster to the spacecraft's mission, the levels of fault tolerance and/or redundancy available, and the impacts on the mission should the thruster fail to perform as specified. Data is your friend and the lack of it will only lead to guesswork. While the decision you'll eventually make may need to accept risk, don't accept any more risk than necessary by obfuscating it with insufficient data. If time is short or insufficient information available, get more of both if you can.

The Decision: Understand the criticality of needing a decision right now. What is the driver for having to make this decision at this time? Question whether this is driving a decision appropriately or forcing a decision prematurely. If the time is right and the data is available, then have the discussion.

Need advice for how to make the decision? Well, simply put, you weren't elevated to the position of Chief Engineer just because you dress well or keep your boss laughing with your poignant sense of humor. No, you got this position because of your experience, and that experience will lead you to the best decision. Relying on your experience and judgement is about the only advice that I can offer on this subject. Even if you don't have direct experience with attitude control thrusters, the counsel of your team and your engineering judgement will carry the day.

Importantly, though, when a decision is required, ensure that it actually gets made. Having an hours-long discussion on a technical trade that leads to no decision is the bane of most engineers. Make a decision. After you've heard all the data and once the decision is made, be confident in that decision so that you and the team can move past it and on to whatever the next discussion calls for.

The Team: Of course, this is the part I'm really trying to focus on in this chapter. Many times, the team ends up being the forgotten part, cast aside as unimportant compared with the "fun" technical discussion and the perceived need to make forward progress. But I'm telling you, this is how you build and maintain productive teams who can promote (or impede) success just as directly as can good or bad engineering.

First, during the discussion, hear both sides equally. If one side of a debate has been given time to make their argument, give the other side an equal amount of time. That doesn't mean giving both sides as much time as they want—you can control how much or how little time is given, but at least give it equally. Perceptions of favoritism, whether deserved or not, can cause harm to a team's cohesiveness.

Once a decision is made, remain empathetic to the side that "loses." While happiness and satisfaction are not a guarantee when bringing forward a technical issue for decision, it does not benefit the team to recriminate, belittle, or otherwise demean those whose decision did not go their way. They brought forward a position with as much professionalism and desire for the project to succeed as did those who "won" their desired decision and bringing it forward in the first place may actually have been an act of courage on their part. Compliment both sides for raising the issue, give credit to all for a good debate, and remain cognizant that some may be disappointed with the result. The thing that I try to remember is that a disappointed engineer who has a management team willing to listen and who is treated respectfully is an engineer who will be willing to bring issues forward in the future. The opposite, a disappointed engineer who feels stonewalled or otherwise shut out, will likely not bring issues or concerns forward in the future, and that's not good for the project.

One of the best examples I've seen of skilled negotiation was again during the Constellation program. (Hey, it was a big program that left a lot of examples!) The Orion spacecraft was having a weight crisis—it was too heavy for the assigned launch vehicle, the Ares-1, and months of work to get it inside the box proved fruitless. Finally, in desperation, the project undertook a drastic solution: They began by cutting out all redundancy, starting with zero fault tolerance on critical functions and eliminating all noncritical components, leaving only the critical functionality necessary to do the job. Would they ever fly such a vehicle? No, but their strategy was to make everything in the spacecraft single string and use this configuration to establish a baseline, a "zero mass" configuration, if you like. Then, they would open the door to everyone who wanted to increase their subsystem's redundancy or add back noncritical functions and capabilities. They assigned someone the role of the spacecraft's "Mass Czar," who oversaw management of the spacecraft's mass. Through debate and negotiation, this person would provide the critical recommendations to project management on what to add back and why. I'll tell you, the line in front of this gentleman's door was a mile long. Everyone wanted to get their time and make their case.

I don't know the exact number of requests that came to the Mass Czar, but it ran into the hundreds. Some requests were obviously necessary as they provided mitigations to critical hazards and were required by safety policy. Those were easy. Others were, alternatively, obviously unnecessary as they didn't directly support the mission or the spacecraft. Those were easy, too. But the remainder of requests composed the majority of decisions facing Orion management, necessitating the Mass Czar to find the right set of solutions. Almost daily, he would conduct meetings on a litany of trades. Think about it, how do you decide between redundancy of two different subsystems in which both are required to accomplish the mission, both control critical hazards, and both add essentially the same mass. These decisions may be functionally equivalent in terms of need and impact to the spacecraft, and yet the vehicle may not be able to sustain both. So, he began to pair off decisions, this vs. that, have a detailed discussion, negotiate between parties, develop a recommendation for project leadership, and then move on to the next trade.

On a few occasions I sat in on these discussions and the Mass Czar was masterful. Advocates on both sides of the trade would defend the virtue of their respective proposals, and the Mass Czar listened to both sides with full attention. He would ask the occasional question to ensure he understood the situation but avoided inserting opinion. He was welcoming and listened extremely well, making both sides feel comfortable and keeping a potentially adversarial situation professional. When all the data was on the table, he would look for ways in which the situation could be turned from win-lose to win-win, even if the winners didn't get 100 percent of what they were asking for. He looked for small concessions on both sides, areas in which each advocate could back off their full solution and yet still feel like they had gained. He remained reasonable, calm, appreciative of the work involved in collecting the data, and respectful of all parties. Ultimately, all were aware that the solution he would end up recommending to Orion management was fair and with the best interests of the project in mind. Like I said, masterful. Most folks did indeed leave happy or at least confident that the best solution really was being brought forward to management. I don't know if this person received any recognition or acknowledgment of his negotiating skills and the fact that those skills, employed correctly, played a huge role in fixing the Orion mass crisis, but I sincerely hope he did. I learned a lot from watching him.

Another good example of where negotiation comes into play in our business are the always enjoyable Review Item Disposition (RID)

Reviews, something quite common to the culture of my original home, Johnson Space Center. RIDs are comments or suggested changes made to documents and design concepts at significant milestone (such as life-cycle reviews during development or flight ops reviews during operations). They are a means of soliciting feedback from the community to help ensure appropriate maturity of products. A document may be undergoing a revision and a draft of the changes released for review. Reviewers parse the document and generate a list of alterations or changes they would suggest making. This list is sent to the office in charge of the revision and each comment, or RID, is reviewed and dispositioned. Feedback is provided to the person or organization who submitted the RID with an Accept, Accept with Modification, or Reject. The RID provider then can accept the disposition or push back and request additional discussion (something commonly referred to as a "reclama").

In 2015, I was leading an effort to revise the *NASA Systems Engineering Handbook* (NASA-SP-6105) and we used the RID Review process to adjudicate the comments we received. This revision included significant changes to the handbook and added well over 300 pages of new content. As such we received over 1,200 comments, each one requiring a separate and dedicated disposition. It took the better part of 2 months to wade through all the comments and provide dispositions, but we knuckled down and got the job done. To our great pleasure we discovered the majority of our dispositions were accepted, but one commenter, a very experienced systems engineer from Goddard Space Flight Center with a long previous career in the military had some issues and requested additional discussion. As it turned out he had about 30 dispositions he disagreed with, and this metastasized into almost 10 hours of negotiation over 2 weeks.

This gentleman was vociferous in defending his comments. His arguments were always logical and well presented, but we often found them to be out of scope of the handbook or contrary to how NASA performs systems engineering. He would defend his original viewpoint and we would defend our disposition and associated rationale. At every step, reaching a common solution or consensus that would allow us to move forward with all parties happy was at the top of my mind. That wasn't always possible. Sometimes I needed to stand our ground, as the comment, if we included it, would compromise the integrity of the handbook. But other times the discussion was much more philosophical and not so clear cut. There were occasions when I "let" him win, that is, have his way when the debate only differed over philosophy and either solution would have been acceptable. I did not want to push him too hard and have him walk away frustrated and disgruntled. Over one topic I would stand my ground and in the next gave ground. In the end we found agreement on the content that represented the best that NASA had to offer on systems engineering given our diverse approaches. At that point we considered the negotiations successful (and for both of us, thankfully, concluded).

Sometimes solutions require compromise and finding one can be an art. Compromise doesn't necessarily mean splitting the difference down the middle. The compromise solutions still necessitate technical merit and must be within acceptable risk for the project. They still need to be based on data, analysis, failure history, and other artifacts that are proven and demonstrable. But within those parameters there remains a lot of latitude for the Chief Engineer to negotiate. When you find yourself in the middle of an argument, trust that you're not completely alone. More often than not, both opposing parties can constructively partner with you in finding a compromise that works, likely wanting the project to be successful more than they want to get their way. Appealing to the good of the project can be an effective motivation to get folks to agree. Try it.

And heed the words of former NASA HQ Chief Engineer David Mobley—the first solution you hear may not always be the best one for the task: "I have told some folks in the past that 'I appreciate your input and the work required to develop that input, but while it is a very elegant solution I need the second-best solution with the impacts of not accepting your first solution.' Almost always the first solution is the most elegant and most costly. It's amazing how many times the second-best solution is the one agreed to."[*]

---

[*] David Mobley. Peer-review correspondence with the author.

One final point on the subject. When you have engineers who are resolute in their viewpoint, attempt to attain an understanding of what may be motivating them to be so. Rarely do you get someone who is out for personal gain (financial or reputational) or holds an animosity against the project and is actively trying to grind it to a halt (although I suppose that can happen). Rather, someone who holds fast to a position is more likely motivated by past experience and a desire not to repeat it. Failure is a great teacher, the best I know, but those lessons should be applied in context. Someone may take a hard-learned lesson and apply it far too broadly, perhaps out of context. They are likely to do this not out of malice but out of conservatism born from the experience of the original failure. If this is true, being aware if that can help interpret their motivation.

It's also possible they may be just plain stubborn. In that case, benchmark a local farmer to understand how they deal with stubborn goats.

CHAPTER 9

DEALING WITH ENGINEERING CHANGE

The only constant in the universe is change. I don't know who said that or their understanding on the science of the laws of conservation, but in general this is true. Change happens all the time and continues to happen in spite of our efforts to constrain it. As engineers, we apply constraints to the forces of change, commonly known to us as configuration-controlled baselines. While these in actuality doesn't constrain change but instead help us understand the impact of those changes, they can act as braking forces and slow the inevitable onslaught of change. We can build a boundary on a project's scope, we can freeze a requirements set, we can lock in a design, but I can guarantee that they will not completely stop the onslaught of change. It's something a Chief Engineer needs to contend with and develop the ability to respond to. And sometimes, on rare occasions, it can even illuminate opportunity that wasn't apparent before. Change is an inevitable force that threatens to wreak havoc within your project, but it can be managed.

Change will happen throughout the life of a project's development. Toward the beginning of the process we identify the system's requirements, which jumble around for some months. We add some requirements and delete others or alter and reconfigure them because they are infeasible, or the boundaries of the project's scope dictate that they are no longer needed. The requirements get thrown into a cauldron where they brew collectively in a dynamic swirling mixture. Finally, around the time of the Systems Requirements Review, they get fixed into a more static characterization through the magic of configuration management. But even after being declared fixed, there will be pressure for change driven by a variety of causes. It's possible that new mission goals or objectives get added to a project. Sometimes a technical requirement, once considered to be a good idea, proves in fact to be infeasible and is removed. Or, perhaps, cost or schedule limitations might preclude further development of a capability and that requirement, summarily, gets cast away. Every time each of these changes occurs, it induces the potential for ten times the impact to a project since the implications for removing or adding requirements must be thoroughly assessed before the change can be made.

During the design phase of a project, change continues to make its presence known. We may advance down one technical path and, finding it unattainable, opt for a different solution. We establish our original schemes for redundancy through the requirements process, but once in design we might find that a solution is impracticable in some circumstances, necessitating a new redundancy scheme. Some new technologies that were intended to be introduced on the project may not pan out, requiring a Plan B use of a heritage component that can be quickly introduced. Some functional capabilities may prove to be constraining in terms of mass or take too much power or require too much active cooling, and the design needs to be altered to accommodate that hardware.

Even late in the development process—during assembly, testing, and verification—we can discover inherent incompatibilities with the "as built" design that could necessitate a different approach. A component may not pass qualification testing, or outgasses inappropriately during environmental vacuum testing, and needs to be swapped with something that is more compatible. Potentially, we could discover that the launch date has changed and now we must arrange for compatible long-term storage of our system, placing new requirements on the project.

Change is ever-present. It'll be your constant companion. In the same way that entropy is inevitable, you'll have to face the headwinds continuously and develop strategies to prevent change from causing your project irreparable harm. It can be managed, but it can also overwhelm you. What happened with engineering drawings in the Shuttle program is a great example of change threatening to overcome a system. Due to its size and complexity, the Shuttle program had drawings for everything. These were originally mid-twentieth century vellum paper drawings produced on drafting tables, but as the program matured and new technologies became available, they were eventually scanned into digital formats and utilized electronically. The drawings covered all the aspects you might expect—installation of components, assembly of piece parts, configurations and tolerances—all the technical matter that engineers and technicians required to build and maintain the Orbiter fleet. Many of the drawings were ascribed and referenced by the venerable VO70 series of nomenclature, a designation that might be familiar to you if you worked on the program. When, say, a technician needed to change out an avionics box, or replace a valve or quick disconnect, they would refer to these drawings. When they removed and installed the Space Shuttle Main Engines, they had these drawing on their work bench. When they torqued bolts and set screws, there were the drawings. Almost everything that occurred on those vehicles were governed by drawings.

Over time the drawings become a liability. As the program progressed and the vehicle matured, the drawings needed to be altered to account for every new part or procedure, each new technical tolerance, and the multitude of standard configuration changes that occur over the years. Many of these changes were small and incremental, but over time they piled up. Unfortunately, as the program was focused intently on processing the vehicles more quickly and turning them around to fly on their next mission, not a lot of attention was given to synching up the drawings with the growing burden of changes. Eventually, some drawings had dozens of changes to them. In one egregious case, just changing out an avionics box necessitated the technician to refer to a set of drawings with over 50 changes listed in the margins, an almost impossible task to get right. And what's more, 20 years after the beginning of the program, the cost of incorporating all those changes to the drawings became prohibitive. You can guess what happened; ultimately, the program decided to live with all that ambiguity because of this immense cost. When the Shuttle flew its last flight in 2011, the situation remained, an unfortunate legacy of a proud program.

So how do you as Chief Engineer stay on top of all of this change? Well, as mentioned, configuration-controlled baselines are an obvious solution, but one that only can be part of the answer. You can establish a technical baseline, a schedule baseline, a cost baseline, whatever; it doesn't matter. What does matter is that at some point you establish a fixed configuration and then track and control changes to that configuration. As with the Shuttle drawing example above, when the number of changes gets large and it becomes difficult to discuss a configuration given all that individual uniqueness, you can synch it up and establish a new baseline and then track and control changes to that new baseline. You don't want to do this too often as, for one, it takes a lot of work to establish new baselines, but also it can disrupt your ability to track certain metrics associated with any specific baseline. Additionally, a lot of our technical analyses are tied to a specific configuration baseline, so changing the baseline too frequently can make it difficult or impossible to keep track of what configuration each analysis is based on. No, instead, keep it simple. Don't make things harder than they need to be. But do use the configuration-controlled baseline to help you keep abreast of the tsunami of change that commonly behests projects.

I always get asked the question, "When should I establish a configuration-controlled baseline"? Doing so either too early or too late can be problematic. I suggest not seeking "easy" answers for this. For example, I have seen in engineering guidance manuals the suggestion of establishing configuration control of requirements at Systems Requirements Review (SRR) and of the design at PDR. In general, that's good guidance and can be thought of as a generic solution. But every project is a little bit different and, even accepting this guidance, the Chief Engineer always needs to consider the specifics of his or her project to implement configuration control when it is most beneficial. Establishing control too late can lead to chaos as no one knows what baseline the project is working to. Establishing control too early can lead to huge amounts of change traffic (in the forms of Change Requests [CRs]) because the design is still fluid, and change continues to occur rapidly.

So, when should you establish a baseline? Well, it's best to maintain a balance between too early and too late (I know, engineers hate answers like that, but darn if it isn't true!). Early in the process change is happening at a constant pace and keeping track of every element of that change would be unreasonable. Trades and studies are being performed that will eventually lead to configuration decisions, but those trades have not yet completed. Much remains up in the air and still to be determined (just think about how many TBDs you may still have!). Allow this change to occur. At this point in the life cycle, considerations for change is good—it removes the wheat from the chaff and putting too many limitations on change can inhibit creative thinking. At some point, though, the amount of change has slowed down and the design settles more or less, at which point a baseline can be effectively established. Change will still occur, but the burden of effectively tracking them is manageable. When exactly this transition occurs is a judgement call and will be yours to make.

Throughout all this change traffic, the Chief Engineer is the clearinghouse. Technical change moves predominantly through the Chief Engineer as the maintainer and owner of the technical baseline. In this capacity you might chair some sort of panel or other forum where technical changes are approved—these are sometimes referred to as Engineering Review Boards. Discipline engineers will assess the need for changes to the system's configuration and those change requests are brought in front of the panel or board for consideration. The requests should include all the technical information needed to make such a decision, like the existing state of the item under question, a problem statement including the need or driver for the change request (ostensibly, but not always, a technical need or driver), a detailed description of the proposed technical change including rationale for why this change will solve the problem, impacts to the system for making this change (alterations to vehicle mass, power, cooling, performance, etc.), any identified hazards that this change will create, and so on. No change should be considered as a "no-brainer"—that can lead inexorably to unexpected consequences (that are usually bad). Instead, each change should be considered in detail with both pros and cons discussed and debated. Finally, after all the information is on the table, it will come time for a decision that, as you knew, is yours to make. When you make that decision, a useful arbiter of a good change is one that doesn't make an unacceptable impact to the system as a whole and its ability to perform its mission.

Technical Performance Metrics (TPMs) are also useful in maintaining an awareness of whether the changes are allowing the design to converge on the desired solution or, alternatively, diverge from where you want your design to go. TPMs can be tracked on any aspect of system design—mass, communication bandwidth, engine performance, power output—and provide the Chief Engineer with a window into the effectiveness of the changes being made to the baseline design. The example of tracking vehicle mass is among the most common TPM within the NASA corps. A vehicle design can be assigned a mass bogey, or a Not to Exceed (NTE) constraint, dictated by, say, the up-mass capabilities of the launch vehicle or the ability of the engine to get the aircraft off the ground. As changes come down the line, even if those changes are justified at the component or subsystem level, they still all have to live within the overall mass constraint of the system. Tracking margin above (we hope it's above) the mass bogey is the function this TPM serves, and the allocation to the vehicle is frequently proportioned in synch with the maturity of design. For example, the overall mass could be (just picking a number here) 25 percent below the NTE constraint at SRR, 20 percent below at PDR, 10 percent below at CDR, and so forth. Every change to the mass of the vehicle is calculated and monitored by the ever-watchful Chief Engineer. If the mass is growing too rapidly, then the TPM would reflect that and the frequency of change can be altered. A mass TPM can also help predict the future as it would indicate where the system should be at major reviews or checkpoints. If the mass TPM looks good, changes can then be managed according to that plan.

And since we're on the subject of configuration management, here's something I've seen that you'll definitely want to avoid. As Chief Engineer for Aeronautics I witness a large variety of projects over the course of their lifetimes. The one project I'm thinking of was performing mid-TRL research and technology development on aircraft jet engine combustors, trying to verify that they could reduce engine exhaust emissions and increase "fuel burn" (essentially, engine efficiency) through new methodologies of combustion. The project tested about a dozen configurations in a laboratory over the course of 2 years and then downselected to a single most-promising configuration to be integrated into an aircraft engine, with the hope of advancing the technology to TRL 5. They developed a 3-year plan to perform this research including additional refinements to the combustor and testing at the component level prior to insertion in the test engine for an integrated test. This was hard, technically challenging research, doing things that had never before been done.

We were watching their progress from HQ and something about their progress just wasn't making any sense. During our weekly status telecons we kept hearing about a panoply of technical difficulties the team was experiencing in getting the technology to work, and yet they routinely reported their status as Green and on plan. They were missing milestones, they were changing configurations, the technology's performance wasn't meeting the research goals, and yet week after week their reported status was Green and on plan. Something was amiss here.

So we dug in a bit and discovered what was causing the dissonance. Essentially, every time they missed a milestone or faced a technical hurdle, they changed their baseline. If they slipped past a milestone then they changed their baseline to reset the milestone for a new date. If they had planned to demonstrate to a certain TRL level and couldn't accomplish it then they changed their baseline to accommodate that failure. They would change their baseline almost on a weekly basis to the point that—you guessed it—their baseline became essentially meaningless and irrelevant. In their desire to "stay Green," they lost sight of the baseline as a management tool. Instead it became a façade for a charade. My advice: don't do this! It's not only bad form (and it is that!), but these tools are put into place to help us achieve success and if we don't use them properly then our success is handicapped.

When change gets out of hand (as in the Shuttle drawing situation) it's not desirable, but there are times when change is constructive and beneficial to the project. One example, used often when exploring unproven technologies, are off-ramps. Many of NASA's projects endeavor to do new things, pushing the boundaries of what has been previously accomplished and exploring new ways to accomplish our goals. It is not uncommon for a NASA project to begin with new and unproven technologies initially on the critical path. This is sometimes necessary to obtain the mission objectives since existing or heritage technology may not provide for full success. And so, early in a project, while establishing its requirements base and defining the ConOps, the team may simultaneously be developing and maturing unproven but important technologies. We see this frequently on new science instruments that can lack the maturity of the proven spacecraft bus it will be attached to. The cutoff point is generally accepted for these new technologies to have been matured to TRL 6 by PDR for them to be considered acceptable risk for the project and stay on the critical path. If they haven't attained that maturity, we employ the off-ramp.

An off-ramp solution can come in the form of a heritage, proven, flown, off-the-shelf technology, previously certified and able to fulfill the primary function of the new technology but perhaps not at the same resolution, performance, or other desirable attribute that the new technology would have provided. Should the new technology not pan out, the project can cease its development and insert the proven technology in its place, thereby maintaining the critical path. Some secondary or tertiary mission objectives may fall by the wayside with this concession, but the mission as a whole can still be successful. This technology replacement, ladies and gentlemen, is change, but it's change that can save a project.

Change also can be beneficial early in a project's life, as allowing the trade space to stay open can allow for the identification of potentially better ways of achieving a function. New technologies get invented all the time, and old technologies are evolved and updated continuously. You wouldn't want to lock in a design for a radiation-hardened microprocessor too early, for example, as a better, faster, more lightweight, or more reliable computer may be just a few months from being introduced and made available. Or a thruster with a two-fold specific impulse (ISP) increase might be just around the corner from completing qualification testing, and if you pull the trigger on thruster selection too soon you miss out on the opportunity to use it for your system. Of course, at some point you need to lock in the design, but don't close out your options right from the start. Keep the trade space open for a while and allow yourself the flexibility to broadly consider your options. After the trades have been completed, if you decide to make a change it'll be change for the better.

Finally, managing this change is a bit like being a car buyer with a salesperson looking to maximize his or her commission. Folks will be trying to sell you everything they can, whether the system needs it or not. There's nothing nefarious going on here (well, normally there isn't), but many advocates for new technologies can provide a million reasons why you should accept inserting their prize into your design. Motivations might include researchers looking for greater amounts of science data (thus necessitating a groundbreaking instrument), or technology developers searching for the right home for a technology they have spent the better part of their career shepherding from birth to maturity. Operators may push for capabilities that make the system more user-friendly, and of course every once in a while, we come across the salesperson actually plying their company's wares. All will have great reasons why the change is necessary or at a minimum desirable, and all will be equally passionate about its benefits. And you will be right in the middle of it all.

In the end, your pursuit of the right systemic solution to fulfill the mission will guide you through this morass of change. All this will take negotiation and integration, two topics previously covered, and a host of other skills I've yet to mention. But I can tell you from experience that it does all come together. Change can be managed, avoided where necessary, and be made to work to your advantage. Through it all the Chief Engineer can stay balanced on top of this mountain and still navigate the project to its goal. It's work, but hey, what isn't?

CHAPTER 10

SHOWING ENTHUSIASM

"**M**an, this is going to be the best damn project NASA has ever had!" was once heard, accompanied by a healthy portion of fist bumps, high fives, and back slaps. Cheers of "huzzah" made the office echo like a Renaissance festival. The atmosphere was electric as the project Chief Engineer, giddy with enthusiasm, brandished the smile of someone who had just been informed they won the lottery.

OK, I just made that up, and I'm not sure we'd ever see an outpouring of enthusiasm quite like that one. But one thing is pretty much true about those who work at NASA—we love our jobs. We love doing what we get to do, and we get paid for it to boot! We're enthusiastic about NASA's mission of science and discovery, about pathfinding and being explorers unlocking the mysteries of the universe and advancing humanity's level of understanding. I would think many of us sparked this passion as kids, spending hours in make-believe play sessions pretending to be astronauts or scientists, living aboard spacecraft en route to distant planets, or traveling to Stockholm to accept a Nobel prize for our discoveries. As we left childhood behind, we all may have taken different paths to get where we are now doing what we always dreamed about doing.*

In a leadership position, Chief Engineers get to be cheerleader, endless supporter, advocate, and biggest fan of whatever the project is doing. They are always onboard as to why NASA is investing in this project, how NASA (and the world) will benefit from the work, and the countless attributes of the project that will make it successful. Chief Engineers can be one of the project's biggest spokespersons, communicating to whoever wants to listen exactly why they should be listening about this project in the first place.

Why is this important? Well, in part, because what we do is terrifically hard and can at times be disheartening. Developing a complex system or experiment is difficult and the path to success is not always easy to navigate or even easy to see. Problems, hurdles, and challenges are

---

* While the Nobel Foundation hasn't yet created a prize category for Engineering, I haven't given up hope.

inevitable in any project and it is very easy for project staff (technical and otherwise) to lose sight of a path forward given those challenges. When this happens, the project can lose momentum, hurdles can become dead ends, and seemingly solvable complications can become insurmountable. And yes, we want to avoid that if we can. When the going gets rough, the project Chief Engineer can always be counted on to raise the team's heads high, motivate them to keep on pressing forward, work the issues/solve the problem, and auger towards success. Again, why is this important? Because project teams consist of people, and people need to see their leadership maintain hope and enthusiasm, especially during times of challenge. The technical team will draw off the enthusiasm (or lack of enthusiasm) of the Chief Engineer. As the Chief Engineer goes, so will the technical team.

At this point I'll ask you: does this all sound a little hokey? Are you thinking to yourself, "This stuff is important but not as important as whether we're converging on our TPMs or whether we're achieving three-sigma performance on the frangible separation nut standard initiator output voltage?" Please be advised—this stuff is important! Ensuring three-sigma performance is important, no doubt, but you have staff and discipline engineers who can maintain the development of your project's NASA Standard Initiator pyrotechnics (a component) and elevate it to you if or when it becomes a concern. Converging on TPMs is important too, but likewise your systems engineers watch these and report on their status at periodic meetings and reviews. I hate to tell you, but there's no one to whom you can delegate the health and attitude of your technical team. That's partly why they hired you and why all projects need a leadership team. It's a people thing, and it's part of your job.

You may be surprised at how much your own attitude can affect the emotional state of your team. There is a spiritual alliance between you and the folks around you. Let's say you come in one morning having not gotten much sleep the previous night. The water heater in your house was leaking and you spent hours emptying buckets of water placed below the unit. If that wasn't enough, your cat caught a stomach virus and deposited multiple "presents" all around the house. You're tired, irritable, and, to top it all off, when you arrived at work the coffee was cold! Thirty minutes later you hold a team status meeting. As you go around the table all you hear are issues, concerns, and problems (which are, incidentally, mostly what you're supposed to hear at a status meeting). So, you respond to these challenges by losing your temper, denigrating your hard-working team, doing some of your own complaining, and cutting the meeting short so you can find some darn hot coffee after throwing up your arms and declaring the project "hopeless!" Understandable, right? You had a sleepless night and you're irritable. Your team is composed of professionals and certainly they understand this and will cut you some slack. Perhaps they will, if you have an experienced and close-knit team. But there's also an equal chance that your negativity will rub off on those around the table. They will pick up on your (momentary) lack of confidence in the project and bring that back to their office, which can affect the enthusiasm of their coworkers.

Let's replay that scenario again, with the same broken water heater/cat throw up/cold coffee Chief Engineer entering the status telecon. You're irritable and short-tempered, but this time you admit that to your team. Recounting the previous night's trials and tribulations, you telecast your emotional state so that they will understand your behavior's origin. Some will commiserate, others will pat you on the back in sympathy, and one precious person even goes out and finds you an actual hot cup of coffee! You bond with your team. At the end of the meeting, you let them know that even though your mood is black you believe in the project and in them, and together you will be successful. Confidence is maintained.

In 2015, we began development of the X-57, the first piloted X-plane developed and flown by NASA since the early 1990s. It is an all-electric aircraft, originated to explore the technologies of electric aviation, identify the manufacturing and operational challenges of such a vehicle, and hopefully foster a new era in aviation. The project began life, interestingly, as a low-TRL feasibility demonstration intended just to see if the darn idea would fly (literally). Originally it eschewed basic project management and engineering practices with an eye to rapid development and "light" management practices. Great, they thought, this is going to be easy! But, of course, someone pointed out that a pilot crew would be aboard—real, honest to gosh human beings—and as such some aspects of airworthiness and safety rigor would need to be built in.

They procured an off-the-shelf airframe from a commercial provider (to save time and money) with plans to fill the fuselage with batteries, remove the two gas turbine engines and replace them with low-torque, high-efficiency electric propulsors. Then they would detach the wing and, in its place, install a composite, high-aspect-ratio airfoil, and line the leading edge of this composite wing with 12 small electric motors that would be needed for takeoff and landing. It was a good plan, but after approximately 18 months of effort the project discovered that this would be harder than they thought. There were no existing aviation standards for the electric propulsors so the project would need to develop their own. The batteries, 270 volts of lithium-ion energy filling three quarters of the fuselage, proved a significant development challenge. More problems arose when the solid-state controllers that would mediate the engine operations wouldn't work properly and required frequent trial and error. Even some of the components that were purchased and didn't necessitate development were problematic, arriving on dock showing evidence of poor workmanship and having to be brought into spec by the NASA workforce themselves. Challenge after challenge after challenge.

But the technical team pressed through all these hurdles, in part (perhaps not a small part) due to the continued belief in the project and unshakable enthusiasm expressed by the Chief Engineer. As I was monitoring all this from HQ, at no time did I see him give up. Instead he remained a steadfast champion of the project even with this chaos swirling around him. He would stand in front of the engineering leadership at Armstrong Flight Research Center and Langley Research Center—the two NASA Centers performing the majority of work on this project—calmly discussing the technical status of the project and what was being done to mitigate the challenges. He always remained upbeat, optimistic that the issues were not insurmountable, and when challenged by his engineering leadership he defended the value of the project and the integrity of the team supporting him. When he came to NASA HQ for a critical milestone briefing, he clearly was the project's biggest fan. In the end, he told a very compelling story about what was needed to get back on track and the plan for getting there, filling the room with confidence that the project was, in fact, in good hands. Man, this guy was good. I took out my notebook and jotted down a few lines about the power of an enthusiastic advocate.

For me, I always try to inject a certain amount of dry humor in my interactions with project, program, and HQ leadership. Certainly, there are times to be serious and eschew humor when it would be inappropriate; you have to tread carefully in those circumstances. But those times are infrequent and in the majority of cases humor can be a powerful elixir for maintaining a positive atmosphere in the room. Most people enjoy the simple pleasure of laughter—it generates endorphins that make us feel good, and the spirit of humor is frequently contagious and can cascade from one person to the next. In short, people like to laugh, and laughter is an effective tool for the Chief Engineer to maintain team spirit and cohesiveness. It's not necessary to offer an unending barrage of jokes or go to comedy school to be an effective Chief Engineer, but the injection of a small amount of humor or the elicitation of an occasion laugh from the team can work wonders. Have you ever been to recurring meetings that were humorless? I have, and while they can effectively convey information, they are also no fun to attend. Alternatively, meetings where humor is allowed and laughter is encouraged are much more enjoyable and satisfying experiences. I dread the former, but actually look forward to the latter.

In Chapter 5, "Demonstrating Knowledge of Systems Engineering," I mentioned the revision to NPR 7123 that we conducted in 2017. If you recall, upon releasing a draft of the revision to the NASA Centers and requesting comments, we were rewarded with over 600 of them. Now, I can tell you going line by line through over 600 comments can be time-consuming and tedious. Ultimately it took us well over 6 weeks to wade through this mountain, breaking it up into 2- or 3-hour sessions spread over a few sessions each week. The "us" in this case was me and two of our contractor supports, brilliant managers and engineers who were involved in the original creation of the NPR and have watched its evolution over the years. Since this review just consisted of the three of us, it was done pretty much informally. (We would occasionally go off on tangential discussions and have to force ourselves back to the subject in question—you know, that kind of informality!) At the beginning of this process I decided to make our tedious task as much fun as possible, and I did that by frequently injecting humor. I found I could make my two counterparts laugh, and I enjoyed doing so just as much as they enjoyed laughing. I did this as often as I could, and the positive affirmation I got from laughter was as nice as any reward for hard work could be. The laughter made a potentially very dull task much more enjoyable, and I truly believe they enjoyed having to sift through these comments because we made it fun. It could have been a laborious job and sometimes it was, but ultimately it was a fun one, in part because I consciously helped make it so. Our enthusiasm never wavered.

Sometimes what you see on the surface is not always an indicator of what's occurring beneath. While at HQ, I often had the occasion to work with one Deputy Program Manager responsible for a sizable portfolio of small, finite-duration technology development projects. This gentleman had been at HQ for many years, was well-experienced, and intimately knew the world of technology development. He was a good man, a very competent manager, but always seemed to be passed over when leadership opportunities opened up. The immediate impression one would get when meeting with him was that this gentleman was blessed (or cursed) with a quiet, no nonsense disposition. He spoke in pure monotone, his voice never rising or falling or indicating any emotion (happy or sad). His face remained resolute, never offering any sense of satisfaction or displeasure. He was a rock; a competent rock and a good, decent rock, but a rock nonetheless. But here's the thing: once you got to know him a bit and saw him when he was more relaxed you came to realize that he actually had a fantastic sense of humor—a bit dry and sardonic, perhaps, but capable of making almost anyone laugh. That humor was hidden behind his rocklike façade, but it was there and accessible if you only invested a bit of time to know him. He seemed dour on the outside but was actually optimistic and hopeful on the inside and often spoke in those terms even if his face and voice denoted a different perspective. His surface persona said one thing, but the individual inside said something very different. Once I got past what was on the surface and got to know the individual on the inside, my perspective of him changed dramatically.

Enthusiasm is both a stimulus for excitement when plentiful and an emulsifier for apathy when lacking. It can work in both directions quite effectively, which is partly why it is so important a characteristic for the Chief Engineer to manage. Plentiful enthusiasm can draw a project out of the doldrums, elevate it to high achievement when problems occur, and maintain esprit de corps throughout all the peaks and valleys. Lack of enthusiasm can de-escalate excitement, compound simple issues into complex ones, and result in slowing progress. Enthusiasm is a commodity that must be allocated, portioned, managed, and maintained. It is a measure not of the technical performance of the system under development but of the potential for effectiveness of the team.

Chief Engineers need to monitor the levels of enthusiasm in their projects just as studiously as they do mass margin or other technical measures. Margins and technical measures are an objective assessment supported by data and demonstrable facts, while enthusiasm is a subjective assessment based on perceptions and empathy. That alone makes this a difficult task for many Chief Engineers who are used to working in the objective, fact-based world. But difficult or not it has to be done. Look, think about it this way: it's a risk, so manage as you would any other risk.

How is this done? What signs should a Chief Engineer look for that may indicate the lack of enthusiasm on your technical team? Here is a list of warning signs to watch for.

- **Your team members stop taking initiative.** While not everyone on your team will be a highly self-motivated go-getter, enthusiastic teams generally solve their own problems. They don't wait around for leadership to mitigate or fix the issues they are contending with, but rather take it upon themselves to find those solutions and bring recommendations to their leadership for consideration and decision. An enthusiastic team will offer you solutions (or a variety of solutions) and then your task is to approve or disapprove. But if you see your team sitting back, not solving their problems or bringing forth solutions or options, it may be an indication of the lack of enthusiasm.

- **Your team members withdraw or uncouple from the work at hand.** Enthusiastic technical teams stay engaged with the project and the work they are to perform. They get up each morning looking forward to the challenges awaiting them and arrive ready to make progress. Some may even show up early or stay late because it's hard for them to disengage. A warning sign in this area is if you notice people wandering into the office an hour after they arrive to work, take frequent leisurely lunch breaks, or start to call in sick. If you find folks avoiding their work, it may be an indication of the lack of enthusiasm.
- **Your team members stop offering ideas and/or opinions.** Enthusiastic team members are contributors. They relish the opportunity to provide input, make suggestions, improve how things are done, and offer alternative solutions to vexing problems. Enthusiasm spawns creativity and a desire to share what that creativity produces. Additionally, contributing team members feed off each other, acting as built-in filters to sanity-check ideas. That, to many engineers, is just as enjoyable as providing the input itself. The willingness to provide input and opinion is a marked indication of an engaged team. If your team stops offering ideas or opinions, it may be an indication of the lack of enthusiasm.

Last, take the opportunity to celebrate successes, even small successes. Doing so doesn't mean throwing a party every week simply because you and your team have survived another 5 days. But successes will come to your team in the form of passing milestone reviews and receiving authority to proceed to the next development phase, or delivering on a product that necessitated near constant negotiation, or clearing a demonstration test that truly tested the mettle of your entire team. Don't pass up the opportunity to celebrate these significant events or wave them off as "just part of the job." Recognize the team and their work, show them that hard work and persistence is rewarded. Perhaps, after a successful test, take a piece of the test hardware and distribute it to your team for them to proudly display. And yes, hold a party occasionally to give them a chance to relax and catch their breath. To quote Ralph Waldo Emerson, "Nothing great was ever achieved without enthusiasm."[*]

---

[*] Ralph Waldo Emerson, "Circles," in *The Essential Writings of Ralph Waldo Emerson* (New York: Random House, 2000), 262.

CHAPTER 11

LEARNING CONTINUOUSLY

Life is like a painter's canvas that is never fully completed. The colors go on, forms appear and come into contrast, but the full extent of the picture is never completely revealed. There is always more room to paint, more modifications and elaborations to make, more variations in color scheme to experiment with. The painter gains more and more experience but never completely reaches the level of mastery. Even if the painting appears to be nearly finished, the painter continues striving for greater perfection, greater clarity of subject, and further mastery of the art. The painter, like the painting, are a continuous work in progress. So are we.

In engineering as in life, our competencies and experiences provide the basis for how well we conduct our job. We combine these competencies obtained through our work, along with the experience we gain every day to produce a Chief Engineer who is knowledgeable, competent, a purveyor of critical skills, and an accumulation of wisdom.

But the fact of the matter is that while we strive for excellence and hope to attain a level of competency marked by that excellence, we can't ever expect to fully reach that goal. There is no "relax and just coast" moment. Yes, experienced Chief Engineers don't need to ask for permission to offer an opinion or make a decision, they already contain the knowledge required to do both. But there is always more to learn, more experience to be gained, more wisdom to obtain. We are never complete in this category, and we should never expect to be complete. We can always improve, always get better, even up to the day of our retirement. We must continuously learn.

Chief Engineers do a lot of learning. At the beginning of our careers many of us start as discipline engineers, focusing on one specific area of vehicle design or operations and spending years getting so familiar with that area that the understanding is almost intuitive. Overlaying that discipline knowledge, we learn design principles, engineering standards, best practices and procedures, and found ways to put that knowledge to work. As we mature, a number of us stretch beyond that discipline knowledge and learn how to interface with other disciplines. In the process we get exposed to design principles, standards and best practices beyond our field of expertise. We learn more about what works and what doesn't and why. As an interdisciplinary engineer we expand the boundaries of what is possible and add new constraints and limitation. We evolve to understand engineering at the integrated system level, learning at each step along the way.

While Chief Engineers spend most of their days concentrating on the technical aspects of the system under development, we also get some exposure to the other legs of the project management stool—predominantly cost and schedule. We learn about critical path, about the benefits and risks incumbent in make/buy decisions, and about the project management and decision-making processes that our technical baselines feed. We get exposed to ideas beyond just our engineering responsibilities and become more competent NASA assets because of that knowledge.

Along the way we learn about leadership, team-building, and interpersonal skills, and we get more experienced at being a Chief Engineer. Wisdom is gained through that experience, and wisdom pushes us to want more. To feed that desire, we start seeking knowledge from others outside our fields of expertise, even outside of NASA, searching for commonalities and differences, comparing and contrasting, and better understanding the art of the possible. We attend conferences and symposiums, we read trade journals and textbooks, and we talk to peers across the engineering community sharing knowledge and experience.

We learn, and we grow, and we never stop learning and growing. Occasionally we may even reinvent ourselves, jumping to a new task or responsibility that requires a whole new set of skills. And we never get satisfied or complacent with where we are, but continuously strive to improve and to better understand the world, ourselves, and the roles and responsibilities handed to us. It takes a lifetime to become an exemplary Chief Engineer, and even then we can still learn more.

While the responsibility for continuous learning may not be on your position description, it is an expectation for any Chief Engineer.

When I was supporting Shuttle missions in Mission Control, I noted two varieties of flight controllers. Earning your certification to work on console in Mission Control is an arduous task, necessitating years of training in a high-stress environment leading up to rigorous evaluations before being considered certified. The first variety of flight controller perceived this process as a long set of stairs to be climbed with a door at the top. Get certified and you pass through the door. You've arrived, tired and beat up from the arduous climb, but you've arrived. While that view is understandable, this perception is actually self-defeating. The second variety of flight controller, alternatively, viewed the process again as a staircase and a door, but in this case the door was situated at the bottom. Getting certified opens the door, but then the flight controller is faced with a long climb of stairs that can be thought of as the experience, seasoning, and learned judgement that produces a good controller. The first variety of controller will be adequate, the second variety will be exceptional. The point here is that certification, allowing you to conduct the responsibilities in Mission Control, is just the beginning of the process. Yes, it took a year or two of constant training to get to this point, but having reached this level the "exceptional" flight controllers recognize that they still need to learn, to get better, to attain experience and improve upon the minimal baseline that is established through certification. The adequate flight controllers didn't understand this; the exceptional ones did.

I think you get the point. Learning is a lifelong activity. Don't stop. Ever.

The need to continuously learn doesn't stop when you get to NASA HQ. Here, I have interacted with any number of senior leaders from across the Agency and have found some who value and abide by this continuous learning expectation. But others (a few anyway) fail to live up to that standard. My guess is that they feel they have reached a point in their career at which any additional learning would be wasted. They are a sponge saturated with experience and anything additional would be either redundant, superfluous, or non-value added. They may even be insulted by the suggestion that there is more they can learn. And when faced with opportunities for additional learning they may become hesitant and can actually walk away from opportunities. This viewpoint is, of course, self-defeating and is born of a twinge of arrogance. Eventually, these folks may get presented with a new challenge they are not prepared for, one that requires a different skill set, and then these leaders come face-to-face with the recognition that a long career may not prepare them for all eventualities. There is always more that can be learned.

There are multitudes of opportunities for continuous learning at NASA. At the Agency level there is the APPEL Knowledge Services, which offers a large catalog of formal and informal training courses on project management and systems engineering. SATERN (System for Administration, Training, and Educational Resources for NASA) is where you can sign up for even more courses covering technical, management, and even leadership topics, many of which are available online or as computer-based training. Most NASA Center training curricula are based on both APPEL and SATERN courses and all NASA personnel should avail themselves of these learning opportunities.

Opportunities outside of NASA can also be fantastic means to increase your acumen on just about any subject. This can include coursework outside of those available on APPEL or SATERN, conferences, symposiums and lectures, or even opportunities to witness management and engineering in practice throughout industry, academia or other Government agencies by participating in temporary assignments or work exchanges. These opportunities can offer you the chance to expand your experience base, witness alternative practices, and gain new perspectives. Furthermore, mentorship (see Chapter 4, "Getting a Mentor/ Being a Mentor") can similarly provide fresh perspectives.

Taken collectively there is an ocean (maybe a galaxy?) of learning opportunities out there. You'll never run out of opportunities and new one gets added all the time. But you have to make an effort to seek them out, reach towards that available knowledge, and become a better and more experienced engineer and manager. If you stop learning, you stop improving.

One of the greatest learning opportunities I had the chance to participate in was the Project Management Challenge (PMC). The PMC was an Agency-wide symposium held each year at a different location near a NASA Center. It utilized a conference format and, lasting 3 days or so, offered numerous lectures on a wide variety of project management topics. Most topics were presented by existing NASA project managers, engineers, or scientists, who crafted their discussions around their ongoing projects and the lessons learned from their experiences. PowerPoint charts were made available to all who registered for the PM Challenge and could be reviewed even if you missed the presentation itself. However, it was far more effective listening to the presentations real-time, hearing the speakers and witnessing their enthusiasm. Every year I would attend the PM Challenge and every year I would learn something new about project management, risk management, cost/schedule management, political management, personnel management—just about everything needed to be an effective manager at NASA. I never left these conferences without obtaining some new knowledge or transferred wisdom. Regrettably, due to budgetary and political considerations, NASA ceased to conduct these multiday symposia. The PMC exists today only as a virtual activity focused on a single topic. I've always felt we lost a lot of ability to communicate experience and best practices when we stopped holding the annual PM Challenge conferences.

Sometimes learning opportunities come to you and sometimes you have to go to them. A number of us use Individual Development Plans (IDPs), which can include designated—occasionally required—training activities available through SATERN or Center training curricula. The majority of these are focused training activities, formal courses with specific learning objectives, with some even offering college credit for having taken the course. They are structured, repeatable (everyone gets the same message), and available on a regularly scheduled basis. Alternatively, other training opportunities can come with little to no warning and maybe once-in-a-career opportunities. For example, a famous author on spaceflight history came by NASA HQ for a single-day discussion on the organization causes of some of NASA's greatest tragedies. There was little notice of this event, and once I became aware it, I had to rearrange my schedule for that day (which I did gleefully) so that I was available to attend. It impacted my schedule and some of my tasks, but boy did I learn a lot from the discussion.

In 2017, as we were preparing to initiate the revision effort of NPR 7123, I had the opportunity to attend a presentation given by a former NASA HQ Chief Engineer. This person, by this time already long retired, returned to the fold for a few days to reflect on NASA systems engineering. (As a side benefit, he threw in a few tidbits on leadership as well; I took notes.) I had been responsible for NPR 7123 and its associated handbook for almost 5 years and over that time I had learned a lot about our Agency's expectations on programs and projects. I was intimately familiar with the content of both documents and I thought I knew everything there was to know about NASA systems engineering. Boy, was I wrong.

Within 15 minutes of this gentleman's presentation it was clear I was largely ignorant of one critical aspect of our engineering policies—the original intent of the policies when they were first established. The presenter was around when NPR 7123 was first created and he regaled us at length on why the policy requirements, many of which we still had on the book, were originally established. He explained that the policy was created within the NASA culture of the late 1990s and early 2000s, and the intent of creating it was to drive out certain undesired behaviors evident at the time. Many of those deleterious behaviors had in fact been eliminated over the course of the years, and yet we still maintained those same requirements on the books. After listening to his presentation, our revision team took another look at our engineering policies and sought to validate their relevance. Clearly, I didn't know everything there was to know about NASA systems engineering policy, and what I learned made me better able to continue owning the responsibility for its management.

Beyond the benefits that continuous learning bestows on us as leaders, we also need to encourage it among our team. It's within your ability to make it easy for your team to partake in learning activities by lowering any barriers that may be inhibiting them. While each member of your technical team performs critical tasks, many of them time-critical, it is up to you to ensure that the overall technical development doesn't grind to a halt just because one of your team is participating in a multi-day class or attending a technical conference in a different city. You have it within your control as Chief Engineer to ensure team members have the opportunity to pursue continuous learning. And further, there is no better way to encourage continuous learning within your team than by attending some yourself. Be seen attending learning opportunities, and your team is likely to emulate that behavior.

You know how passionate and dedicated our technical teams can be concerning their work. Some of them have to be shown the door at the end of the day so that they go home. That same passion for their work can inhibit the need to occasionally drop what they're doing and avail themselves of learning opportunities. Let them know, nicely, that the team will get by in their absence for a short while. Just as you would shepherd a hard-working team member out the door after a long day so that they can get some dinner and enjoy quality time with their family, you might equally need to herd a team member toward a learning activity. This small act not only matures your team but also shows them that you care about their development. These are no small acts of empathy.

In fact, there's no reason why your technical team has to break their rhythm and leave the confines of the project to learn. Make learning a part of their job. Assuming you have a matrixed team, this is partly the responsibility of your team members' direct supervisors. But the Chief Engineer can play a role as well through counsel, encouragement, and the example you set. When any of your technical team comes across information worth sharing, be it a new discovery or a lesson learned, an unexpected test result or a critical decision, encourage them to share the information. It's likely that everyone can benefit (i.e., learn) from the information. What's more, it is also possible to stand the team down occasionally to facilitate learning. This doesn't need to take the form of formal courses or lectures but can instead be informal discussions where any of your team can share something new that they learned. It may be possible to do this too often—the engineering work on the project is important too after all—but this can (and should) be done routinely, not just once. Sharing information increases a group's corporate knowledge, and it keeps the team thinking about new ideas and flexing that most important muscle in the human body (i.e., the brain!). This is the genesis of the idea of Pause and Learn, or PAL, used widely in the corporate world.

When I was a Space Shuttle flight controller, our group would get together once a month for what we euphemistically called "Stump the Chump." During each of these sessions, one or two people would bring in a simulation scenario or failure case they experienced on console during a training session. They would outline the events that occurred, what failed and when, and the other maladies affecting the Space Shuttle during that simulation. Without providing the answer of what course of action they eventually took, we would go around the room and everyone would pose a suggested action. Some were good, some were not (although maybe good for a round of laughs). But we all learned. We would hold Stump the Chump sessions every month and they became a standard part of our job, even though they were learning opportunities.

You might think removing people from the all-heads-down focus our work demands so that they can learn would be disruptive, but it isn't. It's easy to integrate learning into the cadence of your team's day-to-day work. Almost everything can be a learning activity for one person or another, and having a more experienced, more adept team will only reap benefits that will pay off as the project progresses. You can have a junior person shadow a more experienced one, have group discussions in lieu of hallway one-on-ones, widely share discrepancy reports and test failures, whatever! All of these can inform and integrate most technical teams. Don't view these learning opportunities as distractions, taking your team away from their job or immediate task; instead, view such activities as a means to provide a better team.

CHAPTER 12
SERVING AS A TECHNICAL AUTHORITY

Technical Authority was forged from the literal ashes of the Space Shuttle Columbia after that magnificent ship and her beloved crew were violently ripped apart over the western United States and rained debris over Texas and Louisiana. The immediate cause of the tragedy was traced to a sizable portion of foam shed during launch by the External Tank, striking the heat-resistant Reinforced Carbon-Carbon leading edge of Columbia's left wing and damaging it sufficiently to allow superheated hot gases to enter the wing and mid-body structure during reentry. This, of course, destroyed the vehicle.

The loss of Columbia and her crew during Space Shuttle mission STS-107 was a horrific but seminal moment in the lives of everyone who worked on the Space Shuttle program. While the hardware failure that led to the accident was technical, it was the associated organizational (and human) failures that were the real root causes. It was the perception of inviolability, the belief that "it hasn't hurt us in the past so therefore we're OK," that truly prevented Columbia and her crew from returning home. Organizationally, those who knew the vehicle was being operated outside of certification (foam impacts) and tried to raise the alarm were closeted and shut down by elements whose main focus was ensuring the program remained on schedule to constructing the International Space Station. Before STS-107, technical teams reported through programmatic chains, through the program manager. After STS-107, NASA created Technical Authorities to ensure a separate path of reporting for issues of safety and mission success. This process created three Technical Authorities—one for Health and Medical, one for Safety and Mission Assurance, and a third for Engineering. In many projects, the Chief Engineer carries the responsibilities as ETA.

As Chief Engineer you will carry a host of responsibilities, but none might be more important or more sobering than representing ETA. It doesn't get any more serious than this. You are to provide assistance and independent oversight of programs and projects in support of safety and mission success. Independent of whom or what, you may ask? Programmatic authority, defined generally as the NASA Mission Directorates and the program and project offices they fund, have authority over those missions and ultimate responsibility for their success. But there are many forces that impose pressures on programs and projects, not the least of which includes delivering on schedule and at/under cost, including the various political forces that are ever present. As Chief Engineer, beyond managing the technical team and the technical development of a project, you also bear the responsibility of overseeing safety and mission success and have the ability (actually, the responsibility) to elevate issues, ideally within and in concert with the programmatic authority, but if absolutely necessary outside the programmatic authority all the way to the NASA Administrator. You know the saying, "If it isn't safe, say so." Well, that's your job.

Note the wording taken from the *NASA Spaceflight Program and Project Management Handbook*, (SP-2014-3705), The ETA establishes and is responsible for the engineering design processes, specifications, rules, best practices, and other activities necessary to fulfill programmatic mission performance requirements."*

ETA starts with the NASA Administrator and then is delegated to lower levels—first to the NASA Associate Administrator, then to the NASA Chief Engineer, then to all HQ positions. From there the responsibilities incumbent in ETA are normally delegated to each individual Center Director, who further usually delegates those responsibilities to a person within their Center, normally the Center Chief Engineer or the Center Director of Engineering (it differs from Center to Center). From there, ETA lands in your lap as the ETA for the program or project you support. While this series of delegation is normal, delegation does not mean abdication, and those who delegate do not give up the individual responsibility and authority with which they are entrusted. They remain accountable and participate in the TA chain.

Confusing? It really isn't. It just means that the NASA Chief Engineer or Center Director (or even Center Engineering Director)

---

* NASA Space Flight Program and Project Management Handbook, Section 5.2.7.1, *https://ntrs.nasa.gov/archive/nasa/casi.ntrs.nasa.gov/20150000400.pdf*, (accessed October 23, 2019).

cannot maintain insight to everything that goes on to provide sufficient independent oversight. But while they can delegate down the chain (to you, for instance, at the program or project level), they do not give up their accountability in ensuring safety and mission success. Lots of communication has to happen to ensure TA is conducted adequately through the delegated levels, but that's part of the job too.

If or when issues do come up that affect safety or mission success, can the ETA, wielding the banner of TA, just decide on the issue and that's it? Well, no. Remember, the programmatic authority has the overall responsibility for the success of the project and, as such, gets to decide all matters affecting the project. But that doesn't mean the Chief Engineer has to agree, and if he or she determines that the decision in fact does inappropriately affect safety or mission success, or if one of his/her technical team strongly disagrees with the decision, ETA then makes it the responsibility and obligation of the Chief Engineer to elevate the issue to a higher organizational authority. This is where the TA chain comes into play. Issues concerning safety and mission success can be elevated all along the TA chain, from the project to the Center Chief Engineer or Engineering Director, and then to the Center Director, and if required to HQ and all the way to the NASA Administrator. The TA provides for this conduit to the top of the Agency if necessary to ensure that these critical issues are adequately heard, understood, and adjudicated. At NASA, this is called the Dissenting Opinion. The process does not guarantee satisfaction, it does not ensure that ETA always gets their way, but it does ensure that all parties are heard and that critical issues and concerns can be elevated all the way to the head of the Agency if required. As I said, that is both a responsibility and an obligation, and it's a heavy one, to carry particularly when issues may be contentious. But it is a vital one for the Chief Engineer to understand.

The "authority" in the TA does imply some final say. While that's not necessarily true in project decisions (which can be elevated through the Dissenting Opinion path), ETA does provide for authority in approving waivers of or deviations to technical standards. This occurs many times in projects when existing technical standards may not be applicable and might be waived, or when circumstances such as design limitations, insufficient schedule, or unavailable resources might result in managers seeking relief. It is the ETA, the Chief Engineer (or higher if it is not delegated) who "owns" these technical standards. Any waivers or deviations to these technical standards need to get the approval of the applicable ETA, who can approve the request or may reject the request if they feel the rationale or risk is not substantiated.

So, what are the day-to-day responsibilities of an ETA within a project? First and foremost, they are expected to keep their chain of authority informed on issues as they arise. This could be a program Chief Engineer, your Center's Director of Engineering or Center Chief Engineer, or all of them, depending on how ETA is implemented at your Center. But awareness and communication are the keys here—these folks need to know what you know, maybe not in the exquisite detail or level of understanding you have on an issue, but of sufficient understanding to grasp the elements of the concern. Remember, your immediate superior has the same responsibility—to keep their superior informed—so don't cut corners here. Beyond that, responsibilities include the following:

1. serving as a member of program or project control boards and change boards;
2. working with your Center management and other TAs (S&MA, H&M) to ensure the quality and integrity of project processes, products, and standards related to engineering reflect the standards of excellence of the NASA TA community;
3. ensuring that requests for waivers of and deviations from TA requirements are submitted by the program and project and are acted upon by the appropriate level of TA;
4. assisting the program or project with making risk-informed decisions that properly balance technical merit, cost, schedule, and safety;
5. providing the program or project with your views based on your knowledge and experience; and

6. raising or elevating a Dissenting Opinion where significant, substantive, and appropriate disagreement exists.*

Performing the above ensures you serve as an effective part of NASA's overall system of checks and balances.

And checks and balances are what it's all about. Prior to the loss of Columbia and her crew, the program or project managers had the final say over everything. Well, they still have final say over everything, NASA policy places ultimate responsibility for the success of missions in the hands of our program and project managers. But the pressures of delivering a capability on time and on cost obviated and previously overcame some other very important considerations, such as safety, so now there are alternate paths to elevate concerns. For example, for the Space Shuttle program, there was political pressure by the early 2000s to reduce the tremendous infrastructure and workforce costs that the program was facing. This reduction was being driven from the highest levels of Government, from appropriators in Congress and from the Office of Management and Budget (OMB), so the pressure on the program's managers was palpable. Various measures were taken, some effective and some less so, but one measure that was enacted as a cost reduction was to cap and reduce the size of the Safety, Reliability and Quality Assurance (SR&QA) organization. These reductions were draconian to the extent that there was a real threat that SR&QA couldn't adequately perform its function. Did this directly cause the Columbia accident? Of course not. But it did contribute to a culture of prioritizing cost and schedule over safety, which was the main reason TA was put into place.

Today, the three Technical Authorities have more say over things like the approval of waivers to and deviations from technical standards, but also now have direct conduits to senior Agency decision-makers for elevating concerns. Before the accident everything had to go through the program and project managers—now, if a concern is critical enough, it can be elevated beyond the PMs so that thorough, risk-based

---

* Paraphrasing from the *PM Handbook*, Section 5.2.

discussions can occur. Would occur. Will occur. That, my friends, is a check and balance.

Does TA work? Pretty well, in my mind. It doesn't prevent all problems from occurring, but it does provide organizational resilience such that our success as an Agency has improved. It is a safety net, to some extent, and difficult to quantify in terms of accidents or mission failures prevented, but it has helped ensure that anyone with data and concerns can have those concerns heard and discussed.

The fundamental principles of TA aren't just focused on project management vs. TA interactions; these principles can also work within and among the three TAs. A case in point is the X-59, the Low Boom Flight Demonstrator supersonic aircraft NASA is developing to show that the noise on the ground created by sonic booms can be attenuated to the point of acceptability by the general public. During design of this aircraft the Office of Chief Health and Medical Officer (OCHMO, the Health and Medical TA) pointed out that human systems integration (HSI) wasn't being properly considered. For example, there were no specific requirements for HSI or HSI standards for the project to meet, nor were there any designated HSI experts on the design team. OCHMO raised the concern that many aircraft accidents have been caused as a result of overlooking HSI considerations and questioned why more focus wasn't being applied to this for X-59.

The design (that is, engineering) teams, on the other hand, observed that the historical aircraft design processes did include HSI considerations in their own way through qualitative discussions with pilots and ground technicians, and that it's always worked pretty well. As Chief Engineer for Aeronautics, while I have a huge amount of respect and trust in NASA's cadre of aircraft designers and researchers (I mean that, I do!), I also thought the OCHMO folks had a point, so I helped them elevate the issue above the level of the X-59 project. Ultimately, a gap analysis was performed by an independent engineering organization (the NASA Engineering and Safety Center) that identified a number of design and operational shortcomings, and those were fed back to the project. To their credit, the project took those findings to heart and incorporated a number of recommendations, including the assignment of an HSI-lead to the project who is responsible for continuous oversight of HSI. Did this sequence of events prevent an accident or loss of mission objectives? We may never know. But did we increase the probability of success of the project? I'm pretty sure we did. And did the process of elevating technical concerns of safety and mission success work here? I think it absolutely did! The point is that this issue was a concern not between the project office and ETA but between OCHMO and engineer (both TAs).

As a Chief Engineer, many of your technical team members will defer to you on critical decisions. You're the Chief Engineer, after all, you didn't get there playing pachinko machines in Tokyo (an old joke, sorry). You got there because of your experience and abilities. While that deference is true for your technical team, it's not always true for the other elements that make up a project (such as project management, program planning and control, procurement, legal). Many of those elements carry responsibilities for project success not related to the technical, and many of their concerns may run in conflict with yours. While TA doesn't ameliorate all these potential conflicts, it does provide some amount of organizational authority for your decisions, specifically where they affect technical standards and maintenance of the project's technical baseline. Because of the importance of accepted NASA or industry technical standards, a project manager can't simply dictate that the project won't follow a standard because it costs more or other such rationale. TA puts you in charge of adherence to the technical standards applied to the project. In short, you own them. No Project Planning and Control person can mandate that a standard be waived, and, more important, no project manager can do so either. A project manager certainly can elevate their desire to a higher authority for discussion and dispensation (back to Dissenting Opinion), but they can't simply waive a project technical standard. As a TA, you have the responsibility of determining what the system will adhere to and what it should not.

In that light, however, it's necessary to remember that attaining technical performance is not the only objective to be met. A project runs on resources and lives by a schedule, neither of which are infinite. Sensible trades must be made between technical performance and the resources allocated to the project. Adherence to a technical standard might make complete sense from the standpoint of the system's meeting its technical requirements but try to keep in mind that doing so will require funding and schedule that the project may simply not have. It's a balance, all of which equate to mission success in the end. A Chief Engineer carries much responsibility in ensuring the technical solution produces a system that meets mission goals but is also a team player and understands that projects can fail just as well because they ran out of money as because the system didn't perform adequately. Be judicious on which technical standards you hold fast and firm.

It's also important to know that there are limitations on what TA can accomplish. As I said, the existence of TA doesn't guarantee the satisfaction of those raising an issue or concern. It doesn't guarantee that they will get their desired result. All it does guarantee is that they will be heard. The Orion propulsion system is a good example. During the long development of the Orion spacecraft, it was determined by the technical team that a serial prop tank design would be established as the baseline; that is, one tank feeds into a second tank that then feeds the engine system, as opposed to both tanks feeding the engine in a parallel design. Previous human spacecraft utilized a parallel propulsion tank design for reasons of redundancy and reliability, but Orion selected a serial design because of mass limitations and other technical factors. The designers of the spacecraft felt that a serial design would still meet the reliability requirements, even though there was now only a single path from tank to engine, and the project leadership bought the solution (a parallel design would have increased mass and extended the schedule considerably, risking the project delivery commitment date). Well, the astronaut office (who, admittedly, would ultimately bear the brunt of this risk), did not agree and elevated their concern over this serial tank design to the program and then to Headquarters.

The "serial vs. parallel" discussion went to the highest levels of NASA and involved considerable discussion, both technical and programmatic, held over many months. Ultimately, once all sides had their say, the decision was to stick with the serial design and accept the additional technical risk that this design would create. Normally, the discussion would end there and we would applaud the process for working. But, in this case, it didn't end there, and the crew office continued to dissent, elevating the issue again and again. I can't blame them, because absolutely no one had more to risk on this then the eventual crews flying onboard the spacecraft. No argument there. But, the dissenting opinion process did what it was established to do, it allowed for differing viewpoints on issues of safety and mission success to be heard and discussed. And that happened, maybe not to the satisfaction of the crew office, but it happened; all parties were heard by the top of NASA leadership and a decision was made.

Remember, there are two other organizations that make up TA. It's not all about Engineering. The Office of Safety and Mission Assurance (OSMA) and the OCHMO are the other components that make up the TA triumvirate. They, like Engineering, also are responsible for their technical standards and play an equal role within TA to that of the Chief Engineer. They are your peers and partners, collaborators and siblings. When a question comes up that requires TA resolution, it may not always be obvious to your associates on the programmatic side which of the three TAs to go to, so you may have to work this out among yourselves. Still, I have always found my counterparts in OSMA and OCHMO partners in this endeavor, each recognizing the importance of TA and the burden of responsibility placed on us by NASA governance. You may not always have the same viewpoint about every issue, but they are your partners in this grand endeavor called TA. Work with them.

Similarly, get to know your Center's Engineering Director (ED) or Center Chief Engineer. They are typically in the line of authority for issues concerning ETA and are your first stop when elevating issues and concerns. They can advise and consent, can help work issues within the realm of ETA, and also act as a conduit to the higher levels (particularly the Center Director and the NASA HQ Chief Engineer). You may interact with your Center ED through status reporting at monthly engineering reviews or at other forums, but regardless, get to know them. They are part of the epoxy that holds the TA infrastructure together.

Lastly, while serving as ETA is a responsibility, it isn't one that should frighten you. Yes, there are authorities incumbent in being a TA and there are many elements of "the buck stops here," which admittedly can be intimidating. Also, TAs carry the burden of being the front-line defense on safety and mission success and that's no small responsibility. But, don't sweat it. Most of the time being an ETA runs in the background to everything else. You do it without even realizing it, and only occasionally do circumstances dictate that you have to reveal your TA label. Know that the authority is there but keep it in the background until it is necessary to brandish the TA label. Then, do so with resolve.

CHAPTER 13
MAINTAINING FAIRNESS

What does it mean to be fair? When members of your team come to you with recommendations, you are open to their ideas and give them full consideration based on the merit of those ideas, limiting any biases you might have that would impede impartiality. When negotiating between two solutions you actively listen to both sides and allow each adequate time to make their case. When your superiors give you an action that you decide to delegate, you hand that action off responsibly and without motivation of retribution or favoritism. When you are praised and you want to focus that praise on your team, you find ways to recognize the entire team. When you act, you act in an equitable fashion based on what is good for the project, the team, and the system under development.

You are fair. You are impartial. You seek evidence from objective data. You give everyone an equal opportunity to have their say and make their case. You don't allow your internal biases to get in the way of rational and effective decision-making. You are ethical. You lead fairly, you decide fairly, you delegate fairly, and you choose fairly. Furthermore, you have no less than the same expectations of everyone among your technical team and you strive to enforce that impartiality. You are the exemplar of fair.

Those are great ideals, but let's be fair. See what I did there? It's not always easy to be completely fair in every circumstance. Sometimes, conditions dictate taking sides or making a decision based on your personal judgement. Fair enough. (OK, I'll stop.) But, whenever you can, strive to be fair and impartial, if for no other reason than Chief Engineers are expected to be fair. But more important, because fairness is an attribute of good leadership.

Why is it important to be fair? Well, simply, exemplary leaders maintain fairness in their decisions and their interactions. Fairness is a critical (maybe the most critical) component in building and maintaining functional and high-performing teams. The inability to be fair is one of the greatest hazards to a functional and high-performing organization. Think about teams you have been on in the past in which leadership didn't promote or demonstrate fairness. Resentment builds, trust diminishes, team dynamics become caustic, productivity decreases, and work slows (or in the worst case, actually stops). My guess is that at some point in your career you all have been in this sort of dynamic and it's typically not difficult to pinpoint the failure to the leader's lack of fairness. A lack of fairness on the part of leadership can be toxic to a team.

How do you go about being fair? Well, not to be glib, but simply, don't be unfair. Check your favoritism at the door. Understand what biases you may have in a situation and eliminate the influence they may exert over you. Know the people on the team and treat each of them devoid of any negative interactions you may have had in the past. Understand how politics or external influences may be driving your decision and tempter those influences. Recognize any negative implications of your decisions on your team before you make them and consider the impact. Finally, know yourself and how these causes of unfairness may be leading you to unfair decisions and insulate yourself from those forces.

Easy, right? Of course it's not. It's completely consistent with human nature to be influenced by those subtle (sometimes not-so-subtle) forces that drive our behavior. But the key is preventing those influences from dictating your behavior. It means recognizing when, where, and how you may be dealing with a situation unfairly, and cognitively correcting those impulses so that you can remain fair. Does this mean not trusting your gut? No, gut feelings and intuition are all the result of your life's experience and should not be ignored. But even decisions made on gut feelings can be fed through the fairness filter to ensure they are impartial and objective.

Now, what does this mean in an engineering sense? Here are a few examples.

- You're working through generating your project's requirements, heading to an eventual Systems Requirements Review, and NASA HQ sends a high priority request for your project to investigate adding a new instrument to your system. You need someone from your team to assess the capability requirements for this new instrument, the new demands this instrument will place on your system (e.g., mass, power, thermal), and the feasibility of integrating the instrument. You have any number of qualified technical members on your team to hand this task to and it's your job to select one. If you always hand high priority tasks to the same person because they're your drinking buddy and you want constant recognition to come their way, you are not being fair. If you avoid handing a high priority task to someone who annoys you, you are not being fair. If you give the task to someone who clearly communicated to you that they are struggling to keep up with their present workload because that person is friends with the guy who annoys you, you are not being fair.

- You're chairing the project Engineering Review Board and the team is deciding on whether to add additional redundancy to a critical component. The discussion is rich with debate on the criticality of the component, fault tolerance, reliability, and possible penalties on the component if this additional redundancy is added. Everyone is participating. If you disparage the input of one of your team because that person didn't like a previous decision of yours, you are not being fair. If you choose one design and reject others because the advocate of the design went to the same college as you, you are not being fair. If you reject the recommendation from someone on your team who resides at a NASA Center you've never particularly respected, you are not being fair.

- A technology your team developed is being recognized as an especially innovative solution. Praise is extended from your Center Director and from the highest levels of NASA management. You can select one person from your team to travel to NASA HQ to receive the recognition on behalf of the others. If you select that person because they are also on your after-work softball team, you are not being fair. If your team collectively nominates the person who came up with the idea of the technology, but you select someone else, you are not being fair. If you choose yourself because you've never been to NASA HQ and relish the opportunity, you are not being fair.

- The project risk manager is discussing with you which of the project technical risks should be included in the "top risk list." The risk manager is tracking 110 technical risks, but you want to narrow the list to just the top 5 or 10 for communication to the project manager. If you reject the risks your risk manager suggests because of his technical expertise you are not being fair. If you select a low-likelihood or low-criticality risk because the mitigation would result in some personal gain for you, you are not being fair. If you discard certain risks out of hand without even listening to the rationale from your risk manager, you are not being fair.

These examples may be extreme, maybe even comical, but they provide a window into circumstances in which fairness might be compromised. Sometimes it can be compromised intentionally, other times it may be compromised without intent. But either way, the process results in a solution that was not fair or fairly attained. The repercussions can be more detrimental to the team than had you, as a leader, not gotten your way. Conversely, if fairness were maintained, the benefits can significantly outweigh the exact decision because the team will witness fairness and be motivated by it.

Promotions are a good example of where fairness is an expectation. Everyone expects the promotion process to be fair, and, when it's not, it's usually apparent to all (except maybe to those doing the selecting). This happens across the Agency, even at NASA HQ, where I became aware of one such instance. Attrition in one HQ organization had resulted in an opening in a Senior Executive Service position and they advertised to fill. The process proceeded quietly (as it should) and after some time an announcement was made that an existing member of the organization was selected. This person had no previous management or supervisory experience and had served previously in a relatively modest position in the organization's hierarchy. But they had been in the organization for many years, performed their job adequately, and, conspicuously, just happened to be available. After the selection was made the inevitable hallway scuttlebutt began as other members of the organization (and those outside of it) questioned the promotion. Clearly, their perception was that this individual, while admittedly a nice person, didn't exhibit the Executive Core Qualifications expected from a Senior Executive Service person and they assumed they were selected because of internecine reasons. That is, they were "part of the family" and were elevated from within that family. They were familiar to the selecting official, a known quantity, ostensibly a coworker and a friend, even if they lacked the specific qualifications for the position.

The impact that this selection had on the organization was predictable. Selection and promotion without merit does not infuse trust in an organization, and certainly did not in this case. The blame went to the selecting official, who of course led the organization, and this unfairness diminished that person's reputation to the organization's rank and file. Complaints and concerns about management and leadership were already present in this organization and this selection just compounded those. This exacerbated the organization's loss of faith in its leadership.

If you think about it, situations like these are easy to avoid. The selecting official could have considered the impact this selection would make to an already dispirited organization. Whether the scuttlebutt assumption for the selection was true or not is irrelevant—the action solidified a perception of unfairness by the organization's leadership, and that perception became truth to the rank and file. That's all that really matters. A fairer selectee, one chosen through a fully open competitive process and who embodied the qualifications expected from such a Senior Executive position would certainly have been better, both for that position and for the organization as a whole. As mentioned, situations like these are both predictable and avoidable.

The same can go for you as Chief Engineer when selecting members of your technical team. When faced with these decisions, just apply the precepts of fairness to those selections and you should avoid these sorts of issues. Does that mean you can't bring in someone specific given a strong individual experience or skill through a noncompetitive selection process? Of course not, that happens when the situation justifies it. But in general, and for the majority of your team, select and promote people with an eye to fairness.

Which brings us to the subject of diversity, admittedly sometimes a sensitive topic. Diverse teams, in general, are stronger, more resilient, more innovative, and more productive than teams that lack diversity. And by diversity I'm not talking simply ethnic, gender, or racial diversity, but diversity of skill set or experience, of origin (home NASA Center), and even of personalities. A team that lacks diversity can be perceived as unfair; it can appear that many people were excluded from being considered because they fall outside of the desired demographic. And that's not fair.

As to gender, NASA historically has had some inherent difficulties ensuring a gender-diverse workforce, as in the past few women pursued engineering or scientific degrees. Of course, this produced a predominantly male workforce. That has changed considerably and today the demographics show almost equal numbers of qualified male and female candidates. In today's world there really is no excuse not to have gender diversity in your team. If your team is lopsided with respect to gender, in either direction, you should consider the fairness of your selection process.

When I first arrived at HQ there was another organization that had a reasonably diverse staff from the standpoint of gender. Not completely equal, but not lopsided either. A good mix. The year before I arrived that organization attained new leadership. Things didn't change immediately, but over the next 5 years there was a slow exodus of most of the women from the organization. Soon enough very few women were left, so few that it gained the notice of HQ Human Resources, who track such things. There was a pattern there, they decided; ostensibly, given the exodus, the organization may not be a good place to work for women, and they did not fail to notice that no women were replacing those who left. Fairness in hiring and in the workforce became an issue and eventually word got all the way to the NASA Administrator's level (which, believe me, is something you never want to happen). The point here is that it happens, consciously or otherwise, and organization/team leaders need to remain cognizant of the fairness of their processes.

But back to engineering. In your role as Chief Engineer you'll be placed in a position to make any number of decisions. How fair is your decision-making process? Have you ever thought about it? And even if you have, how often do you give it consideration? Making decisions is both an internal and an external activity. The internal part relies on all the thought processes that happen, the internal debate, the reliance on intuition and experience, and occasionally biases and prejudices—all the calculations that go on inside every one of us. Those calculations are rarely fair, and quite frankly don't need to be, as we all arrive at initial conclusions based on how we feel about a situation. But the external activity, the interaction with your team and other stakeholders should be fair.

First, let others speak and have their say. You may not agree with them, at least not initially, but allowing all parties to have input into a discussion is an exercise in fairness (and, you never know, something they say might actually resonate with you or even change your mind). Even the people most passionate about a subject will usually not declare a process unfair if they feel they've been heard. Second, when people are speaking, don't cut them off or if you do cut them off, ensure that it's because there's something factual they said in error or because they have become disruptive to the conversation (it's actually not unfair to do this as long as it was preceded by a fair opportunity to have their say). If you're tempted to declare they are full of "horse hockey," try to rein in that temptation. Keep the discussion going until everyone who shows an interest in participating has had a chance to offer their opinion. Third, at least externally, show openness for alternate perspectives. Even if you are adamant about something within your own head, your façade should show a willingness to consider different views (hopefully you'll be open to alternate perspectives internally too, but at a minimum ensure the side you present to others is open). Fourth, when arguing a position, maximize your use of data, facts and real-life experiences and avoid using guesses, theories, blame, or invective.

Finally, when ready to declare your decision, lay out the rationale so that others can understand it. Charges of unfairness can be easily raised when rationales for decisions are hidden, obfuscated, or otherwise unclear. This, in fact, may not be fair to you, the decision maker, but it can easily be avoided by communicating your rationale. In this context it's not critical for the team to agree with the rationale, and once a decision is made it's appropriate to close off further discussion and move on, but if your team doesn't understand how and why you came to a decision they will fill in the blanks themselves and the rationale they assume may not always be favorable to you or represent your actual thinking. Head this hazard off at the pass simply by outlining your reasons for reaching your decision.

NASA doesn't legislate fairness. There's nothing in NASA policy that says decisions have to be fair, there's no processes that managers follow to ensure fairness, and no organization that monitors decisions to ensure they were made fairly. Largely, it is up to each of us to conduct ourselves with integrity and maintain fairness in our actions. There are a few quasi-exceptions to this, the Dissenting Opinion process (discussed in Chapter 12, "Serving as a Technical Authority") is partially an attempt to ensure fairness in airing alternate perspectives. But in the end, we're left to our own recognizance. So, what makes fairness happen? Well, for Chief Engineers anyway, the expectation of fairness that underlies the integrity of the position is strong. The leadership that is expected from our position demands fairness in its execution, and the fact that the bar is held high for every NASA Chief Engineer drives some of this behavior. As a member of the corps of NASA's Chief Engineers, I have high expectations for myself and for my peers and counterparts and will call out my colleagues when they fall below the bar. That bar doesn't maintain its position through magic, but by the example demonstrated by other Chief Engineers. If we fail individually then we fail collectively, and the failure of any of us to meet those expectations is a blemish on all of us. Tough words, I know, but being selected as a Chief Engineer is an honor and the responsibilities incumbent in it are not always easy ones. Those looking for easy paths should avoid this position—we hold ourselves to a high standard.

As a Chief Engineer, if I am not being fair I expect someone to challenge me on it. While my intentions are always to follow the path of fairness, I may not always recognize when I diverge from that path. My actions may not be intentional, but that doesn't matter much to the person to whom I am being unfair. I have had, on occasion, a friend or colleague pull me aside and state they felt a recent decision or action was unfair. I appreciate and rely on that kind of feedback and welcome it, too. Particularly within the fog of war that is our day-to-day work in developing complex systems and managing teams, I don't always see the ramifications of my decisions or the rectitude of my process. So we help each other maintain that bar, help each other keep to that path, and the integrity of Chief Engineers remains the highest in the Agency.

CHAPTER 14
MANAGING YOURSELF

After making the decision to move from Johnson Space Center in Houston, TX, to NASA Headquarters in Washington, DC, I made my intentions known to my colleagues. As with any change of station, my remaining weeks were filled with congratulations on the promotion mixed with regrets on my departure. Many had been colleagues for my entire 21 years in Houston, with a good number having become close friends, almost family, and the separation would be hard. On my last day at JSC, more than a few of those friends and colleagues bade me farewell with the admonition, "Take care of yourself."

I'm sure you've heard that expression, it's a common salutation given to those one cares about, and I've used it on countless occasions myself. It's so common that our society offers it without much thought—it's almost an intuitive reaction to the stimulus of a person's departure. "Take care of yourself!" But there is a deeper, almost hidden meaning behind the comment, particularly in the context of job transition. Moving from one locale to another, from one set of job responsibilities to a different set, can impose a great deal of stress on an individual and that stress has to be managed effectively. The implications of not managing stress can be catastrophic to the person undergoing the transition as well as to their family, as their lives unravel into chaos for a time.

Once in place at their new destination, the task of taking care of yourself continues. New jobs and new environments can be unsettling, as all the rules to which you've become accustomed have changed. That can be quite disturbing and the process of understanding and formulating a new set of rules takes time. New people, new office environment, new relationships, new hierarchies, new organizational politics, even new food (places to eat lunch). Everything is new. And with this newness comes uncertainty and a loss of foundation or grounding. Boy, that's tough, I know. And through all this change and the focus required to keep it all together, what typically gives? It's our ability to take care of ourselves. It's not uncommon for those moving to a new job to sleep poorly, eat insufficiently, and at random times lose emphasis on the personal appearance and other "housekeeping" chores we all do routinely. That's understandable, and it happens more times than you may think.

But taking care of yourself still remains a priority, and must remain a priority, as leadership demands nothing less. The reason is not simply for your own wellbeing (although that is extremely important, too) but for the wellbeing of those under your charge. That is, your team. See, here's the thing. In a fundamental way, your team needs a leader who has their act together, in large part because that persona inculcates a sense of strength and security to the team through the perception of stability. And stability can be everything in a team environment. It's stability that allows team members to focus on their responsibilities and maximize their performance without the worries and complications that an unstable team can bring. Unstable teams lack cohesion, purpose, vision, and focus and spend exorbitant amounts of time seeking stability rather than whatever task they are supposed to be performing. Without stability, a team can fall apart, which brings us back to you and your ability to take care of yourself.

If your team sees you are not (or cannot) take care of yourself, they may question how you can stay on top of all the responsibilities incumbent in taking care of the them. Which, in fact, they will want you to do. In this case it's not the need to establish a firm foundation that could erode from below, but the need to place a strong horse at the front of the wagon who knows the way.

How do you take care of yourself? Well, I probably don't need to answer that, you guys are smart. Just do the things you need to do for yourself to enable you to also take care of your team. Oh, you want a list? Well, off the top of my head:

- Get enough sleep.
- Eat sufficiently, and healthily, too, if you can manage that.
- Do your laundry.
- Shower, please!
- Work hard but also take some time for yourself outside of work.
- Participate in a hobby you enjoy (or more than one).

Simple stuff, nothing too complicated. Just living healthy and happy. The opposite to any of the above, of course, could indicate you're not taking care of yourself. If, for example, you are tired from insufficient sleep, lethargic and lacking from not enough food (or a diet of nothing but junk food), disheveled from wearing the same worn clothes again and again, stinky from lack of personal hygiene, or have bags under your eyes from working 16-hour days week after week, you'd be a poster child of someone not taking care of themselves. Fortunately, this isn't rocket science, but pretty much just standard life practices to most of us. So, do it, and keep it up. It's important for both you and the team you lead.

The best example that comes to mind is, unfortunately, a personal one. Between the end of 2001 and mid-2003 I was going through a divorce from my first wife. At the time I was the Technical Assistant for Shuttle in the division that provided the majority of systems flight controllers in Mission Control. While the TA position didn't include any supervisory responsibilities, it did require leadership skills through the vast amounts of technical integration and relationship building needed to represent our Systems Division to the larger MOD, and the MOD to other elements within the Space Shuttle program. Without going into details, this time period was not a happy one for me. I largely stopped eating and lost more than 30 pounds (great from a physical health standpoint but, man, that's not the way you want to lose weight). While dealing with a collapsing marriage and seeing much of the life I had known end, I found myself losing my temper quickly and really struggled with making sleep a priority (as with eating, it just wasn't important to me at the time). What's more, as many who have gone through these sorts of experiences can attest, my stress levels were off-the-scale high. Outside of work, the yelling, crying (by both parties), loss, and disruption had an extreme effect on me. It was bad.

But what's more important here is that it affected my ability to do my job. Not only was I royally distracted, upset, shaken, and without a sense of grounding, but people began to take notice of it in my performance. In all honesty it assuredly wasn't that hard to see (I don't think I hid it well), but this losing of myself began to affect the professional relationships that I had built and were necessary for me to perform my job. I can recall closing myself in my office one day when my wife called, filled with vile anger and invective at me. The ensuing argument lasted maybe 45 minutes and the decibel level in the room would have been sufficient for acoustic qual testing of a payload on a new launch vehicle (in other words, it was loud). When the conversation mercifully ended, I opened my office door and walked out into the adjoining Division Office where I was met by concerned (and maybe disappointed) stares. At other times, I remember losing my temper over mundane and reasonably minor situations where tact and good relationships were requisite. Finally, my appearance was dreadful, so much so that my bosses were hesitant at one point to have me out in front representing the Division. Was I taking care of myself during this time? No. Did it affect how people perceived me and my ability to perform my job? Yes.

There were many things I learned from that experience—much of it about myself as a person—but one thing I learned was that in times of crisis you can self-medicate either with destructive behavior or constructive behavior. At first, I did the former: I drank a lot of wine (keeping the local liquor store happy but not, so much, my liver); eventually I shifted to the latter in that I threw myself into a daily exercise regimen. I had always enjoyed running short distances for my general health, but now dealing with this maelstrom of divorce I started going to the fitness center almost every day. I ran, I swam, I rode the stationary bike and elliptical trainer and found it was a fantastic way to work through the stress in my life. Soon I moved on to sprint triathlons and eventually to half-marathons and full marathons. I found that I could pour my sorrows into these activities and constructively work through them. I found solace, health, and discovered a path to renewal. It was unfortunate that I had to go through something horrific to make this discovery, but I also learned that constructively dealing with trauma is better that dealing with it through destructive behavior. It's possible.

But enough of the confessional. This chapter is titled "Managing Yourself," so let's broaden the discussion to other aspects (of which taking care of yourself is just one component). Managing yourself represents maintaining practices of self-organization so that you can operate at expected levels of efficiency. That's a pretty dry definition, but it captures the essence of the subject. What I'm talking about here are the other aspects of managing yourself, things like time management, the limitation or elimination of clutter, self-organization, self-awareness, and maintaining work-life balance. Let's explore each of these and what they may mean to a Chief Engineer.

Time Management: Some of us have administrative assistants to help us keep our schedules straight, prevent us from planning two meetings on top of each other, and help ensure that we are at the right place at the right time. But many of us don't and have to accomplish these tasks ourselves (my hand is raised as a member of this group). Regardless, managing our time during the workday is essential to managing ourselves. It organizes our activities and ensures we keep to our commitments. Imagine our busy schedules and the number of meetings we have to attend each week, and how impossible it would be if our calendar were a mess and we had no idea what constituted our day's activities. Furthermore, practicing time management also ensures that we have enough time in each day to accomplish all those tasks and we're not overburdening ourselves with too many activities. I have seen schedules in which a person is supposed to be in three places at the same time. While that's occasionally unavoidable given our responsibilities and the demands on our time, it should certainly be avoided when possible (and is a strong reason to have a deputy). Much of what I'm discussing here are basic ideas and may seem obvious, but I still see many leaders overcommit themselves or lose track of their commitments, and the result is disorganization and a less effective team. I'd also note that our society in general and NASA culture specifically expects punctuality, and failure to demonstrate that quickly draws a reputation of unreliability. While that might not always be fair, it is nonetheless true, so try to stay punctual. If you need help ensuring this (I do, to be sure), get some help with an administrative assistant who can keep track of your time commitments. This is not an unreasonable expectation for a Chief Engineer, so don't be afraid to ask for some help.

Limiting or Eliminating Clutter: Evidence of clutter indicate disorganization. If your office desk is buried under stacks and stack of... well, you have no idea what exactly is in those stacks because they have been there so long. As you file through all that paper intent on finding a specific meeting agenda or that hazard report you printed but ultimately give up trying to find after 10 minutes of searching, that person in your office politely waiting for the information is apt to think to themselves, "Man, this is our Chief Engineer?" Imagine, instead, knowing where all your information is or how to locate it, and the impression you leave will be a very different one. In today's world this notion of clutter is not limited to the physical detritus we maintain but also in our digital information. More often than searching for some information on my desk I am searching for information on my computer. You can get lost in the avalanche of digital information you receive and waste just as much time as the aforementioned stack searcher; however, it is possible to organize this information in efficient ways such that locating a specific element is achievable. There are hundreds, if not thousands, of web articles recommending solutions for organizing email and digital information, so I won't suggest any here, but the point is to limit, or better even eliminate, that which you don't need—that is, the clutter. Stay vigilant with this or it will consume you.

Self-organization: "Where's my phone?" "I had a pen but now I can't find it." "Here's my business card... Oh where did I put those?" "Have you seen my car keys?" I suspect you've all encountered this person before and can probably identify someone you know who fits this personality. While lovable and endearing (maybe), the person who struggles with self-organization is one who runs the risk of having people lose confidence in them. Chief Engineers don't actually cut a lot of metal or solder actual circuit boards, but instead manage information—a whole lot of information—much of it kept inside our little noggins. The teams they lead expect that information to be organized and readily available, so the image of someone who constantly loses their car keys or other acts of absentmindedness serves to diminish the perception of competence.

In the end this isn't about knowing where your stuff is but in maintaining awareness of your surroundings.

Self-Awareness: And speaking of awareness, a Chief Engineer is self-aware. They are cognizant of their appearance, of their health, and of limitations of their abilities. They know who they are, their strengths and weaknesses, and when they may be pushing themselves too hard (or conversely, may need to turn up the gain). They know when they are dressing nicely or dressing sloppily and when either is appropriate. They know when they are in good health or when they are as sick as a leaking battery under load. And they are aware of when they can handle a situation or when they need help (and they ask for it). Maintaining awareness of yourself is vitally important to a leader, not only in projecting that aura of competence but, more importantly, in recognizing when you don't. Some lack this awareness, and while it's understandable that we can occasionally get so involved in our work that we lose ourselves, we should never completely lose sight of who we are and how we appear and act. This isn't a task you can delegate to others; this is something you'll need to do yourself.

Work-Life Balance: Finally, and this may be the most difficult task to accomplish for some of us, we need to maintain a healthy and proportional work-life balance. Our work is very important and is critical to NASA's mission, but to ensure that we stay at maximum efficiency we need to occasionally get away from it. That, admittedly, is hard for some of us to do as dedication to and passion for our job can keep us at work hours way past when we should have gone home. But that balance of life away from work, whether focused on your family or on your hobbies, is a necessary ingredient to ensuring that what you do while at work is productive and effective. You may be so busy that you feel you need to work constantly just to keep on top of all the demands placed on you. It's a challenge, to be sure. But if you don't maintain this balance you run the risk of losing something even more critical than the work you perform—you may lose yourself! And that's not good for anyone, and especially not good for your project. Get away occasionally. It's OK. It's healthy!

Some on your team might find disorganization comforting, as it validates their own inability to maintain order in their lives. Some may find it endearing, personifying you as a cuddly character because of your idiosyncrasies for clutter. But in my experience, most of your team will view this behavior for what it is—unnecessary disorder. It's like the guy or gal who never washes their car and allows the dirt to build to the point that some good Samaritan (or irreverent friend) finger paints "Wash me" through the grime on the back window. It's funny, for a bit, but ultimately, it's an indication that the individual lacks the ability to take care of fundamentals. There could be good reasons for this, legitimate events happening in their life that prevent them from maintaining basic order, and for most people that's OK. But not for leaders. When you ascend to leadership, the expectations of maintaining basic functions is elevated, even when events in your life would normally prevent taking care of fundamentals. Team members want their leaders to be the embodiment of good practices. They want their leaders to personify exemplary behaviors. Leaders are expected to set the example, to go above and beyond, and to be the exemplar of what each team member should be. Unfair? Well, unfair or not, it's a reality. Welcome to the role of Chief Engineer!

But fortunately, in this aspect at least, attaining your team members' expectations is not an impossibility, or even hard really. Just take care of yourself, manage your time and efforts, and Voila! You've done it.

It should be noted that the bar being established here doesn't mean you need to dress immaculately, have your schedule memorized in detail months into the future, or demonstrate a photographic memory of events years in the past. Expectations of self-care and self-management don't extend to the sublime, but just to the adequate (or maybe slightly above adequate). The expectation doesn't mean you need to recreate yourself into a superman or superwoman. All it means is that you show you can care for yourself and manage your commitments reasonably. If you do that, you will have met expectations. My present boss, the NASA

Chief Engineer at HQ, is a fantastic engineer. His engineering sense is second-to-none, developed from years of plying technical engineering practice and gaining a career of experience, including both spectacular successes and heart-wrenching tragedies. When he speaks on technical matters, people listen, whether it's a Center Engineering Director, the NASA Administrator, or members of Congress. His expertise has earned him the respect of his peers. Now, does this level of proficiency extend to managing his schedule? No. But he is fortunate to have one of the best administrative assistants I have ever met, one who not only manages his schedule and time but also looks forward in time to ensure conflicts are resolved before they occur and to ensure that he remains fully aware of upcoming schedule commitments. With the help of his assistant he never gets blindsided. Does being the NASA Chief Engineer mean he has to manage his own schedule in the exemplary fashion that he conducts his other responsibilities? No, in this case he has someone to do that for him. And that's perfectly OK.

Of course, not everyone has the luxury of an administrative assistant. So, for the tasks that you have to do yourself, do them like a Chief Engineer! Stay on top of them, stay ahead of the curve, understand the incumbent hazards, understand your options, and show competence in this worthy of emulation.

CHAPTER 15

EMPLOYING SOUND ENGINEERING JUDGEMENT

Space Shuttle flights, from launch through wheel stop, were governed by Flight Rules. The Flight Rules provided guidance and limitations on every aspect of Shuttle operations, every flight regime, and every subsystem on board the vehicle. They constituted much of the collective knowledge and wisdom of Shuttle operations and were revised frequently as new knowledge was gained. These Flight Rules consisted of three elements: 1) A title and unique identifier number; 2) the rule itself, explaining what should be done, when, and under what circumstances; and 3) the rationale for the rule. The rationale would be in narrative form and include as much historical information, precedence, and factual background data as required to ensure that any flight controller referencing the rule firmly understood the rule and its application. It was always desired that the rationale included actual supporting data from ground testing or previous flight history to provide further substantiation of the rule. We don't like to shoot from the hip in Mission Control and, like most engineering organizations, preferred quoting from data. But sometimes, on rare occasions, the ops community would agree that a certain procedure or practice was warranted for a given situation in which there was no supporting data to back it up. These procedures or practices would be thoroughly discussed through informal and formal meetings, bent and folded and thoroughly wrung out to ensure that the practice was safe and sound for Shuttle operations and widely accepted by the community. Even with no supporting data, these procedures and practices could find their way into Flight Rules. Generally, in these cases, the rationale would consist of two simple but seemingly contradictory words—"engineering judgement."

What exactly does "engineering judgement" mean? And why is it acceptable rationale to substantiate Space Shuttle operational rules in lieu of hard test or flight data? Well, I've never seen a formal definition for engineering judgement and you probably won't find one (many of you will now go off and likely prove me wrong) so I won't try to offer a formal definition, but in a nutshell, it is your best-informed guess given your accumulated experience. It's collecting all the facts available (however many or few there are) and factoring those into a situation.

CHAPTER 15 • *Employing Sound Engineering Judgement*   159

Engineering judgement includes understanding the situation's parameters and limitations, the environment in which the system is operating, the known or unknown hazards or risks present, and a clear understanding of the mission goals and objectives you are trying to achieve. And still with all of that, it's ultimately having to make a guess.

As you can see those guesses are not simply a WAG (wild-ass guess) or cavalier attempts to solve a situation without thinking it through, but instead are an application of collective wisdom and experience necessitating use of all the information available and still lacking the certainty needed to fully eliminate risk. If the data available can't do that, then engineering judgement will either have to fill the remaining gap, or the action will not be performed (which is a perfectly acceptable outcome in some cases).

In the Mission Control world, one of the comments frequently applied to the Flight Directors (who lead and manage the flight control team while on console) is that they were trained to make decisions with less than 100 percent of the data. I've always liked that expression and have thought it a perfect characterization of the job. That is, they had to make decisions with uncertainty, and those decisions could affect the safety of onboard crews, the health of a national asset, or very expensive and important mission objectives. A Flight Director would collect as much information about a situation as possible, but if that alone couldn't get them over the threshold of acceptable risk, then it was up to engineering judgement to get them the rest of the way. Or, they would stand down on the problem (which, again, might be the right decision in some cases).

Engineering judgement's foundation is the collected knowledge and experience that a person or organization accumulates over the years. It relies on that foundation. It is not infallible and can't provide absolute certainty, but it can allow a team to proceed forward in the face of uncertainty. Think about mountain climbers pursuing a difficult summit. They may have to cross ice fields and crevasses, traverse difficult vertical rock terrain, ascend and descend by rope hanging on to uncertain anchors, and other activities with obvious potential hazards. Occasionally a mountain climber will reach a particularly difficult juncture and have to make a decision on whether to proceed or not. Do they have the skill and strength? Are the hazards and risks of the upcoming maneuver understood? Will the snow give way, or the ice anchor pull out? With all of these considerations, ultimately, a mountain climber will use his or her experience to answer these questions and in answering these questions they will never reduce uncertainty to zero. The decision to proceed or not to proceed relies on their judgement of the situation and what their experience is telling them. Engineering judgement is no different.

In February 1962, NASA was conducting the first orbital spaceflight mission for America: John Glenn's historical Mercury Atlas 6. Already in orbit for a short time, telemetry from the spacecraft indicated that the landing bag had deployed. This inflatable bag, contained underneath the heat shield required for reentry, would cushion the impact of the spacecraft once it returned to Earth and landed in the ocean. Upon surviving the extreme heat of reentering the atmosphere and just before landing, the heat shield would separate and allow the landing bag to deploy and inflate, preparing the spacecraft and its occupant for the impact on the ocean. Unfortunately, on John Glenn's flight those monitoring in Mission Control saw that telemetry indicated the heat shield had separated and bag deployed prematurely while the spacecraft was still in orbit. If this had in fact happened, the spacecraft would have burned up during reentry and its occupant would have perished. Rounds of discussions immediately commenced to figure out what to do. There was no way to know with any certainty if the heat shield and landing bag had indeed deployed or if the indication was false, due to a bad sensor or some other erroneous indication. After some time, with John Glenn continuing to circle Earth and oblivious to the discussions on the ground, Mission Control recognized that the heat shield was being held in place by the retrorocket package used to deorbit the spacecraft, secured to the bottom of the spacecraft by metallic straps. Normally the retrorocket package would be jettisoned immediately after firing, but in this case, it was decided to leave it in place throughout reentry by inhibiting the pyrotechnics that would separate the metallic straps. Keeping the package in place would, it was hoped, also maintain the heat shield in position if indeed the landing bag had deployed. Once the decision was made, they informed the orbiting astronaut, who asked for a reason for this action. The communicator on the ground replied simply, "This is the judgement of Cape Flight."

As I said, in this situation there was no way to definitively ascertain the actual status of the heat shield and landing bag. The only insight those on the ground had was that one piece of telemetry indicating the bag had deployed, but they didn't know if the indication was real or in error. All the while our first orbiting astronaut was in space and the responsibility of bringing him home rested with the Flight Director on console in Mission Control. That Flight Director, Christopher Kraft, had built his career performing aircraft flight testing, providing him with years of experience monitoring high-performance vehicles being tested in unforgiving environments. Spaceflight was new, but flight testing was not, and Chris Kraft utilized this previous experience to make a judgement call—a call in which an astronaut's life was at risk, with the world watching, and one he had to make with less than 100 percent of the data he needed. He used engineering judgement. He considered the circumstances, the system involved, the environment, the hazards and risks, and pulled from his years of aircraft flight testing to come to a solution. He could have been wrong, but a decision needed to be made and he made it. Fortunately for us, for NASA, and for John Glenn, he made the right call. But the point here is that he filled in the gap of available information with his engineering judgement.

So, is engineering judgement simply experience? In part, yes. Every day we make decisions, engineering or otherwise, based on our life experience. We use that experience to help inform our decision-making, whether it is crossing a crowded parking lot, buying a new car, investing in the stock market, accepting or turning down a job offer, deciding which restaurant to eat at, or any of the tens of thousands of other decisions that come our way. We use our experience, in part, to guide us toward desired outcomes. But we also do other things. We observe our surroundings and the situation at hand. We note what's in and what's out of the equation, what assists us and what impedes us. We consider how much money we may have to spend on a purchase (constraints and limitations), the advertised reliability of the product (risks and hazards), and whether we want a product with a long warranty or a short one (controls to those hazards). We try to fill in as much information as we can given the data available. And then when that data is exhausted, we use our judgement to make the final decision.

That judgement is, thus, not a simple guess or throwing of some dice. It is an informed decision, eliminating as much uncertainty as possible using available information, and then relying on and utilizing our experience to fill in the remaining void such that we can choose or decide on a course of action.

In your role as Chief Engineer, maybe you are trying to decide whether to upgrade a component within a system—say, moving from a spring-operated valve to one with a solenoid commanded by a computer. In an engineering sense, there's normally lots of available data to assist with this kind of decision. You may have previous test and development data from the system or component, information on its performance in prototype form and during qualification and certification testing. The system or component may have a significant flight and operational history, of which there may be substantial runtime information including anomalies and malfunctions. You may be able to pore through volumes of hazard data, failure modes and effects analyses, and detailed probabilistic reliability assessments that can help quantify whether future anomalies or malfunctions may occur. There may be additional test and analysis data from laboratory testing. And, once a vendor is selected, there is normally a variety of information on that supplier, their manufacturing history, their quality control processes, and their part selection criteria.

All of that is good and important when making a decision. It may be sufficient information to allow you to reduce the uncertainty of making the change within acceptable risk. Or, it may not be. Let's say it is not enough information, either due to the unavailability of portions of the above or, perhaps, poor pedigree of the information itself such that additional uncertainties are introduced. Regardless, the decision of whether to make the change or not may come to you as the project's Chief Engineer, at which point you'll need to tap into your engineering judgement. You may think back to previous projects that used similar equipment or had similar choices confronting them. What did those experiences teach you? You may have learned that solenoid-actuated values are good under ambient temperature conditions but not always so good under cryogenic usage. Or you may have once supported a project in which both varieties of valves frequently failed, although that project operated in a slightly different environment than your present system and used different fluids. Or, you might know that the particular vendor has an immaculate production record except for one circumstance in which they lost quality control (for which the technician was let go). All of this information, while not specific to the case at hand, still can help inform your decision when relying on engineering judgement.

The above example is not theoretical but stems from an actual Shuttle experience of mine. The console I supported was responsible for the Orbiter's onboard cryogenic systems that fed reactants and oxidizers to the fuel cells for production of electricity. The valves that allowed the cryogenics to enter the fuel cells, called reactant valves, and the valves that separated the fluid manifolds in the event of system-wide leaks, referred to as manifold valves, were not always reliable at cryogenic conditions. When in the open position they were designed to be magnetically latched, meaning a magnet held them open. When you wanted to close one of these valves, you operated a solenoid that pulled the valve away from the magnet to the closed position, where it was held by a spring. When it was desired to reopen the valve, a different solenoid was powered, pulling the valve in the direction away from the spring and back to the magnet that then held it open. Pretty simple design. Normally these valves are always open, but occasionally there was a need to close them. Unfortunately, every once in a while, as the Shuttle was in space orbiting Earth, these valves would fail to close when commanded.

On STS-57, we were conducting a test of the ability to shut down a fuel cell and restart it later. The plan was to shut the unit down, close the reactant valves (considered a safer configuration), and then reopen the valves and restart the fuel cell 24 hours later. The shutdown of the fuel cell went smoothly until the crew attempted to command the reactant valves closed. One closed but the other stayed stubbornly open. My counterpart on console at the time had two choices: 1) Leave the fuel cell shut down and live with one reactant valve open, or 2) reopen the closed valve, restart the fuel cell, and call the test off. In the end, he decided to recommend the second option to the Flight Director, who accepted the recommendation. The fuel cell was restarted and the test was called off. In reaching this decision he used his engineering judgement, considering the history of these valves, the off-nominal configuration of a fuel cell shutdown with a reactant valve open, and the potential impacts if a leak developing downstream of that valve (which would have been undetectable with the fuel cell shut down). He considered all of these things and probably a dozen other experiences taken from his engineering career and came to his decision.

See, here's the thing with using engineering judgement. Given the exact same situation, I probably would have opted for leaving the fuel cell shut down and continuing with the test. In my mind I could make a risk trade that considered all the same particulars but come out with a different solution. Did the flight controller on console at the time make the wrong decision? I guess the best way to answer that is that he made the best decision for him. The point here is that engineering judgement is subjective. It is based on personal experience (which is different for everyone) and may not always provide the same solution (that is, it may not be repeatable). This is why you need to be careful when using engineering judgement. You need to use it judiciously, as it will never be verifiable in the same way that test data is. It will always be open to question and based on individual personal experience. Engineering judgement will rarely stand the rigor of a mishap investigation and should never be inserted into reliability, qualification, certification, or other means of ensuring risk is appropriately accepted. Engineering judgement will always be a gap filler, nothing more.

Which brings me to the last point on this topic—the need to ensure that your engineering judgement is sound (remember the title of this chapter). As a Chief Engineer, when utilizing your engineering judgement, ensure that it is based in reality, good engineering practices, reasonable assumptions, and can be supported by previous experience. If you're just spitting wads or shooting from the hip, you're not using engineering judgement. In those cases, you're just guessing (which is not a good engineering practice). Just guessing on something can be acceptable as long as you clearly advertise it as just a guess during the discussion (that is, don't disguise a guess as engineering judgement). Sound engineering judgement is normally defensible through historical precedent or anecdotal experience. If you're using engineering judgement, there should be something tangible in your past that you can point to as precedent. The specifics may be different than the situation you're dealing with now, but there is still some tangible experience you can point to that provides guidance on the current event. Sound engineering judgment should be based on factual experience and, more importantly, not based on bias, prejudice, or emotional response. If the majority of your rationale for a decision is because a similar component burned you and made you look bad on a past project, that's not engineering judgement. A Chief Engineer has the latitude to use that as rationale for a decision, but don't call it engineering judgement, call it what it is (the old "I'll be damned if I ever do that again" rationale).

You made Chief Engineer because of your experience. It has taken you far, vicariously into some extraordinary places (Earth orbit, around distant planets, peering into the depths of the universe, or to the outer boundaries of aeronautics), and that experience defines you as an engineer. It is probably the largest asset you own, and many actions you take or don't take over the course of your career will be informed by that experience. It has been tested, verified, and become imbedded in your practice. It forms the basis of who you are as a NASA engineer. It is like an old friend, familiar and occasionally quirky, but still something you trust. Continue to do so. But use it with caution and validate it each time it is used.

CHAPTER 16

BEING GOOD AT BOTH TACTICS AND STRATEGY

Most engineers enjoy getting down in the weeds, as we say. We relish the opportunity to get our hands dirty with details, with the minutiae of a technical subject, burrowing down to the piece part and really understanding the physics of a phenomena at the most discrete level. We strive to get our hands around the specific, the one-on-one interaction; our objective many times is to solve an immediate problem. We often get accused to getting lost in the details, an accusation that we are frequently guilty of, to be honest. It's where we thrive.

Engineers are problem-solvers and many problems exist at the level of details. If a transmitter on an interplanetary spacecraft is unable to hold its expected bandwidth a day before critical transmission of data back to Earth, send in the engineers. If a hydraulic actuator on an experimental aircraft is leaking fluid for seemingly inexplicable reasons, send in the engineers. If a new carbon dioxide scrubbing technology fails to reduce CO_2 to acceptable levels in a laboratory demonstration and needs to be redesigned, send in the engineers. If a propellant valve on a commercial crew visiting vehicle to the International Space Station is not commanding to the desired position and preventing deorbit, send in the engineers. Resolving these sorts of tactical issues, those pertaining to specific items or events and requiring near-term resolution, are what most people think of when they think of engineering.

And yet, while we live in this environment as discipline engineers, Chief Engineers have a greater challenge and need to see the big picture, the whole, the system-level perspective, and consider long-term needs and implications. Yes, Chief Engineers enjoy getting down in the weeds (come on, admit it, it's fun), but we also must elevate our perspective to ensure that the larger framework of our system under development or in operation is being considered. We are faced almost daily with problems and issues that immediately need resolution, while at the same time we have to maintain awareness and cognizance of issues and problems that will be around for much longer, perhaps for the life of the project.

If the previous examples were characteristic of tactical issues, what would a strategic issue look like? Well, for example, if during the design of the above-mentioned interplanetary spacecraft it was felt that an optical communication transmitter would serve better but also carried more risk than an off-the-shelf heritage radio frequency (RF) unit, send in not just any engineer but the Chief Engineer to evaluate that trade. If the same leaking aircraft hydraulic actuator was found to have been procured with the wrong specifications and an entirely new procurement activity using correct specifications was required, send in the Chief Engineer. If the development CO_2 scrubber was found to be not physically capable of meeting its requirements and new requirements need negotiating with the project manager, send in the Chief Engineer. And if a short-term workaround for the valve failure was found but a long-term redesign is required, send in the Chief Engineer. Resolution of these sorts of strategic issues, those pertaining to long-term resolution requiring a vision for the life of the project, may require the unique skills of the Chief Engineer.

Chief Engineers need to have a level of technical understanding to help resolve the tactical issues. But Chief Engineers also need to have a strategic perspective to help resolve the strategic issues. In short, Chief Engineers need to be good at both tactical and strategic thinking. As Chief Engineer, you will be master at both levels (piece-part and big picture) and timeframes (short-term and long-term). You will also need to be able to separate the tactical from the strategic when focusing on only one is required. A Chief Engineer works at all levels, the detailed and the overall, over all timeframes, and can do both with precision and vision. Tactical and strategic. Sound hard? It's not, really. The tactical should be familiar to new Chief Engineers, and while the strategic may necessitate some new perspectives, it's still all engineering. Imagine yourself as putty, being stretched and pulled. You may now cover more area than you did before, but you're still putty.

The tactical is important. It's the day-to-day activities that constitute a large portion of what we do. It's the nuts and bolts, the specifics and the details, whether we're talking component integration, near-term schedule milestones, specific life-cycle review entrance criteria, or whatever. No system was ever developed without a focus on the individual items, and each has to function individually for the system to function as a whole. It's critical we get the details right because entire systems have the potential to fail if we get any single critical detail wrong. We can't verify higher-level assemblies until we verify the lower-level components. And the sheer number of individual issues that come up can be overwhelming if they are not each dealt with, mitigated, or controlled.

The strategic also is important. It's the long-term, full life-cycle activities that consume our time. It's the big picture, the system-wide perspective, whether looking at the entire outer mold line, considerations for the life of the system, planning a fully integrated assembly or test, or whatever. Systems engineering was developed to provide a holistic, integrated scheme taking the entire system into account and optimizing at that level. During the process of being focused on individual items or issues, it's vital to remember it all has to operate as an integrated system.

When working a tactical issue, it's possible that resolution of that issue may impose penalties for the system once it is integrated. Few things are free. You might congratulate yourself and the team for resolving a particularly vexing technical issue on a component or figuring out an innovative way to schedule a difficult test within the short timeframe allocated, but remember that the resolution of the technical issue may impose penalties on the system once it's integrated and that the test is likely to be followed by further integrated testing that may show it not to be compatible with the system overall. Tactical and strategic.

During my time as Chief Engineer for Aeronautics at NASA HQ, I have learned that most folks at the Centers expect HQ to be involved predominantly in the strategic. That is, establishing the policies, vision, and overall strategies for the Agency's programs and projects and leaving it to the implementing Centers to figure out the details of execution (i.e., the tactical). That's not to say that HQ doesn't deal with tactical concerns—maintaining oversight requires HQ to remain aware and apprised of many tactical issues, and since the HQ Mission Directorates provide the funding to programs and projects, resources remain an HQ tactical concern. But, to a large extent, the expectation meets reality and HQ stay pretty much in the realm of the strategic. So,

CHAPTER 16 • *Being Good at Both Tactics and Strategy* 171

many of my responsibilities focus on engineering policy, such as figuring out governance for NASA's piloted X-plane projects, working with the Aeronautics Research Mission Directorate on strategic objectives, outyear budget planning for NASA aeronautics research, and the like. But once in a while, I'll get the opportunity to attend, say, an X-plane design review and get to ask detailed technical questions on things like design changes made since the last major milestone review, stability and control of the aircraft, and vexing component selection or procurement issues that may be vexing the project. I have gotten to the point in my career where I can discuss both sides of the coin easily, narrowing to the tactical details through specific technical discussion or staying in the stratosphere on areas of strategic concern. I'm bilingual in that respect, if you think about it that way.

Project Chief Engineers have to do similarly. Many of them provide statuses each month to the respective Center Engineering Reviews, appearing before the Center Chief Engineer on technical status for their projects. These presentations normally review near-term milestones recently completed or soon to be conducted, major or significant technical issues or concerns, status of subsystems, and maybe some insight into Technical Performance Margins, risks, and current technical trades. It all stays pretty much in the tactical. But once removed from these reviews, it's entirely likely that they may get called into a planning meeting on the long-term budget for the project or a session with procurement experts on developing a strategy for how the system will be acquired. At the beginning of a project, the Chief Engineer may be developing needs, goals and objectives or negotiating Key Driving Requirements with the program or with HQ. These Chief Engineers have to bounce quickly between the tactical and the strategic, jumping from one audience immediately into a second and doing so without skipping a beat. And they have to provide representation for their technical team in both discussions. Tactical to strategic, strategic to tactical.

In Chapter 10, "Showing Enthusiasm," I mentioned the X-57 electric aircraft and the technical and programmatic issues it ran into that necessitated a replan. During the briefing to HQ personnel, the project

Chief Engineer did a masterful job dancing this do-si-do. He went into comprehensive detail on the technical challenges faced by the project in developing new electric motors, motor controllers, wire harness routing, and other challenges never before faced on an aircraft. He discussed impedances, electromagnetic interference, bend radiuses, circuit board production and acceptance testing, and other technical details to give us a perspective on what challenges the project was facing. We got the picture. Then, he jumped into the replan, the schedule realignment shifting milestones to the right, the addition of environmental testing to ensure allowable performance was attained, and the impact to staffing of the technical team to ensure adequate Government oversight and acceptance. His presentation was not a mash-up of tactical and strategic jumbled together, but a well-thought-out story that covered both. He did not have to shift gears when jumping from one to the other but spoke to both with competence and alacrity. Nicely done!

Risk management is another area in which Chief Engineers can express this tactical-strategic dance. Risks can be discrete, describing the likelihood and consequences of specific areas like issues to hardware under development or concerns affecting testing, design, or procurement. At the same time, a project may have risks to the ability of the system to meet mission objectives, on the performance of source providers over time, or the availability of long-term stakeholder interest or participation. Risks fall easily into both the tactical and strategic bodies of concern, and Chief Engineers often face risks in their registries that cover both.

Another example, a theoretical one. On one particular sunny and clear day, a project Chief Engineer walked into a conference room for her weekly status tag up with her technical team. She went around the room, person-by-person with each of her subsystem managers, who reported their most recent status and their top issues and concerns for the forthcoming week. The project was within a couple of months of their Preliminary Design Review and most efforts are on maturing the design to be ready for that review. The last week had been a bad one for the mechanical subsystem, as development of the vehicle's articulating antenna pointing mechanism had run into significant problems. The requirements on this mechanism to point the antenna alternately between its science objective (a rocky asteroid, let's say) and communication receivers on Earth, and to do so every 0.1 seconds, was proving very hard to meet. Not only were the analyzed stresses on the attachment bracket connecting the antenna to the vehicle body showing vastly negative margins, but the articulating joint kept on freezing after only 10 minutes of operation in brassboard testing. The team was beginning to question whether the design they choose was even viable. So, the subsystem manager brought this up as his top concern.

Our illustrious Chief Engineer sat at the head of the table, dispassionately but empathetically listening to the description of the issues, nodding occasionally, until finally the subsystem manager was done. And then, she began to ask questions:

- What assumptions on materials were used in the attachment bracket analysis?
- Had they verified the stress margins were appropriate for this use?
- Did the articulating joint test accurately simulate expected environmental conditions?

Good, tactical questions. They discussed each point, the subsystem manager acknowledging where they had data and where causes for the issues were left to speculation. More questions followed and the picture began to become clear that, in fact, the design was inadequate. Once the team ascertained this, the discussion shifted to a different nature. The Chief Engineer posed some questions.

- What would it require, in terms of time and resources, to redesign the mechanism?
- Were there existing heritage mechanisms that could be incorporated in the design, even if they did not meet all the requirements?
- Could they renegotiate the requirement itself with project management and stakeholders?

In this case, good, strategic questions. The flow of the conversation went from tactical to strategic, but I'm guessing it seems very familiar to you. While there was a pause in questions between the transition, the issue required both consideration of tactical and strategic issues. The Chief Engineer here was thinking both sides of the coin: 1) How do I fix what's going on? and 2) If I can't fix it what options do I have to keep the project on track? That frame of mind is exactly what a Chief Engineer needs. Of course, this example is fictitious, but I suspect it is reminiscent of numerous similar discussions you've been privy to.

If in the past you've focused pretty much on the tactical and haven't had many opportunities to flex those strategic muscles, how can they then be developed? I'd suggest that opportunities abound. First, spend some time around your project or program manager. Project managers deal with tactical issues certainly, but they also have to contend with the strategic in terms of initially formulating the project and getting it approved, and then ensuring adequate funding for the life of the project. They may deal directly with stakeholders who aren't interested in the fine details of developing the capability, but rather simply in what they want the capability to be and in when it will be ready to deploy. Things naturally gravitate more to the strategic at the program level (you will find the higher you go in any hierarchy the more strategic the responsibilities and concerns become). Program managers can delegate almost all tactical demands to their project managers to spend their own hours and days managing the long-term viability and relevance of the program. You will also find strategic discussions at Center Management Councils (CMCs) that are normally chaired by your Center Director. Some details of project implementation might be discussed here, particularly issues that the project cannot resolve on their own and need Center-level interaction, so many of the topics at CMCs tend to be strategic in nature. Finally, if you also get the opportunity, spend a bit of time at HQ or even volunteer for a short detail there. The insight into strategic discussions can be very insightful.

In fact, on this point, the Aeronautics Research Mission Directorate has dedicated entire reviews to the question of strategic vision. Early each calendar year, in preparation for the upcoming annual budget request to OMB, the Mission Directorate holds 3 days of nothing but strategic discussions. Termed the Strategic Planning Management

Review (SPMR), this series of meetings brings in project managers and researchers to discuss proposals for research in the coming budget planning cycle. The presentations are each focused on specific topics, but the discussion they generate revolves around the potential for ARMD investment in these areas. Questions are raised on how the research will benefit the aeronautics community or U.S. competitiveness in a world market, why NASA is uniquely positioned to conduct this research, what feedback the aerospace community has provided on the need for this research, and other purely strategic perspectives. There is no discussion on proposed project timelines or implementation details—that will come later if the proposals garner interest. Instead, these discussions center on whether NASA should invest in these research areas. As an example of a strategic discussion, they serve the purpose extremely well.

If you got selected as a Chief Engineer to a project after it was already formulated, you missed a fabulous opportunity to experience strategic thinking. The entire formulation process, especially during the very early stages such as pre-Phase A, revolves around developing a concept, finding advocates and selling the idea to those who might fund it. At this point in a project's life there is little discussion on *how* to execute the project, but rather on *what* the project should be about and perhaps even *why* NASA should have such a project. These are all strategic questions. The process of answering these questions is not an engineering one, but it is developmental, logical, and in some ways repeatable. But more important the process forces you to think long term, to consider a project throughout its entire life cycle, and to answer the more philosophical questions incumbent in these sorts of decisions.

Strategic thinking doesn't come easily and its ability in a person has to be cultivated. I have observed that most people, even many who are responsible for thinking strategically, think tactically. Maybe it comes more naturally to engineers who are always being charged with coming up with solutions to problems. But the ability to think broadly, on solutions writ large, with a long-term (maybe generational) vision is a talent reserved for few of us. It is an ability that Chief Engineers need to be successful. If you feel your ability to think strategically could use some maturing, pursue opportunities to affect that maturation. Educate yourself, read, attend meetings such as those suggested, and find ways to do it yourself. Train your brain to think strategically and over time it will do so.

Finally, get good at mixing the two (tactical and strategic thinking). Find ways to think about an issue through both lenses. Many times there are both qualities to an issue if you look for them. The tactical is usually easy to identify, the strategic may be somewhat more obtuse or seemingly irrelevant. As a discipline engineer you can comfortably live in the former and only be pulled into the latter on rare occasions. But as a Chief Engineer, you'll need to live in both worlds and speak both languages.

CHAPTER 17

MAINTAINING AN AWARENESS OF CULTURAL DIFFERENCES

Merriam-Webster carries a few definitions for "culture." One states "the customary beliefs, social forms, and material traits of a racial, religious, or social group." That's pretty good but not quite what I'm looking for. A second definition is "the characteristic features of everyday existence (such as diversions or a way of life) shared by people in a place or time." In this context I think they're referring to the accoutrements of popular culture; again, not quite what I'm looking for. The third definition is "the set of shared attitudes, values, goals, and practices that characterizes an institution or organization."* Perfect!

My guess is you are probably thinking this chapter will be about how to handle differences in our society's various ethnic, socioeconomic, and community cultures in the conduct of your work as Chief Engineer. And it will, in a bit. But for starters, I want to begin with a culture familiar to you all and much closer to home—our very own NASA culture.

Yes, NASA has a culture. Many cultures, in fact. As a Government Agency populated predominantly by engineers, scientists, technology developers, and researchers, NASA's inherent technological and engineering culture sets us apart from most other agencies. We tend to be meticulous, data-driven, and ever so passionate about the work we do. We live for the mission—to explore and discover—and absolutely love the process of building and creating. It's the epoxy that binds us together as an Agency.

But within NASA we are separated by a number of unique cultures, each augmenting and potentially conflicting with another, that can partition (and, unfortunately, sometime outright brand) us into distinct groups. They affect how we work, communicate, and approach problems together. These internal cultures can be geographic (each NASA Center has its own culture), discipline or position-based (engineer vs. manager vs. researcher culture), or even seniority or pay grade (early career vs. SES culture). If you've spent any time at all inside NASA you have undoubtedly encountered many or all of these.

---

* *https://www.merriam-webster.com/dictionary/culture*, (accessed October 23, 2019).

CHAPTER 17 • *Maintaining an Awareness of Cultural Differences* 179

Let's start with Center culture. I "grew up" at Johnson Space Center outside Houston, TX, having spent the first 21 years of my career there before moving to NASA HQ. Because JSC has been the home of so many of NASA's most visible endeavors (humans in space, the Apollo missions to the Moon, the Space Shuttle and the International Space Station) it has a reputation among the other Centers as a behemoth, sucking up funding, resources, and whatever oxygen might be in a room at any time. Some of this is earned and some of it is unfair. But the reputation exists. Because it is one of NASA's largest Centers based on its number of civil service employees and contractors, it operates similar to many large organizations with enormously deep hierarchies and considerable internal processes. Things don't happen rapidly at JSC, and a sizable majority of personnel have only ever seen the Center Director on TV or in the newspaper. Even within JSC there are cultures, largely broken into lines defined by the Center's directorates (e.g., Flight Operations, Engineering, Life Sciences, etc.). Each of these internal organizations has been steeped in a history of human spaceflight and has been around for decades, producing imbedded cultures that can be beneficial to the pursuit of spaceflight but also resistant to change. JSC tends to like large programs and isn't afraid of challenges but can find difficulties working outside of its long-used internal processes.

Compare that with a smaller NASA Center, say Armstrong Flight Research Center in California's Mojave Desert. Like JSC, Armstrong has a long-storied history, having been the home of much of America's aeronautics flight testing dating back to a time even before the creation of NASA. Think of high-speed X-plane research conducted just after World War II, with people like Chuck Yeager piloting the X-1 and becoming the first to break the sound barrier, and Neil Armstrong at the controls of the X-15 rocketing to the boundaries of space. But unlike JSC, Armstrong remains a relatively compact Center with a significantly smaller staff than that of its Houston sister. Because of that, personnel are more familiar with each other across the Center and the organizations are smaller with fewer levels of hierarchy. It's not uncommon for technicians on the flight line to see their Center Director routinely walking the hallways. The groups and teams are more intimate and everyone speaks the same language (that of aviation). Armstrong, I have noticed, also tends to be somewhat insular, viewing outside organizations (even those who provide it with funding) as distant cousins but not really part of the family. They can view HQ with distrust and prefer to keep their activities limited to those "inside the fence." Yet, they are tremendously proud of the work they do and, just as with JSC, feel pride in their history and in their accomplishments.

Every NASA Center is unique, and you'll find unique cultural aspects at each location. Ames, Glenn, Goddard, JPL, Kennedy, Langley, Marshall and Stennis are very different from each other, their cultures deriving from the size of the Center, their history, their geographical location, and other factors. Those outside NASA might see us all marked by the same stamp, but we are, in fact, very different within the Agency.

And then there's NASA Headquarters culture. I think the biggest cultural artifact I have determined having worked at HQ for 8 years (and counting) is that those at the Centers view HQ much differently than those inside HQ view themselves. The common perception of HQ by those at the Centers (some of which have never passed through HQ's turnstiles and stepped foot inside) is that it is filled with bureaucrats and pencil pushers who have lost touch with the reality of life outside DC's Beltway and should, as much as possible, be kept at arm's length. That's unfortunate and largely underserved, in my opinion, and yet it persists. Still, within HQ, I've found far fewer barriers between its offices than I have witnessed between organizations and directorates at the Centers. Folks in different HQ offices tend to work well with each other and the organizational barriers you find elsewhere tend to be fewer. Perhaps that's due to physical locality of everyone's being in the same building—I don't know. HQ is also composed predominantly with GS-14s and above, with GS-15s and SES making up the largest contingent. Because of that, the average age at HQ is significantly greater than at the Centers. Retirement parties are more frequent, yes, but the advanced age also reveals itself in both greater experience and wisdom and also

CHAPTER 17 • *Maintaining an Awareness of Cultural Differences*   181

greater hesitation to change at the personal level. Conversely, HQ is pretty adept at change as it occurs at the wholesale level each time a new White House administration comes into office.

And yet with all these unique cultures affecting how we think, work, and achieve, we all reside within the same Agency and work to the same common goals of exploration and discovery, building, and creating. This common mission ties us together and allows for collaboration that, despite our disparate cultures, works pretty well. Few achievements by NASA today occur just at a single Center in isolation; most are collaborative team efforts that cross multiple Centers. And maybe that's the first point to make here for you Chief Engineers—use that collaboration, that common mission, to your advantage. When disparate viewpoints arise or different approaches to solutions are suggested, remind yourself and your team that we are all working to the same goals. That is a strong gravitational force that can help dislocated teams come together.

A good example of this was the Crew Exploration Vehicle (CEV) Smart Buyer effort that occurred in 2006. This occurred right at the very beginning of the Constellation program, the "CEV" being the generic name for the forthcoming spacecraft, later designated as Orion, that would carry astronauts to the ISS and the Moon. The Smart Buyer activity was created by the NASA Administrator at the time, Michael Griffin, as an exercise with two purposes: 1) To get more informed about what we wanted in a crewed vehicle prior to beginning acquisition and selecting a prime contractor, and 2) showing that NASA human spaceflight, which had been largely focused on operations for many years, hadn't lost its ability to also do development. The team that was formed comprised approximately one hundred managers, engineers, and technicians from across the Agency (all 10 Centers) for 2 months of focused, dedicated work. I led the Mission Operations contingent from JSC. This was, for many of us, the first opportunity to work with some of the NASA Centers not routinely involved in human spaceflight. Although I had been with NASA for 14 years at that point, I had never worked with counterparts from Ames, Armstrong, Langley, or JPL, for example.

What I found from this activity is that once a team was formed, it didn't matter what Center a person came from. All inputs were valid and openly received because we were working towards a common goal. No "Center perspectives" persisted—it was all one team. And what's more, we found that having the diversity of these different cultures worked to our advantage. For instance, the Centers that primarily develop robotic spacecraft routinely design in what is called a "safe mode," where a vehicle encountering a problem executes a protocol to power down, get to a thermally benign attitude, and point its antennas to Earth for further instructions. Well, human-tended spacecraft don't use safe modes and never have. In fact, it didn't even occur to any of us from JSC that such a mode was even an option. But team members from Ames and Goddard brought that into the design and it was accepted.

Here's a second point. Recognize that your team may be composed of members from different Centers and that those Centers each bring different cultures, perspectives, and solutions. Those differences in culture might be the root cause of disagreements that inform and influence different approaches to problems. That's a good thing, actually. Having those perspectives on your team may allow it to view a problem from a different vantage point and find solutions you might not have thought of. Different cultures can open windows to new options and open your eyes to other viable approaches. Take advantage of that whenever possible; it can make your team and your solutions stronger.

But the opportunity that diversity brings also comes with a caution: Don't get locked into any one culture. While our work conducting NASA's mission can cross multiple NASA Centers, it is typical for a single Center to "host" a project and that Center's culture can predominate on the team. Give this some thought in regard to your team and its composition. Culture can provide advantages in the form of historical processes that work and work well, but it can also blind a team with biases that are rooted within a culture. A culture that predominates can still work and there are lots of examples showing exactly that. Just be wary of a predominating culture and be sensitive to whether its biases may be limiting your team to singular approaches.

The previous example of JSC offers another insight. As a large NASA Center with immense human spaceflight programs in residence that consume entire generations of engineers, it is not uncommon for JSC to propose equally immense solutions in terms of suggested organizational size and complexity. JSC can do things small, though: the Morpheus lunar lander technology demonstration is one example of agile, rapid development conducted by a small team. But for complex projects or entire programs, JSC normally brings large solutions. In itself that's not a bad thing, as certain complex activities mandate large solutions. But it might not be the right solution for your specific project. Each team and each solution need to be right-sized for the project, given such factors as the issue's cost, complexity, risk, and national importance. The point is that JSC's culture generally is to do things big and that this inbred bias could prevent a team from seeing a more appropriate, less-sizable solution. The same may be true for other Centers who routinely practice rapid or agile development with small teams, recommending a similarly small team when a larger, more rigid organization might actually be called for.

Operators and developers bring their own community cultural biases. We ran into this as flight controllers in Mission Control as we, representing the ops community, would not always see eye-to-eye with the Engineering Directorate or Program Office representing the hardware owners. Two communities, two cultures, two perspectives on how to solve a problem. Is it unworkable? Of course not, we could work together and reach good solutions given the common mission, but we did bring in different perspectives on how to solve a problem.

Another source of cultural bias is between project managers on the one hand and scientists/researchers on the other. I have observed that scientists and researchers naturally abhor process, paperwork, and policy. Their primary desire is to conduct their research and the associated project wrapped around it is just a means for them to do that. The prescription of 1) Give them resources and funding, 2) leave them to do their work, and 3) come back when they are done makes for a happy scientist/researcher. Of course, the world doesn't work that way and responsible managers want to see progress and evidence of their investment. Plus, those managers themselves are accountable to the higher-ups who mandate the policies and procedures the project follows. In my position at HQ, as the Chief Engineer to a research organization, I see this conflict all the time. Again, does it prevent people from working together? No. But it remains important to recognize that both communities bring their respective cultures to work, which can lead to some conflict and differing perspectives.

So, different perspectives forged by cultures can be of benefit in that they offer potential alternate solutions to problems and "outside-the-box" thinking, but they can also bring in the potential root for conflict and disagreement. In case you may have been hoping to avoid such culture clashes, be aware that there's no way to completely do so. We can't get away from them—even homogeneous societies have minor cultural differences—and NASA works within a country with diverse cultural influences beyond those mentioned above. Those influences are part of humanity and will be around as long as we work with people. (Someday, in the future, it's possible that even automated machines and robots will develop cultural differences between them, but that's for speculative fiction right now and, anyway, I'm getting off point.) Since we can't get away from cultural conflict, all we can do is recognize that it is part of any team's dynamics. Having an awareness of its existence may help you make sense of some of your team's behavior.

And while we're here, let me just say the obvious about cultural diversity. We in the United States live in a multicultural society with residents coming from a vast array of countries, religions, ethnicities, professions, socioeconomic classes, languages, belief systems, and experiences, living in vastly different cultural geographic regions. We talk differently, act differently, celebrate differently, worship differently, eat differently and view the entirety of life differently. And on top of all that, we also fall into two genders, which overlays everything with additional complexity. Cultures are inherent in all of us, and most of us carry the effects of many different cultures. It makes us all different, and yet it also binds us all together. If humanity has at least one thing in common it is that we all are influenced by our cultures. These cultural influences bring diversity to a team, and that diversity is most definitely a strength. I cannot imagine any technical team being stronger with a homogeneous complement than one with considerable diversity. Look for diversity and make it part of your team, not for diversity's sake but to augment and strengthen. And a special note to the guys out there. NASA has made lots of progress in increasing the number of women in our ranks over the last few decades, but the Agency still remains a largely male-dominated workforce. If your team is composed entirely of men, get some women on it, damn it! Your team will be stronger, better, more adaptable, and more competent for it. Plus, women make great leaders!

So, let's say you have a diverse team already, composed of members from across the Agency, a mix of genders, experience bases, seniorities, and backgrounds. And then a disagreement arises that you credit to cultural influences. How does a Chief Engineer manage that? Well, first of all, fall back to some of the foundational practices we've already covered in this book, things like giving everyone the opportunity to speak, listening empathetically, avoiding accusing anyone of anything less than having honest intents, things like that. But let's say, given all of that, you still recognize a cultural influence in one (or more) of your team. First, do a self-check. Make sure that your observation doesn't carry with it any cultural bias or, dare I say, prejudice, of your own. I'm personally not beyond the occasional bias based on my own cultural upbringing, but I do try to examine and catch myself before making any conclusions based on that bias. The objective is, of course, to act objectively and not allow yourself to give in to biases or perceptions (we're data driven people, remember). So, check yourself first.

If then you feel that you are being objective and that the observed behavior is the result of culture, go ahead and give the competing ideas consideration. Even with a cultural influence, good ideas are good ideas. If one of them seems reasonable, appropriate, and fits the situation, then it doesn't matter whether it was influenced by culture. If it makes sense and has merit, go with it.

Similarly, if you see others in the team discarding ideas due to culture (either their own culture or the one of the person suggesting the idea), turn the conversation toward the idea itself and have a debate on the idea's merit. No idea should be thrown out simply because it's imbued with a Center or organization's culture. Ideas can be either good or bad, but measure them on the merits of the idea itself and recommend that your team do the same.

If you witness people "stuck" in their culture and unable to think outside of their predefined box, don't chastise them for doing so. Recognize that cultural influences are strong and people may be used to groupthink within their home organization. Again, focus the conversation on the idea itself and its applicability to your project. If it doesn't fit based on that measure, reject it, but make sure your team knows it is being rejected for the right reasons.

Also, recognize that culture and experience are mostly different things, with both likely to influence individuals. A project manager who had a project go off the rails and fail for whatever reason may be hesitant to take similar risks again. It's possible that the hesitancy is due to his or her previous bad experience and not due to any cultural influence. Consider a person's experience as a possible motivator to their actions. You may have caught that I stated at the beginning of this paragraph that culture and experience are "mostly" different things. Sometimes, when experience is widespread and gets thoroughly imbedded within a community for a long time, it has the chance to evolve into culture. Take, for example, the human spaceflight community's experience with the loss of Columbia on STS-107 and the associated observation that NASA had become risk-adverse. Those who experienced the loss of Columbia and her crew were highly influenced by that tragedy (myself included) and this likely drove an aversion to risk, so much and for so long that the aversion became a part of NASA human spaceflight culture. That's speculation on my part, of course, but you get my point, widespread and shared experience can morph into culture.

On the positive side, there are many fine cultures within NASA that promote really fabulous practices and raise the bar on rigor, integrity, and thoroughness of the work performed. Most Centers have anywhere from small pockets to entire programs that perpetuate these best cultures across the entire Center. Look for these and take advantage of them. It's my view that some of the most productive cultures in Government (or outside) are NASA-bred. One of my favorite positive cultures stems from my days in Mission Control. Twenty-three years before I walked in the door as a new hire, Flight Director Gene Kranz and his White Team were sitting on console monitoring a routine test of the Apollo 1 spacecraft with the crew inside. On that eventful and tragic January afternoon, NASA lost three heroes when a flash fire erupted within the spacecraft, killing the crew—and Gene and his team were there in Mission Control to hear it happen. The impact of the deaths of astronauts Grissom, White, and Chaffee struck the community like a hammer blow, stopping the program in its tracks and caused everyone to reflect on what they could have done better. In what has now become a famous missive, Gene wrote a memo to his flight control community, intending to raise spirits and build esprit de corps, about how flight controllers need to be "tough and competent." Those two words went on to define how the community felt about themselves and acted in the course of their jobs. His memo directed everyone to write those two words at the top of the blackboards that adorned each office, and to never erase them. Consequently, when I came in the door 2 decades later, "tough and competent" was still being written on the office blackboards. Today, there are no longer blackboards in each office, but those two words still remain an identifying moto of the flight control community in Houston's Mission Control. It's become part of the culture and is a constant reminder of the positive qualities expected from that group.

CHAPTER 18

SHOWING ACCOUNTABILITY

Remember when ISO 9000 was all the rage? OK, maybe it was before your time, you can look it up on the internet. In the early 2000s, companies and businesses were getting their management practices ISO 9000–certified as an incentive to prospective customers, and that expectation of compliance extended to the Government as well. NASA spent considerable time training internal auditors to assess our Agency's compliance with the standards set out by ISO, the creatively titled International Organization for Standards. ISO 9000 was about a simple concept, encapsulated in what would become the motto for the entire endeavor: "Say what you do, and then do what you say." In a nutshell, ISO 9000 was about documenting your management (or other) practices, and the implementing those practices per the documented procedures. It was about "talking the talk" combined with "walking the walk." It was about meaning what you say proven through your actions. ISO 9000 was, when filtered down to its basics, fundamentally about accountability.

Accountability is absolutely essential to the credibility of any leader. Like ISO 9000, it's about meaning what you say and proving those statements by the actions you take. It is following through on the promises you make and, on your word, counting for something by the promises you keep. Some leaders can get far initially through charisma and charm, but if they are not accountable to their word, eventually people stop following them. In any relationship trust must be built and earned, and trust cannot be built right from the beginning if the leader proves to be unaccountable. These are basic, fundamental tenants of leadership (or development of any relationship, really). Absolutely foundational stuff, the first cardinal rule of leadership (or it should be). If you find you cannot be accountable, that your actions don't follow your words and that what you say is, in fact, meaningless, then maybe leadership is not the right job for you.

Sorry, I hate to be so negative, but it never ceases to amaze me that this concept is so often broken by poor leaders. Promises are easy to make and making them is compelling because we all want to be liked. But if you make a promise then you simply have to keep it if you want to build trust, develop relationships, and lead. If you don't, well, then you lose trust, destroy relationships, and how can anyone do that and be a leader? Rhetorical question—the answer is you can't.

The number of people Chief Engineers must remain accountable to is daunting—their team, their bosses, project management, and their stakeholders, just to name a few. They must build trust among and throughout all of those groups and keep that trust throughout the life of the project. In fact, when dealing with external stakeholders, Chief Engineers are often representing the project itself, so if they don't demonstrate accountability the entire project loses credibility. If they fail in demonstrating accountability to individuals or groups outside of NASA, the entire Agency loses credibility. There's much to lose here if this is done poorly.

Fortunately, accountability is easy to accomplish. If you say something that requires action, do it. If you promise something, keep that promise. If you claim something, substantiate that claim with data or proof. Do the things that make your word the gold standard. Think about it from the opposite direction. If you exaggerate, you'll find it hard to remain accountable. If you accuse unjustly, same thing. If you make unattainable promises, accountability goes out the window. And once accountability leaves the building, you cannot be effective as a Chief Engineer.

Let me repeat that so there's no confusion on this—If you lose accountability, you cannot be effective as a Chief Engineer. Yes, folks, a lot is riding on this.

When starting out as a Chief Engineer you get the opportunity to establish your accountability among your team, management, and those you interact with outside of the program or project. Whether you are a known quantity or brand new to an organization, you can always establish accountability at the start. Do so. There's no better way to begin in the role of Chief Engineer than by establishing your accountability (you'll find much of your reputation will flow from the accountability you establish). At these early stages you'll have many opportunities to establish accountability, even before you get into the details of the project itself. For example, if you set up or agree to meeting with people, you can either keep those appointments and show up on time or you can blow it off and leave them waiting. Or, if you promise to deliver an early draft of the project's NGOs or Key Driving Requirements, you can deliver as promised or you can ignore the commitment and hope someone else will eventually do it. And, even if you do develop a draft of the NGOs or Key Driving Requirements, you can offer capabilities that are feasible (even if they are difficult to achieve) or you can suggest clearly unattainable deliverables that defy the laws of physics and laugh to yourself that they actually bought it or hope that someone else can magically deliver. Any of these things can establish or destroy your accountability right from the start. I suggest you establish accountability. Yes, that would be a good thing!

As the project continues into Formulation and eventually through to Implementation, from concept to requirements to design and on to manufacturing, assembly, integration and test, and finally to operations, you will have literally hundreds if not thousands of opportunities to maintain or tarnish your accountability. Every day you will be met with opportunities to make promises on your time, your efforts, the project's technical capabilities, your team's commitments, the resources under your control, the project's deliverables, and on and on. The window of opportunity will be open every day. You may not jump through that window each time; you may decide instead to hedge your bets and not make a promise this day; and that's entirely OK. But if you do make promises, each one will be a test of your accountability.

Here are a few examples.
- The Principal Investigator (PI) for the project is negotiating with you on what resolution an optical sensor should be specified to. As a researcher, the PI will push for as much capability as can be delivered. As the Chief Engineer, you need to keep it within the realm of the feasible. What resolution do you tell the PI can be developed?
- You've just completed Systems Requirements Review (SRR) and have received authority to proceed to Preliminary Design Review

(PDR). Your project manager shows you the schedule they project working to and reveals the time from SRR to PDR is 9 months. The PM asks you if your team can in fact be ready for PDR in 9 months. Do you commit the team to being ready for PDR in that amount of time?
- A member of your team has been working on structural analyses but has fallen behind the curve because of illness and a death in the family. She requests you inquire if you can shift some their work to other colleagues to help catch up. Do you give the proposal the OK?
- During build, the prime contractor was informed that NASA quality oversight would have fewer people than originally planned and, as a result, their fabrication schedules are now at risk. Quality is managed from a different organization than yours, but the contractor needs an answer today so that they can report to their boss. How do you respond?
- A critical technology is needed to pass component qual so that it can then be incorporated into the higher level assembly for more qual testing. You need to have the hardware manufactured and delivered, passed by quality assurance, develop the test procedures, ensure that the test facility is available and ready, and dedicate a sufficient number of personnel to conduct the testing. What sort of commitment do you make?

With all of these scenarios, if you respond with a commitment, the firmness and level of confidence you put into an answer is likely to be taken as an indication of concurrence. If you concurred with a plan, or even were interpreted as concurring with a plan, then you'll be responsible for delivering. Are you really that confident when you make the commitment? If you are, and can base it in fact, realistic timeframes, and resources, then great, go for it. You don't have to be 100 percent sure, there can be some uncertainty or risk remaining on the issue. But once you've made the commitment then you need to stand behind it. If, on the other hand, you know you can't deliver, then it's probably not a promise you should be making. If the question is in the middle ground, potentially achievable but with lots of challenges and risk, then that should be your reply and the commitment should be negotiated.

Here's an area where the lack of accountability routinely gets projects into trouble right from the start. During early formulation, while the project is looking to secure funding and eventually gain approval, it's not uncommon to advertise optimistic schedules, grandiose technical capabilities, or aspirational technology advancements. This is one reason why so many projects can't meet their cost or schedule commitments, because they underestimate the complexity of the challenge or the time required to develop the system, or the level to which the technology has to be advanced. Sure, it's a game, getting projects approved and funded, but it's one that's fraught with risk and almost always ends up with the project unable to deliver on its promises (necessitating a replan, reporting to Congress, and other clearly messy consequences). Are the project proposers trying to consciously pull the wool over the eyes of the approving authority? Generally, no, there's rarely active malfeasance going on. Simply, they want their project to be approved and fear that if the approving authority knew the reality of how difficult it would be to develop, it might not receive that approval. OK, maybe a conscious action, but not really malfeasance. Or, the proposers may not have sufficiently researched the development time, cost, and complexity and made their proposal sincerely but out of ignorance. Anyway, the point is that should this happen again and again by the same proposing organization, they eventually lose credibility because they cannot stay accountable to their promises. It happens, unfortunately.

Accountability equals reputation, and that's a commodity that is very difficult to replenish if it's lost. It is much easier to make sure that you stay accountable than it is to dig yourself out of an avoidable situation because you promised more than you know you can deliver. Which brings us to the subject of truthfulness. If you're not being truthful, by definition you're lying. But it is possible to make an unattainable commitment without lying. As mentioned in the proposal scenario above, the proposers may not have knowingly made an unattainable proposal, but simply had been naive to the situation and didn't study the development needs sufficiently to get an answer that had a high probability of success. They weren't lying in their proposal; they just didn't have a good answer. But as for accountability, even if they weren't lying, they were still accountable for delivering on their promise. Being accountable, therefore, necessitates knowledge of the achievability of the commitment you're making. Some promises are easy to make without a lot of research—say, you promise to make a meeting the following day because you know your calendar from memory. Other promises may require substantially more study, such as your promising to deliver a new technology in an accelerated timeframe. That's going to take some research. Whichever case it is, just make sure you're pretty confident you know what you're promising.

So far, everything we've discussed in this chapter concerns your accountability with others. But there's also someone critically important that you need to stay accountable to—yourself! Your commitments to others are important, but also are the commitments you make to yourself. Perhaps you have set some personal development goals to take training courses or improve your competency in some area. Maybe you really need a bit of time off and scheduled a vacation to let off some steam. Or, even more intimately, maybe you recognize that you need to leave work earlier to spend more time to your family or spend less time responding to email when home. These commitments to yourself are no less important than those you make to others. And your accountability to yourself can equally be tarnished by making promises you cannot keep. Just as you need to be honest with others, you need to be honest with yourself (see Chapter 14, "Managing Yourself").

And here's another challenge: Staying accountable even when those around you are not. The situation can come up in the course of your responsibilities as Chief Engineer. Let's say that others in your team are responding to the project manager that 9 months to PDR is definitely doable but your analysis says "no way." Or the program makes a promise on instrument resolution because the PI is very influential with the project's stakeholders, but you know that promise cannot be accomplished. Or maybe your component developer promised the test chamber manager that the hardware would be ready when the chamber's availability window opens, right after a meeting in which he told you it would not be possible to deliver on schedule. These are not easy cases to handle by any means, but they are realistic ones you might see. What to do?

Admittedly, these questions are in areas that verge on the realm of ethics, to be sure, and this really isn't a book about ethics. Plus, these are situations that can affect relationships, touch on politics, and have wide-ranging effects on aspects that have nothing to do with engineering. Many of them have to be handled with discretion and finesse, which, again, is beyond the scope of this book. But I can offer one simple suggestion—stay true to the ideals of being a Chief Engineer. While I can't really provide guidance on what you should do in these situations, I can tell you what I would expect of myself. In each of these scenarios I would opt to be on the side of truth. If I knew something was untrue, I would say so. Exactly how that message would be delivered can be complicated, but I know, myself, the direction would be to ensure that the true situation became known. Others may not have a commitment to accountability, and I can't control others, but I can ensure that I remain accountable. At least to the commitments that I have control over. I understand all of that is easy to say and much more difficult to do, but again I point to the ideals of leadership incumbent in being a Chief Engineer and use that as a measuring stick. What's more, adhering to ideals makes you a suitable role model for the rest of your team—another role you serve as Chief Engineer.

There are mechanisms that can help you remain accountable. Obviously, maintaining cognizance of your schedule can help you stay accountable for your time commitments. If you have an administrative assistant (hey, some Chief Engineers do!), they may be of some assistance in noting and reminding you of your commitments. And of course, writing things down can be invaluable, particularly if like many Chief Engineers you need to process and retain more than the average brain can handle (you Superperson you!).

But the goal of accountability reaches beyond these routine commitments. Validating (or, in our vernacular, "sanity checking") what you agree to is a good practice. If you can do this yourself, by internal analysis, test, demonstration, or inspection, that's great. Sanity checking yourself takes some practice, but it certainly can be done. More commonly, we ask others to sanity check us, which can be done by a deputy or other trusted colleague. Sanity checking alone may not help us remain fully accountable all the time, but it can help prevent us from making commitments in the haste of a discussion that we may not be able to keep.

Additionally, you can have someone you trust hold your feet to the fire. If you agreed to do, provide, deliver, test, or design something and it was a reasonable thing to agree to, it may still remain a difficult thing to complete. Someone who can remind you that a commitment is approaching tardiness or otherwise give you a heads up that you might miss the commitment is absolutely invaluable. That's not as ideal as keeping track of it all yourself (the best way to stay accountable), but in the lurch it can do the trick.

Ultimately, accountability, like trust, reputation, and credibility, are the most important commodities that you own. These are vital to your success. But if you don't stay vigilant, they can be lost, or extremely difficult to recover. Hold on to your accountability like your career depends upon it, because in all likelihood it does.

CHAPTER 19

BECOMING A MASTER OF RISK

When I transitioned to NASA HQ in 2011, one of the projects for which I had oversight responsibilities was the Environmentally Responsible Aviation project. This 6-year effort was charged with investigating and maturing promising technologies with the goal of reducing noise, fuel consumption, and emissions of transport-class commercial aircraft. The project was separated in to two phases: the first 3 years (Phase 1) would investigate more than 20 individual technologies with great potential, and then during the second 3 years (Phase 2) would down-select about a half-dozen of the most-promising ones to further mature to TRL 5 or 6. The project manager had a long and distinguished research career, but as many research projects are unbounded, this was his first project that was on a limited schedule and a finite budget. At the end of the project's run, after gaining a master-class education in project management, he was noted for stating that he discovered his primary function as project manager was to manage risk.

That's not untrue for a Chief Engineer as well. Risk permeates everything we do. It's constantly out there and has to be monitored at all times. If you ignore it, it is likely to hurt you. Even if you watch it, it may come at you from a completely unexpected direction and make your life miserable. It is a tide you struggle to hold back as it flows and then get to relax as it ebbs. It is pernicious and will give you an education whether you want one or not. The only option you have is to deal with it, and if you want to be a successful Chief Engineer you will master it. In fact, you may even be able to make it work to your advantage (see "Opportunities" in this chapter).

Risk management is actively considering things that might impact your project and determining how these impacts might be avoided or consequences reduced. At its core, that's what it's about. It's thinking through and identifying all the events, occurrences, or circumstances that could bite your project in the butt and then walking through all the ways you might be able to fend them off. Risk management is not a consideration of hazards—that's a whole different area. It is a methodical process—or at least it can be, it doesn't have to be—but it's not so much about the process as it is about the thought and discussion that goes into it. Risk management starts at the beginning of the project during early formulation and continues throughout its entire life, at every stage, until the mission is accomplished and the project ends. It doesn't stop because risks don't stop coming at you.

Over the years NASA has developed both a strong culture of risk management and the associated processes and practices to assist its execution. We have NPRs dictating policies, handbooks offering guidance, management plans from a variety of projects outlining processes, Communities of Practice gathering practitioners to discuss what works and what doesn't, and even workshops and symposiums on the topic of risk management. Resources are also available outside of the Agency in the form of textbooks by professional societies. And all of this is great, really good stuff for both the novice and the experienced practitioner, and these resources should be used, no question about it. But all of this in and of itself won't make you a master of risk. To accomplish that, you have to practice it yourself and train your brain to think in terms of risk.

Risk management is a constant, continuous effort and something that should always be on your mind during every status telecon, every technical review, every meeting with your prime contractor, every discussion with project management, while reading every email and activity report, when approving configuration changes, and on and on. Risk should always be on your mind and you should always stay sensitive to the presence of it. Risk should be part of the equation for every decision you make and every direction you give. Thought of it should be a constant companion, as you do already with considerations for safety. Giving consideration for risk should become part of how you think. I've trained myself to think about risk so much that I've started to bring it home with me. My wife doesn't always want to hear about the incumbent risks before we troubleshoot the garbage disposal. She's probably right, as she is about most things, but you get my point about risk always being on my mind.

Even if you haven't done much risk management before, some of you have probably seen and might be familiar with the 5×5 matrix of risk Likelihood and Consequence commonly used in many NASA reviews.

This matrix shows the likelihood of a risk occurring along the Y-axis, measured from 1 to 5, with 1 being nearly impossible and 5 an almost complete certainty. Along the X-axis are the consequences should a risk occur, again measured from 1 to 5 with 1 being the least impactful consequence and 5 being catastrophic to the project. Risks are then populated into this matrix, each positioned to show its 1–5 score for consequences and likelihood. These risk matrices are very helpful management tools in that they give you a broad perspective of the risk environment for your project in a single snapshot. They are used to the greatest effect when prioritizing which risks need to be actively mitigated and which you can just sit back and watch. (Most projects won't have the resources or time to mitigate every single risk, so you have to prioritize.) On the downside, I've seen far too many risk managers develop 5×5 matrices just for the sake of developing a matrix and it becomes a process for the sake of process. I have been in meetings in which we spent hours debating the placement of a risk in the matrix, with one side advocating for a 3×4 and the other side equally arguing for a 4×3. Remember, that ain't the point of this, folks! The point of scoring risks and populating the matrix is so that you can then have an informed discussion about which to mitigate and which to watch—the discussion is what's important here, not the matrix itself. Sorry, I've got myself all riled up now.

But back to the title of this chapter. Being a master of risk means two things. It means mastering the inherent process that goes into risk management—looking out for and identifying risks (the hardest part), categorizing and prioritizing them, determining mitigations and enacting them when able, monitoring the mitigations' effectiveness and making changes when required, and determining when mitigation is no longer required. Much of this is supported by process and your project's risk manager (if your project is large enough to have a risk manager) can assist with much of this. Second, being a master of risk implies something larger: that you are the master of the risks and the risks do not master you. You control them, not the other way around. You see them before they show up. You minimize them before they damage your project. I know, that sounds great from an idealistic standpoint, all motivational and such, but there are limits to what you can do, right? No one can tell the future with certainty or make things happen at the snap of a finger. That's true. But there's a lot you can do within the wide boundaries of mastering risk, and it is part of your job. If you have to do it, you might as well get good at it, and if you do get good at, it the benefits of mastering risk are enormous from the standpoint of shepherding a project toward success.

So what sorts of things could befall your project that you should monitor as risks? Where to start—there are about a million things that could happen. There could be technical issues with developing your hardware or software (for a thousand different reasons) or the system might not perform as desired. There could be issues with testing or manufacturing facilities, or the facilities may become unavailable. Your contractors could have a whole slew of issues that slow down work. The technical team you lead could lose members, which could also slow down work. Your budget might be cut. You might win the lottery and buy an island in the Caribbean, only to learn that the previous owner was a crook who used the island as a tax write-off illegally and that as rightful owner you now owe those taxes plus interest and they will make you work as a short-order cook in a Jamaican jerk restaurant until it's paid off. Admittedly, that's a low-likelihood risk, but it certainly would slow down work.

Figuring out which events might bite the project on its proverbial rear is frequently the most difficult part of managing risk. No one has a crystal ball, and no one can foresee everything that might happen. Plus, identifying risks requires a certain amount of creativity and that sort of challenge is not easy for everyone. Still, do the best you can and really try to think of all that might strike your project. You don't have to get all the risks identified at the very beginning of your project; you can always add more to the list as time goes on as new ones get identified. But the only way to stay ahead of the curve, which is the main idea here, is to give this thought and respond proactively instead of reactively. If you know your system and its goals and objectives, then you should know what could prevent attaining them. If you know your design, you should know what challenges there may be in producing it. If you know your contractors, you should know what potential weaknesses they may bring with them. If you know your manufacturing plan, you should know what difficulties you might have at that stage in the development life cycle. Knowing all these things doesn't give you absolute clairvoyance, but it should give you enough grounding to be able to predict what could set your project astray. And having this knowledge can help you stay out in front of the risks, controlling and mastering them instead of their controlling and mastering you.

So on to our favorite question: What's your role in this as Chief Engineer? Do you have to do this all yourself? If your project is very small, say only a few people total, then yeah, you might (as well as a plethora of other roles). But most projects large enough to have a dedicated Chief Engineer are also large enough to have someone who can do the day-to-day management of risks. In most cases this is a project risk manager, but the position title varies from project to project. Regardless, someone should be able to do such tasks as day-to-day risk tracking, managing the repository where the risks are stored, updating wording as required, creating the 5×5 matrix if one is used and keeping it up-to-date. This is all done so that the risk story can be provided to you and project leadership on a regular basis, driving discussion on which to mitigate and how and which to just watch. Your role generally comes in prior to these regular discussions when it would be beneficial for you to review the list, become familiar with some of the details on the more critical risks, and be prepared to discuss your and your team's perspectives on the risks. Your risk manager may also ask for your opinion on how the risk owners scored their risks (Likelihood and Consequence) and request your feedback (sometimes changing the score as a result). Then, when the discussion with project leadership occurs you will be ready to provide context and technical perspective.

These discussions occur at the project-level with many in the project's leaders, but it can be useful for you to have similar discussions just within your technical team. You'll get smarter on the risks and you'll hear directly from those who are likely the owners of some of the risks.

And besides, some of the risks may be purely technical and authority to mitigate (or not mitigate) has already been handed to you as the project's ETA.

Note that risk management can be perceived by some as a complete bore. Don't let it be. If it gets boring and pedantic and you're wondering why you're even spending time on it, then you may not be doing it right and clearly, it's not providing you much benefit. Again, don't get too wrapped up in the process. The process is important to queue up the discussion, but it's the discussion itself that is the real value here. When you're reviewing the collection of risks, make sure that the set represents your understanding of priorities in the big picture. That prioritization, figuring out which risks to focus on and which to pay less attention to, is a big part of managing risk. Compare them apples-to-apples so that you get an objective comparison. Once you feel comfortable, you're focusing on the really important ones, then dive into them individually. And here's something critical—make sure everyone has the same understanding of the risk. Sometimes the risk statement, which provides a description of the risk, is ambiguous or misleading. When this happens, you may be thinking one thing and others are thinking something else, and then you're not working the same risk. Before moving to mitigations, ensure that everyone agrees what the risk is. I've seen this both done well and done poorly, and the time (and opportunity to mitigate) wasted by misunderstanding risks can be regrettable.

Your risk manager, if you have one, can help with managing the sheer volume of technical risks you may be carrying, it's really incumbent on you to then get a deep understanding of those risks. If someone has a question on a particular technical risk, they should be able to go to you as Chief Engineer for a thorough explanation. Your risk manager can give a top-level overview stemming from the risk statement but shouldn't be expected to have a deep technical understanding of the risk and the implications to your technical development. But you should. What this means is that you should take the time to familiarize yourself with the technical risks and gain an understanding of them commensurate with being able to explain them to whoever asks.

You never know when this might be required, as questions can arise at technical reviews, management meetings with the project leadership, or at HQ during budget or schedule reviews. At these sorts of meetings, when questions arise on technical risks, all the heads generally turn to the Chief Engineer to provide background, context, and understanding. This is expected of your position. To be fair, some risks may be so low in likelihood or consequence, or affecting such a small part of the system that they simply haven't percolated up to your level yet. That can certainly happen. But it's also unlikely for those "small" risks to come up at the aforementioned meetings, so you can pick and choose a bit on which risks you carry a deep understanding—certainly understand the top technical risks and perhaps the next level down. If you're able, be conversant on every risk in your risk registry, but at least be very conversant on the most critical ones.

And how do you get conversant on all of these risks? Well, for starters, read them. Yeah, I know, that can be boring and time-consuming depending on how many your team has identified. But even reading through them once can set a bit in your noggin that can be extracted later should it become relevant to a discussion. For the top risks, though, some study might be required. Thoroughly understand the risk statement, what the risk is really conveying and what it could affect within your system development, design, or operations. If it's a hardware performance risk, know that. If it's a contractor deliverable risk, know that. If it's a test facility availability risk, know that. If it's a resource or funding risk affecting design decisions—right, know that. Get a good feel for the impact to your system or its development should the risk be realized. Know the impact not just in terms of "moderate," "high," or "catastrophic" catchwords, but in terms of technical performance lost and requirements or mission objectives not attained, or maybe in terms of weeks or months of schedule lost or the potential for redesign and the incumbent effects that could have. If someone asks you, be able to describe all of this at least to the level that they can understand and that is required to support the discussion. Then understand the likelihood of the risk occurring. This will always be a subjective argument, as no one can precisely know the future. A probabilistic assessment of likelihood is great if you have one, but even a subjective assessment of likelihood is normally sufficient for most conversations.

Which takes us to mitigations or what can be done to prevent the risk from occurring. It is at this stage of the process that you will very likely need to roll in the programmatic side of the equation, as many mitigations require additional schedule or funding; not every single one, but many. If a mitigation might be to increase work from single-shift to double-shift to complete fabrication on schedule, that will require additional funding (or at least a shift in its phasing). If reducing the risk of a contractor who has a history of delayed deliveries not meeting their commitment means bringing on a second contractor for the same part, that would require additional funding. Or perhaps mitigating the risk of maturing a critical technology beyond TRL 6 dictates adding 2 months to the schedule, that would be an impact the project manager would want to know about. Developing mitigations can be an exercise in creativity, maybe even an opportunity to think creatively, but whatever you come up with will also be a test of your credibility should the project manager decide to go with it. So, know what you're talking about and provide realistic mitigations with factual data, because you might be called on it.

Throughout all of this, it's your responsibility to maintain an eye on the big picture. Others, like members on your technical team, might know more about any specific risk than you do, but they will be focused on that specific risk and that specific mitigation. You, on the other hand, are responsible for understanding how the risk and its mitigations play into the system under development as a whole. Some mitigations may provide an elegant solution for that individual risk but could in fact place impediments or hurdles on the system writ large. Say, for example, there is a risk that the procured hydraulic actuator won't be able to supply sufficient force to an aero surface because the actuator was certified for a different environment. One risk mitigation could be to increase the power output of the Auxiliary Power Unit (APU) that supplies the pressure to the hydraulic fluid. That could certainly mitigate the issue with the actuator and solve that problem, but it might create a whole different problem because now you might need a different APU than the one you procured, or it might increase the overall mass of the vehicle. That's kind of an obvious example, but you get my point—the Chief Engineer needs to keep an eye on the big picture and understand impacts to the system as a whole.

Finally, there are Opportunities (remember, I promised to discuss this). Just as we can manage risk and reduce the likelihood of occurrence or the consequence on the project should they occur, we can also manage opportunities. Opportunities can help a project achieve its goals and provide benefit. They are the opposite of risk, so as risk is characterized by the impact of its consequence, opportunities are characterized by the advantages gained by their benefits. With risks we seek to actively reduce the likelihood of their occurrence, and with opportunities we desire to increase the likelihood of their occurrence. Both can be managed similarly, perhaps on a 5×5 matrix to compare, contrast, and prioritize. Both utilize actions to affect desired outcomes—mitigations in the case of risk and realizations in the case of opportunities.

An example of an opportunity might be that a technology is under development outside of your project that could, if it were matured and available, solve some significant technical challenges. The technology might require maturing, which necessitates additional resources, but has the potential to solve some really vexing issues for you. It's an opportunity. This technology could be placed on your opportunity matrix. You can assess the likelihood of the technology's being matured to the point that it could be incorporated into your design and you could assess the benefit it would provide if that were to happen. Some opportunities would provide little benefit or be very unlikely to occur—these rate low; other opportunities might offer substantial benefit or be extremely likely to occur—these rate high.

Not many people or projects give a lot of thought to opportunities because they are spending so much time trying to ward off the risks. That's true. And it's probably unlikely that opportunity management would share equal time with risk management. Nor should it. But spending a little time on it, every once in a while, could help your project get ahead of the curve in substantial ways. It would require an investment of your time and thought and might take you away for a short time from other pending matters, but it could pay off in ways that make your life easier.

Again, a last word from former NASA Chief Engineer David Mobley:

> One of the ways I found to help keep a risk or an opportunity is to build into the mitigation plan a decision point (usually one or more are required anyway) with a date for reaching this decision. This greatly helps to keep the risk to my attention and obviously the need for a "new" direction in the mitigation plan.*

Outstanding advice. Identifying risks and including them in a risk registry alone will not increase the likelihood of a project's success. Ultimately, risks are about informing decisions, and few things will improve if no decisions are made. It can be beneficial, as David suggests, to insert decision points into the process. Doing so has the benefit both of maintaining the issue on the decision-maker's radar, and also ensuring that needed decisions are made in a timely manner. Or said another way, when they can be effective. Keep watching a risk for a long time, and you may be too late to actually do anything about it. You can force the process to ensure that reasonably timely decisions are made. As Chief Engineer, it's your call.

---

* David Mobley. Peer-review correspondence with the author.

CHAPTER 20
PROMOTING INNOVATION

NASA has always been a hotbed of innovation. We have to be! On countless occasions, we're handed missions to execute that have never been attempted before with few if any analogs from which to pull. Newer and more-capable instruments have to be developed and new technologies have to be devised to accomplish more and more complex tasks. Just think about the innovation that went into sending astronauts to land on the Moon and return safely to Earth at a time in which our collective spaceflight experience was 15 minutes in a one-person, rudimentary ballistic capsule. To accomplish the Apollo program, almost every bit of the technologies, the techniques, the means to test and verify it all and the actual operations had to be developed from a whole bunch of nothing. And the push for innovation continues today as technology gets more complex, hardware and software more integrated and seamless, and computing capabilities allow us to do more and more. Innovation lies at the heart of what NASA does, not simply for innovation's sake but because we must innovate to achieve our objectives.

Innovation enables. Innovation revitalizes. Innovation allows doors to open and identifies new navigable paths to solutions. Innovation is inherent in what we do as an Agency and little would be possible without its inclusion. NASA is not a community that's comfortable with the static and set. No, we seek to achieve great things in exploration and discovery and new ways of looking at the skies, at the planet, at the universe, and at ourselves. To do these prodigious things, innovation is written into the fabric of our being.

What's more, innovation isn't limited to just new technologies. We innovate processes as well. We invent new ways of managing and funding projects and better ways of monitoring their performance. And, yes, we innovate on the engineering, in how we analyze, assess, verify and validate, and a multitude of other aspects of the job. We innovate on new ways of modeling and analysis, on better ways to test, and on processes that continue to meet the needs of increasingly complex systems.

To keep this moving and continue to meet NASA's goals and objectives, this innovation, of both processes and technology, is something for the Chief Engineer to remain aware of and, when possible, promote within his or her team.

Your technical team will face many challenges along the way and tried and true heritage solutions may not always work. When that happens, when available technology won't fit the bill, or system complexity mandates new methodologies, your team will have to innovate. The ability to innovate, which you'll find is effortless for some but difficult for others, can be assisted and more easily enabled if there is an environment that promotes innovation within the team. Environments that promote innovation allow for and encourage alternate solutions to be proposed and implemented, help facilitate out-of-the-box thinking and experimentation, and avoid discouragement by detractors shooting down suggestions simply because they are new or untried. Open innovation environments reward entrepreneurial experimentation and free thinking.

So, what does that mean for the problems you and your team will likely be facing? First off, I assume you already accept the part about having to face challenges; that's probably rhetorical, you can count on that happening. When it does, you'll have to assess whether you have the tools, technologies, and methodologies needed to solve those challenges or whether something new will need to be invented. For example, let's say your project needs a pressure vessel that has to be four times lighter than anything available on the market. Or, you need to figure out how to test and verify a parachute for a planetary lander that's too large to fit into any available test chamber. In these situations, the process can start by encouraging your team to brainstorm on ideas. Nothing should be considered ridiculous; no idea is outside the boundaries of what can be suggested. Those ideas may generate laughs and snickers, but nothing should produce ridicule. Who knows, one of those ideas may indeed turn out to be your savior once it's more thoroughly fleshed-out. Provide your team an environment in which they feel free to offer suggestions, even crazy ones, and have them considered.

Sometimes, a suggestion might have merit and seem to have potential, but there's a lot of uncertainty associated with the proposal. Some of this uncertainty can be reduced by experimentation. It might be tweaking things in a laboratory or playing with spreadsheets on a computer in an office, but experimentation continues this environment of innovation. People learn through experimentation, they test ideas, reduce trade space, and sometimes realize that the infeasible may actually turn out to be feasible. But what's more, given the opportunity to experiment, people know that their leadership isn't stonewalling their ideas and are allowing them at least a chance to succeed. This experimentation may prove the idea to be a false path, but at least the idea got tested and has shown that it was not viable. That means a lot to most innovators and you can encourage their ability and desire to generate ideas by allowing some amount of experimentation.

One of the best examples today of the need for engineering innovation comes from the world of autonomous systems and the challenge of ensuring V&V of these systems. Verification is primarily an exercise in probabilistic outcomes. You test, analyze, inspect, or demonstrate to ensure that the functional outcome you're looking for has a reasonable probability of occurrence. The functions we typically verify are outcomes that we can predict and determine (thus called deterministic outcomes). But for autonomous systems, where the decision-making is highly complex and outside of the enforcement of standard physical controls, deterministic solutions may not be guaranteed.

Confused? Here's an example: A spring-actuated valve is fairly deterministic. Knowing the spring force, loads, and materials involved, you can predict to a high probability when and how the spring will operate. It's just pure physics and the mechanics of the spring can be predicted through mathematical equations. But then take autonomous systems, where the outcome is the result of machine logic and, possibly, artificial intelligence. In this case the outcome is not so easy to predict. It can be tested, but due to the complexities involved (not to mention chaos theory) it may not be deterministic and when tested again the same starting conditions could give a different result. So, when verifying an autonomous system, our normal methodologies may be lacking since the outcome is not entirely deterministic. The engineering community

CHAPTER 20 • *Promoting Innovation* 215

writ large (i.e., not just NASA) needs a new V&V solution for autonomous systems. This is a well-known problem and many people are working on it. But the point is, since traditional methodologies won't work, innovative solutions are required.

Maintaining an environment of innovation for your technical team, who are a bountiful and fruitful source of ideation, unlocks creativity and gives you a powerful tool for success. But nothing is easy and there are barriers to creating this sort of environment within your team. In March 2017, the NASA Chief Technologist presented to the NASA Advisory Council's (NAC) Technology, Innovation, and Engineering (TI&E) committee its plan for assessing best practices for promoting innovation within NASA, and also ways to address the barriers or impediments to innovation.* The presentation included a particularly insightful chart on these barriers, collected from the members' own research, including benchmarking and discussions with technology developers and innovators within and outside the Agency. It included seven such barriers or impediments, and I'd like you to think about these in terms of the Chief Engineer's job.

- **Risk-averse Culture**—Management/workforce conservatism and oversight bodies drive costs and create more incremental steps.
- **Short-term Focus**—Immediate mission needs (for example, meeting-level requirements) often must take short-term priority over the development of future capabilities.
- **Instability**—Changes in decisions and direction set by external stakeholders as well as tactical decisions have dried up the innovation pipeline and led to a cycle of technology start/stops.
- **Lack of Opportunity**—Fewer flight opportunities have reduced available pathways for infusion of innovations. Technology demonstrations historically come and go yet have spurred some of the revolutions in NASA history.

---

* *https://www.nasa.gov/sites/default/files/atoms/files/nac_march2017_dterrier_oct_tagged.pdf*, (accessed October 23, 2019).

- **Process Overload**—Excessive administrative burdens can stagnate innovators; process owners have become gatekeepers instead of enablers.
- **Communication Challenges**—Organizational silos, "not invented here" thinking, and lack of commonality in IT and communication technologies for linkage.
- **Organizational Inertia**—Cultural tendency to stay the course and a lack of trust often portray innovation as a threat; need to balance the risk with reward.

Let's start with risk-averse culture. Such cultures promote conservatism and innovation is considered the antithesis of playing things conservatively. A risk-adverse culture may discourage innovation and force more "known" solutions. It's OK to be cautious, but a cautious attitude can leave doors closed to what could potentially be good ideas. Risk-adverse cultures generally discourage even trying new ideas because of the fear of failure. Innovation doesn't mean taking gratuitous risk, sometimes all it means is thinking about your problem from a different angle. When even that can't happen, you may have a risk-adverse culture in your team.

Short-term focus is common as managers and leaders keep their team's heads down, addressing only the most immediate problems with tactical solutions. Because there's so much work to do, the intent is to focus on what needs to be solved today and no attention is paid to what the project may need in the future. Looking at the world through only a day-to-day lens is likely to produce band-aid solutions, and innovation can't get a foothold. While the majority of work your technical team will do is short-term focused, going from one milestone to the next, maintaining only a short-term focus can inhibit innovation.

Frequent course corrections, leadership changes, and rebaselines can contribute to instability, resulting in cycles of innovative ideas being started and then stopped. Good ideas are attempted and pursued but are quickly terminated due to the change occurring within the project around them. You can see this when requirements change, or designs undergo substantive alteration. What were challenges before are overcome by events, and the innovation stops in its tracks. There is no follow-through, and the environment can get degraded to the point that innovators become discouraged through the fear that their efforts will inevitably be terminated. In fact, they may get so discouraged that they hesitate from even starting.

Due to budget constraints and perhaps a bit of the risk-averse culture, opportunities that require innovation are getting fewer. Lack of opportunities to innovate can have obvious ramifications on innovators, as there is a smaller pool and need for innovative solutions. While there's nothing a Chief Engineer can do to approve more projects for the Agency, there certainly is latitude to allow opportunities for innovation in the projects we already have.

Process overload is likely a familiar grievance for most of you. There are NPRs, work instructions, procedures, quality inspections, audits, and a host of other paperwork that the technical team has to abide by. When the administrative burden gets to be overbearing, it can extinguish the bandwidth available for innovation. Although much of that overhead is born of best practices put in place to ensure that projects maximize success, they can also quash environments that allow for innovation if leadership is not careful. I wouldn't recommend throwing away the process, it's there for very good reasons, but instead maintain an awareness of where and when it may be inhibiting your environment for innovation.

When people talk, they can share ideas and solicit feedback. When people don't talk, they submit to the standard practice in their area and are not exposed to potentially new ways of doing business. Communication challenges can inhibit innovation by creating silos of parochial practices, and residing within those silos with no exposure to outside ideas can create organizational and cultural hurdles to innovation. An innovative team discusses solutions within itself but also is liberally exposed to ideas from outside itself.

Finally, all of the above can lead directly to organizational inertia. Doing things because "that's the way they are done here" can have obvious effects on the ability for team members to innovate. Fresh ideas are immediately discarded, and developing these ideas sometimes are even discouraged or outright prevented. Organizations that submit to these ideals rarely innovate (and frequently get surpassed by those willing to innovate and change paradigms). Again, as we've discussed in previous chapters, organizational culture can bring strength to a team, but it also may deliver hidden penalties such as diminished innovation. If, for example, someone suggests a testing methodology not used at your project's host Center, don't discard the idea simply because it's from another Center. Give it thought and see if it could make sense for your project. In doing so, you promote an environment of innovation.

Even if you clear these hurdles, you should note that innovation can have its detractors. Not everyone is comfortable with innovation, and you're likely to have a few on your team. "Tried and true" and "invented here" may be barriers to innovation but they are comforting concepts to some. You may get retorts like "It's risky, maybe dangerous, to try new things. We might fail. Let's just stick with what we know, even if it doesn't do everything we need for it to do." Familiarity gives a sense of security for some folks and anything unfamiliar breeds fear. This is understandable: change is hard. But the opposite, remaining static, while it may be comforting doesn't necessarily get the job done when doing the complex and groundbreaking things that NASA does. Managing detractors on your team is not hard, they may just need a bit solace to assuage their fears. But at a minimum, note that they may exist within your team and watch for any effects their inhibitions might have on the rest of your team's ability to innovate.

By the same token, you may find some team members strongly innovative, so much so that they border on the impractical. It sounds silly, but it does happen. These folks, like the detractors above, are trying to help the project be successful in the way they believe is best. There's nothing malicious here, in either case. But it warrants awareness that these influences may be on your team and, as their leader, it's up to you to ensure neither becomes disruptive.

Within NASA, you'll find certain Centers more open to innovation and others more beholden to traditional solutions. Some put a strong focus on advanced technologies and research, which by definition require innovative thinking and allow or even encourage out-of-the-box solutions. Others have strong institutional practices with firm controls in place based on years of usage and may be more hesitant to innovate.

These generalizations don't always apply. You would think JSC would be one of the Centers with strong institutional practices and firm controls, but in fact, when you get down to the working troops level there was a strong desire for innovation when I was there. In 2010, with the end of the Constellation program and commercial crew providers coming online (both existential threats), my home organization (MOD) initiated an effort to see where its skills could best be used in the future, even looking in nontraditional human spaceflight areas. I co-lead a team that consisted of about a dozen midcareer, nonsupervisory personnel. This group spent almost 9 months reviewing the critical skills MOD had to offer and brainstorming on where and how they could be applied. The innovation here was extraordinary. Outside-the-box thinking was highly encouraged and many of the recommendations the team applied were far outside of MOD's traditional roles. For example, flight controller problem-solving abilities and astronaut training capabilities were acknowledged as critical skills and the team considered how those could be applied to customers outside the realm of human spaceflight, something that MOD had never considered over its long history. This group of innovators, having spent their entire career to date at a large NASA Center with very strong institutional processes, had no problem thinking innovatively and coming up with some very unique solutions. The inherent capability to think innovatively was there, we just had to uncover it by initiating this activity.

The point here is that while innovation may not be readily apparent at first glance, it may be there within your team and can be uncovered by looking a little harder or by encouraging it a bit more consciously.

CHAPTER 21

BUILDING A TEAM

You're the boss. Well, sort of. You're not the boss of everything, but you are the boss of your project's technical team, and you own the technical baseline. You have lots of responsibility, a little authority, and the path for success of your project runs through you in part. All true. But only very rarely does anyone accomplish anything by themselves. Even in writing this book, while I am authoring all the words, getting it into your hands necessitates an editor to proofread and correct grammar, an artist to create a book cover, and a publisher to package it, print it, and distribute it. I could try to do all these additional tasks myself, but I'm pretty sure I wouldn't be anywhere nearly as successful if these other experts didn't bring their talents to this endeavor. The book may have my name on it, but it requires a team to produce it.

This is no less true for complex system development. In fact, that's an understatement. Complex system development requiring a team is verifiably, demonstrably, unquestionably true. No system that I am aware of has ever been developed in the absence of a team. It's necessary. You're going to need one. OK, so check that off the list, you're going to need a team. Now, how do you build one, and just as important, how do you as the leader keep it functioning?

Teams can vary widely in terms of size, complexity, scope, complement, diversity, and just about any other measure you may wish to apply. Answering the above questions starts with considering the needs of your project. Is it a complex, integrated system or is it a more discrete technology development or small research effort? Is the project large and costly or small and agile? Is the risk tolerance high, medium, or low? You can generally scope a team with a few of these top-level parameters.

And then, what will this team be doing? Will it be building a new system? If so, which parts are new and which are heritage? You may need specific discipline experts for the new components, while perhaps combining responsibility for some of the heritage parts within a single individual. What are the technical needs of the project? Where do you need to focus and where do you not? Obviously, the focus areas will require some extra eyeballs and the non-focus areas can rely on lesser attention.

Which specific technical disciplines do you need on your team, and can the remainder be ignored or handled by a general practitioner?

How much systems engineering will be required? Do you plan to follow the traditional systems engineering "V" or utilize a more agile, rapid development approach? Will you have a large requirement set to manage or just a few? Will your V&V use formal techniques or something more informal? Will your Systems Engineering Management Plan be lengthy and complex, mandating the need for someone to help develop it, or simple and straightforward that you can do yourself? Will you be needing a dedicated system engineering manager?

How much integration do you expect there to be? If you are developing a complex system, there may be significant integration of parts, components, assemblies, and internal and external interfaces. If you'd developing a specific standalone instrument or component, there may be less integration required. How it all will come together when the parts are fabricated? How complicated will your assembly be? Will you need a dedicated integration manager?

And then there's test and evaluation. Will your project necessitate a vast amount of testing and verification or will it be fairly straightforward? Will the testing necessitate the use of many different facilities or can you accomplish this all in, say, a single laboratory? Will you need a dedicated test and verification manager?

How much emphasis do you plan to put on risk? Will you be approaching the project with a low risk tolerance and a high need to mitigate, or is the project inherently risky and much will be allowed? Will you need a dedicated risk manager?

Given all these questions, and others you may think of, you should be able to get a feel for the size of team you will be needing. Maybe not an exact number, but at least a general estimate of its size. With this in hand you can consider how your team should be organized. Do you want a hierarchical, top-down structure to the team or a flatter, more horizontal organization? Both have advantages and disadvantages, some work well in certain kinds of projects and worse in others. Large projects tend to vector more to the hierarchical and smaller to the flatter, but there's no hard rule. Much of this depends on your particular preferences and how you want to be able to manage the team. The organizational structure of your team will affect how it communicates up, down, and across, and who reports to whom, so give it some consideration. This is not a small matter.

If you've gotten this far and have a feel for the size of your team and how it will be organized, you should validate it with your project manager. Not that the project manager will necessarily have strong ideas on the above list of questions (and a good project manager should defer to you on these details), but they will be concerned about the overall size of your requested team because, after all, they have to pay for it. The final answer should be a negotiation between you and the project manager, a balance between what you feel you need to accomplish the job and what they can afford to provide. Try not to overlook this discussion.

When you get through that, now comes the hard part—actually finding these people. You may be lucky and have inherited your project team from a previous project such that they can just roll over to your new project. That happens, but that would be too easy, wouldn't it? (I'm joking, no, it wouldn't, it would be ideal!) More realistically, you'll have to go out and find the people you need for your team. The Engineering Director at your Center is a great place to start. They carry the mantle of responsibility for the engineering workforce at NASA Centers, hiring and overseeing many of the technical experts you'll need for your team. They may have the data to let you know who is available and when. If there is a capability you need on your team that's not resident at your Center (say, something specific like Entry, Descent and Landing or Aerothermodynamics), they can put in calls to Engineering Directors at other Centers about obtaining those capabilities.

Of course, you may also be aware of good, relevant engineers and technical staff through your previous NASA experience. That's fine, and in fact is how a number of projects are staffed. Be careful to recognize that these people may have commitments to ongoing projects and may be difficult or disruptive to extract, and even if they can eventually support your project it may be some time before they become available. But if there's someone you've worked with before that you've just got to have, sometimes it can be arranged.

Great! So, now you have a technical team, either in part or in full. You have to get them up to speed on the project they've been assigned to and start them working together. Teams are just as complex as the systems they develop, with just as many complicated interactions and interfaces, unique behaviors and occasional idiosyncrasies, even appearing one way when static and another when in motion. The big difference between teams and the systems being develop is, of course, the constituent part of teams is people, and they are much less predictable and deterministic than is hardware. In building a functional team, even one that looks great on paper and has all the parts you need, your team will be unique given the very human attributes that its members bring. This can present you with opportunities but also with challenges.

Each person on your team brings strengths and weaknesses, talents and shortcomings. They all are individuals, and you should make some effort to get to know them as individuals. Meet with them separately as they report aboard your team and get to know them a bit. Ask them about their personal histories, their hopes for the project and for themselves, their families, and their hobbies. Get to know them a bit. See who likes to laugh and who likes to complain, who is talkative or abrasive and who is quiet or submissive. Get to know them as people. When they all come together to form a team they will be working in a group but will still maintain all of their individual traits. As their leader, it will help you to also know them as the individuals they are. This takes time but it will pay off.

I experienced this in Mission Control. When training begins for a Shuttle mission, typically about 4 months before launch, each controller gets assigned to support a specific flight control team, one of three (or four, on longer missions) who will staff the consoles in shifts throughout the flight. Typically, there would be two to cover the hours the crew is awake and performing the mission's activities, and a third to monitor the vehicle and plan the next day's activities while the astronauts are sleeping. The responsibilities of these separate flight control teams were all the same—monitor the vehicles and crew, oversee their activities, and provide whatever assistance possible to ensure the safety of the crew and the success of the mission. But just because the responsibilities remained the same doesn't mean that each team operates without differences. Myriad flight controllers brought myriad personalities to each team. Some of those personalities got overcome by the rote responsibilities mentioned above, while other personalities still shone through. There were controllers I enjoyed working with more than others, and each time I would get assigned to a flight and to a specific team I would always review the roster to see if any of them were on my team. This was particularly true in the case of the Flight Director for the shift, the identity of whom I would try to ascertain first, as they lead the team and have a larger influence over the overall dynamics than just about any other factor. We flight controllers numbered relatively few—a couple hundred in total—but the unique combinations that composed each of these teams produced some very different flight control teams.

Your team will be no different. Even if you have led other teams before, this one will have its own unique flavor. Since we're all engineers and professionals, it will operate according to basic practices that on the surface seem familiar and standard, but just slightly below the surface you will find the individual personalities coming through. Do you remember the diminutive characters in the famous movie *Snow White and the Seven Dwarfs*? Each of the dwarfs mined for jewels, that was their job, but within that mining consortium you found one who was happy, another who was grumpy, one who was bashful and one who sneezed a lot. Individuals, right? You get the point.

So, take stock. Now you have a team and it consists not just of position titles on an org chart but with actual individuals. The responsibility will fall to you to keep that team functioning, effective, engaged, and productive. You will have to set their goals, monitor their performance, direct and redirect as required, investigate when things aren't working so well, negotiate quarrels, and act as mentor and counselor, boss and friend. It's a lot to do but, hey, you accepted this position.

All teams need clearly defined roles and responsibilities. No one likes ambiguity or the notion that they don't know what they or their neighbor is responsible for. Not only is ambiguity ineffective, it can also be the root of some very unfortunate misunderstandings. Instead, make sure that everyone on the team is aware of their responsibility and that those are well understood by the rest of the team as well. Provide clarity, clear up any confusion, and the functioning of the team will benefit. Here's a hint. One of the easiest ways I have found to understand and communicate roles and responsibilities is to build a RASCI matrix. These constructs work particularly well when organizing roles and responsibilities for producing products, but it still works for other roles and responsibilities too. On this matrix (I'm assuming you're already comfortable with matrices) you place the team members' names on the X-axis and the individual team roles and responsibilities on the Y-axis (or vice versa, it doesn't matter to the RASCI). Then, in each intersection between member and role/responsibility, fill in the box with either an R, A, S, C or I, which stand for Responsible, Accountable, Support, Consulted, or Informed.

Need a decoder ring? Here goes: Responsible indicates the person with overall responsibility for performing and carrying out the task. Accountable (or also sometimes Approver) denotes the person who approves the work that is done. Support designates those who help or aid in the production of the product or execution of the task. Consulted marks someone who can lend assistance with skills, knowledge or expertise to complete the task. And Informed characterizes those who need to know when the task has been completed. RASCI matrixes don't convey everything you may need to know about a team, but they are quick and fairly comprehensive overviews that allow for the determination and communication of roles and responsibilities on a team. I use them.

Most teams arrive at conclusions through discussion. When discussing matters with the team, when possible, try to achieve consensus. It's not always achievable, you may end up with disagreements and those alternate opinions might have merit. But when you can, it's good to arrive at decisions that the entire team supports and can get behind.

When disagreements do arise, listen to all viewpoints with dispassion and objectivity. You'll earn points if you can do that. Be a good listener and allow everyone who wishes to have a say. When a decision needs to be made, make one, and communicate your rationale for the decision. We've covered this before, but it's good to emphasize the superb effect these practices can have on a team.

And be a delegator. Many team members enjoy the opportunity to take on a bit of additional responsibility. It validates their sense of self-worth and value to the team. It also shows you have confidence in them, which can be empowering.

But mostly you will need to keep your team focused on the technical work required by your project. You can set the overall pace and establish both near-term and long-term milestones to provide your team a road map of what is to come. This can help them keep on track. They may look to you to determine the general direction of their activities and to decide what in the big picture should be on their plate at the moment. And count on them looking to you for information from the project office on things that are not technical but still affect the project (like budget or programmatics).

This is your opportunity to put into practice many of the behaviors we've so far discussed in this book (more good ones are to come, I assure you). You can demonstrate emotional intelligence and empathy, you can be the voice of many and be the box top, you can show enthusiasm and maintain an awareness of cultural differences. It all comes together now that you have a team to lead. Fantastic!

Doing so means you will have to contend with the team's problems and issues. Don't expect that you'll simply be able to brush these off on your team members' home organization supervisor. You can't. Even if they formally report to someone else who does their timecard and yearly performance appraisal, they are your team and the team is your responsibility. The most common problem you might encounter is interpersonal conflicts with other team members. Not everyone works well together, and this is difficult to foresee when the team is first assembled. It's not guaranteed, but is likely to occur, especially on larger teams.

You can try separating those in conflict by ensuring their activities don't cross each other, but the better solution is to get with them separately and then together to understand the issue. The issue could be minor or really significant, but either way ensure you give each of them some time to explain to you the problem and then seek a solution. Ideally, they can work out the issue themselves and come to an amicable solution, but that's not always the case and occasionally the situation requires intervention.

Intervening between combatting team members is about the last thing a Chief Engineers enjoys doing. As engineers we easily focus on the technical stuff but can tend to avoid these sorts of interpersonal spats. It's uncomfortable, it can be messy, and anyway why can't people just get along and focus on the engineering! Be that as it may, while these unfortunate circumstances do nothing to advance your project's mission, they do have the potential to derail things just as assuredly as an uncontrolled hazard. As the technical team's leader, the responsibility for dealing with it is yours, messy or not. You can be the adult in the room, hear both sides, bridge the differences and reach common understanding, or if absolutely necessary instruct them to stand down (necessitating a cold war that while definitely not ideal is better than a hot one).

So that was a testy topic. Sorry. But not everything in leading a team will be as uncomfortable. I mean, you also get to do some really cool stuff. That's exciting! Your team will pick up on that excitement and it can be a source of encouragement should challenges arise. That excitement can be a rallying point if the technology doesn't mature as fast as desired, if a risk looks like it will be realized, or if budgets get cut. The very fact that you're all working on some very cool stuff also can help bond a group and as a side benefit parlay the notion that "we're all in this together." That can be a very helpful sentiment when things aren't going so well.

When your team does well, acknowledge it, reward it, and even celebrate the success. I've learned that a simple "well done," acknowledging hard work and accomplishment, even when not paired with any other reward, is often extremely meaningful to folks. It means their work and achievement have been recognized by their boss, which makes just about anyone feel good. Similarly, the time and effort invested in thanking a person for their work is miniscule compared with the appreciation and pride it creates. It's such a simple thing, saying "thank you" or "good job," taking just a second or two and a few breaths, that it amazes me leaders don't do this more often. Do it, often, it means a lot to a team! Similarly, when the team achieves a milestone or some significant event, take the time to celebrate it. I don't mean necessarily renting a dance hall, hiring a band, and tending bar. But even small celebrations such as pizza lunches, balloons in the hallways, or other simple recognition can make a small accomplishment feel like a large one and keep the team motivated.

Remember, in the end this is your team and its success can be directly tied to your leadership skills. Be a good leader and you're almost guaranteed to produce a successful, effective team.

CHAPTER 22

HAVING THE AGILITY TO ADAPT

Plus ça change, plus c'est la même chose. "The more things change, the more they stay the same." So stated Jean-Baptiste Alphonse Karr in an 1848 issue of his journal *Les Guêpes*.* A favorite quote of mine. Stated another way, change happens, it continues to happen, and it always will happen. It's unavoidable, an unquenchable force that acts incessantly and, whether good or bad, something we all need to contend with. This is true in life and in NASA development. Nothing stays static for very long, so we need the agility to adapt to changing situations.

The very nature of change is that it's relentless and unavoidable. Change is unpredictable, but the fact that change will happen is extremely predictable. Change can occur through conscious choice or it can be mandated for us outside our control, and when it happens, it can be uncomfortable and disturbing because it invokes feelings of the loss of control. Change can be miniscule or monumental, tweak-inducing or life changing. Fighting change is like trying to hold the ocean back with a broom (an idiom for a futile effort, another favorite saying of mine).

You will find a mountain of change in your role as Chief Engineer. While we maintain configuration control over our baselines to keep track of change, change still occurs. Our requirements might change, leading us to need to invoke different designs. Project schedules change and milestones move around and affect our ability to deliver products. Budgets change, threatening our ability to staff and acquire capabilities. We might have to contend with turnover in our technical team, long-standing members leaving and new members arriving. Contractors may go out of business and affect our procurements. Interfaces within our system might change or elements our system will need to interface with might change, risking our ability to accomplish our mission.

I don't think many of us enjoy this sort of change because, well, to put it bluntly, it causes additional work and makes life complicated. We have to "re" everything (e.g., redesign, restaff, reverify) and that takes us away from the already full-time job of moving our project forward. When change occurs, we feel like we've lost ground because we have to

---

* Jean-Baptiste Alphonse Karr, *Les Guêpes*, July 1848.

go back and fix or accommodate the change. It doesn't feel like progress. I understand. But basic facts of life are that we simply have to deal with change. It can't be ignored or else the project will assuredly grind to a halt and we can't simply wish it away (I've tried, that doesn't work).

Even seemingly static situations may in fact be changing. Back at JSC when I was in the Flight Director Office I once went to my boss, the Chief. I had been working with a contractor at Ames Research Center who had a background and specialty in sociology. We were talking about the way that much of the flight control team in Mission Control emulates the vehicle we were monitoring—separate flight controllers for the individual hardware subsystems. Both the vehicle and the flight control team were divided into mechanical systems, electrical systems, data processing systems, life support systems, communication systems, and so on. This structure was a conscious decision that can trace its lineage back to the original flight testing of aircraft in the early twentieth century, a legacy that continued into the space age, as many of those that created Mission Control had aircraft flight test backgrounds. The Ames contractor and I speculated that in the future, as spacecraft got more complex (particularly in the area of autonomy and intelligent software systems), the nature of how we configure ourselves as a flight control team should change as well. The thought was that no longer would it suffice to have a control team composition defined by different hardware systems, but rather by something new that better reflected how the system was designed and operated. I was intrigued by this and by the opportunity to help NASA meet the future by proactively reaching for it. So, she and I worked up a proposal to take a look at how the flight control team operates, how the controllers interact, and see if anything useful could come out of it that could inform how we should evolve the flight control team. With this proposal in hand we brought it to the Chief for the study to be funded.

He wasn't interested.

Not that he didn't have the funding; he in fact had a hefty discretionary line in his budget. It was that he just didn't think a study was necessary. He explained that he was a firm believer in things evolving to their most efficient form, and after nearly 60 years of human spaceflight operations the flight control team in Mission Control had attained that evolved form. He believed that it was as good as it could get and had been for some time, so he wanted to keep this form the way it was and not change it. We picked up our proposal and left his office empty-handed and the study never occurred.

Later I gave his supposition some thought and decided firmly that I didn't buy it. I think you could make a case for his argument, but only if you also assumed that the environment around it remained constant. Change the environment and that highly evolved form of organization might no longer be the most effective. In fact, at the time we brought forward the study proposal, the world of human spaceflight control was transitioning from a Government monopoly to one in which new entrants (private spaceflight companies) were emerging, giving NASA a run for its money. The environment of spacecraft operations was changing. Change the environment and evolution no longer produces efficiency. So even if the flight control team structure had evolved to its highest form and had attained that form for some years, that evolution was only relevant as long as the environment around it also remained the same. The point to take away from all this is that even when a situation appears stable and static, it might only be so within the bubble of perception. Increase your scope on that bubble and change is apparent.

So, what are you gonna do? Well, like any resilient system, you adapt.

Before we get into that, let's be clear about one thing, though. In discussing change I'm not suggesting that you have to accept every change that comes down the pike. The theories above are to substantiate the point that Chief Engineers need the agility to adapt to changing circumstances, but you do have some control over the pace and volume of change in your project. While change is ever-present, not all change is acceptable or a good idea. Some change may run counter to the precepts of good engineering that you are to uphold. Some change may be recommended for expediency but is ill-advised (or worse, unsafe) over the long haul. As Chief Engineer you have the latitude, even the responsibility, to push back on change that you see as short-sighted or detrimental to the project. In maintaining technical excellence and in your role as ETA, you can do this.

But given that, this chapter's about having the agility to adapt, right? What do I mean by agility to adapt? When change happens within your project or outside of it, a Chief Engineer can work to accommodate that change without undue complication, with professionalism, and without it throwing the project into chaos. Adapting also means having the perspective and attitude to accept a required change and working to make it happen. This is acceptance even if it means a certain amount of disruption and a positive attitude to get it done. You may go through the classic five stages of change as you would with grief—denial, anger, bargaining, depression, acceptance—but eventually you reach acceptance and, hopefully, you get there quickly. Agility can be thought of as nimbleness and dexterity; nimble in making the change fit in to the technical baseline (it may not always fit easily) and dexterous in how accommodating you can be. Both the Chief Engineer and the technical baseline require a certain amount of agility, as excessive rigidity in either can result in failure.

Accommodating change is not always easy, and your first impulse might be to resist. Discounting the circumstances mentioned above when you should resist, such as safety or poor engineering practice, resisting the change only puts a delay on its incorporation. Work will be required to make the change, so why add more work and time by not accepting the change and putting up a wall to its incorporation? This is rejecting change for the sake of rejecting change. It may feel good initially and give you the impression of control, but it serves little benefit as the change is going to happen anyway. Like astronaut Jim Lovell recounted about the crew's reaction on Apollo 13 immediately after one of the oxygen tanks exploded: "[I]f we had panicked, we would have bounced off the walls for about 10 minutes, and we were still going to be back where we started from."* Wasted energy that doesn't perform

---

* Jim Lovell, quoted in the article "Remembering Apollo" by Buzz Aldrin in the July 1994 issue of *Discover*, *http://discovermagazine.com/1994/jul/rememberingapoll396*, (accessed October 9, 2019).

any useful work, solve a problem, or move an effort forward is illogical. Resisting change because the change is troublesome, ill-timed, or otherwise disruptive just wastes time, doesn't perform any useful work, solve a problem, or move the project forward. When it happens, accept it and focus on what is required to make it happen. Attitude, here, is the start of successful resolution.

You will need to communicate this to your team, preferably in a positive, affirming way. It most likely isn't going to be you, the Chief Engineer, who will have to lift an eraser, change a requirement set, modify a design or alter a plan—it will be your team doing the actual work. Even if you can accept a coming change, your team might be hesitant or resistant for all the same reasons you may be. Sympathize with them, or, better yet, empathize with them, let them know you understand the hardship this is causing, but make it clear that the change needs to be made. Firmness touched with compassion wins the day here, in my mind. You know how your team feels, but you are still responsible for moving the project forward. You can play off their professionalism here too, not to invoke guilt but to remind them that in accommodating the change we are fulfilling our responsibility to NASA and demonstrating our competence and commitment to the project.

Here are some scenarios and examples of how to adapt to change.

- Your project approved its Systems Requirements Documents (SRD) at the Systems Requirements Review. The SRD established a baseline for your requirements set, from HQ-mandated requirements through your system and subsystem requirements, including the associated verification methodologies. Your team has already jumped to some high-level design work, establishing system-level configurations that will meet the requirements. Your requirements were all set, or so you thought, when the project office informed you that HQ has added a new mission objective at the recommendation of the National Academy of Sciences. This new objective is not insignificant and will have design implications. First you sigh. Then you get to work. After informing your team you understand the implications of the new objective, you

update your NGOs and ConOps, and then decide how to incorporate the objective into the SRD. What requirements need to be added, deleted, or maybe altered? With this figured out you get the updated SRD approved and then move on to understanding the implications of the requirements change on your design.
- The schedulers in the project office, normally meticulous and detailed, just discovered an error and it's significant. They pick up the phone and tell you that CDR needs to be shifted 6 weeks earlier to meet the launch date. You are 2 months from PDR and in final preparations, so there's time to accommodate the change, but in a snap of the fingers now your margin to meeting CDR has been reduced significantly. First you sigh. Then you get to work. After informing your team, you take a look at your schedule to CDR, the critical milestones, and the interdependencies with those milestones. If you haven't already, you determine the critical path and see how much margin or slack you have. You may decide to accelerate some milestones that are carrying a good bit of margin, or maybe even delete or defer a few if CDR is not dependent on them. You and your team figure out a new schedule, one that is achievable and within accepted risk, and you feed that back to the schedulers along with the notification that they owe you a beer (OK, you don't have to do that last part...well, if it's good beer, maybe.)
- At a weekly project leadership tag up, your project manager enters and sits down with a stern expression. The project manager just got out of a meeting with the Program Office and the project's budget is going to be cut by 5 percent next fiscal year. It is no reflection on the project's performance or value but is to help resource a new contingency fund within the program and all projects are being asked to contribute 5 percent. The project manager will spread (like peanut butter) the impact around and informs you that your technical development budget will be reduced by $750K. First you sigh. Then you get to work. After informing your team, you look at your predicted budget and spend rate for the next fiscal year. Your team helps you identify how much is being

held in margin and where any conservatism resides. To maintain schedule and engineering rigor, your team determines that you can only handle a $500K budget reduction. Doing any more will result in the inability to adequately proceed with analysis and design and would impose unacceptable technical risk to the project. You feed this back to the project manager who, although disappointed in the answer, respects your opinion and lets you know they will find the additional budget from elsewhere in the project.

- The Center's Engineering Director shoots you an email titled "Staff Reduction." Most of your technical staff is matrixed from your Center's Engineering Directorate (as are you), so you know this is not going to be good news. Upon opening the email, you discover that two of your team are going to be shifted to work a high-priority rapid development project that's important to the Center Director. These two team members are not irreplaceable, but their loss will be a significant hit to the team. First you sigh. Then you get to work. After informing your team, you discuss how to shift the workload to accommodate two fewer members. You and your team find a workable solution that allows for the work to continue without overworking those who remain. Part of the solution will be to contract out some analysis work that your team had planned. Fortunately, the Engineering Director can cover that cost.

- The procurement office leaves you notification that the company you selected to provide a critical subsystem just filed for bankruptcy. There was no indication that they might do so, and news reports indicate that they might have been cooking the books. The CEO of the company was arrested and will be indicted for fraud. Meanwhile, you're now left with no one to deliver that subsystem. First you sigh. Then you get to work. After informing your team, you research whether there are any other certified suppliers for the hardware in question. You remember during the selection process that there were two potential vendors, and although the original selection may not have been the right one in the long run, you ask the procurement office to check whether the other company would

be interested in providing the parts. Fortunately, they would, but would not be able to deliver on the original date, so your schedule will take a hit. See the schedule bullet above.
- The system you're developing relies on a commercial satellite provider to get your data from the space-based observatory you are developing back to the ground. They are a new provider and their communication satellite is still under development but were selected because they promised performance that outmatches any other provider. The fact that their system is still under development was considered acceptable risk. On this day, however, you get notified that they have been forced to utilize a different frequency spectrum by the international organization that makes that allocation. They apologize, but it's out of their hands. First you sigh. Then you get to work. After informing your team, you study the impacts of this different frequency and whether it might result in any degradation of your data's integrity. After your RF specialist studies the matter, he determines that the frequency itself won't have an impact but that it will require transmission at a lower bandwidth, which will take longer to get the data retrieved. This could impact the project's stakeholders, the researchers and science community who were expecting the originally promised bandwidth. You notify the project manager, who then has the unenviable task of contacting the stakeholders with the disappointing news. But, hey, that's why project managers make the big bucks, right?

In each of these scenarios the overall goal is to reassert order. Change upsets that order, but a little bit of work can restore it again. Once the change is incorporated, the impacts assessed, the details checked and double checked, then you're back to a sense of order and stability, which is what's desired. The change likely caused a loss of configuration control, but the actions and remediations you take eventually return the configuration to order. With this complete, you can proceed with the rest of the project.

Even if we have agility to adapt to changes, technical excellence demands that we fully understand the change and make sure we identify any impacts to the system. If we make changes to our requirements, we track that change up and down the traceability to determine how flowing down the altered or new requirement will change other requirements. If we make a design change, we need to get our hands around how it might affect other aspects of the design. Our systems are highly interrelated and it's rare that a design change won't impact something else. We may need to do analysis, additional laboratory testing, or even a demonstration in the field to understand the implications of the change. If the change is of software, we can perform regression testing to ensure expected performance and no unintended consequences. In the end, any changes may indeed impact our system or might produce a different operating performance. Hopefully not, but that's always a possibility. Regardless, it is incumbent on the Chief Engineer to understand how, when, and to what level performance degradation might occur and to communicate those results to project leadership.

Change is hard, and dealing with change can be cumbersome, uncomfortable, and disruptive. But you can handle it because you have the agility to adapt to new situations, get the work done, and keep your team and your project moving forward to a successful outcome. Because you're the Chief Engineer: you can do this!

CHAPTER 23

ENSURING TECHNICAL EXCELLENCE

In 2006, Christopher Scolese was the NASA Chief Engineer.* During his tenure as NASA Chief Engineer, Chris authored a series of memos entitled "Message from Chief Engineer," covering a variety of perspectives on subjects falling within his purview. He used these memos (or "messages") as opportunities to establish and communicate his expectations of the engineering community and his vision striving for that community to achieve heights of performance, integrity, and excellence in their tasks. In one such memo, Chris spoke about his views on what he referred to as "technical excellence."†

Within NASA's engineering community we discuss the idea of technical excellence all the time. We throw the term around as a catchphrase, include it in position descriptions, and underline it as an expectation of those carrying the engineering banner. We expect technical excellence from our practitioners and especially from our leadership. But while the term is used continuously in discussion, during hiring and promotion, in group meetings, and at formal events, no one had ever defined exactly what was meant by "technical excellence." Chris's memo put words to the idea.

I'll get to the specifics of Chris's memo in a moment, but first I want to remark on how important maintaining technical excellence is for NASA's Chief Engineers. Whether you are at the project level, program level, Center level, or Mission Directorate level, you've reached a career pinnacle of responsibilities and authorities and are in a position in which NASA is riding on your success. You make critical decisions, lead tremendous teams, and represent both engineering and the Agency both internally and externally. You have been selected for this position from many qualified candidates and you represent the best that NASA has to offer. Along with the responsibilities you carry at whatever level you serve, you also carry the responsibility of representing NASA Chief Engineers and of maintaining the highest

---

* He later was elevated to the NASA Associate Administrator, served as the Center Director of Goddard Space Flight Center, and most recently took over as Director of the National Reconnaissance Office (NRO).
† *https://appel.nasa.gov/2010/02/25/ao_1-4_sf_chief-html*, (accessed October 23, 2019).

standards of performance and behavior. You are a paradigm for excellence, and you are expected to embody that paradigm. I'm not sure if they told you this when you were interviewed for your position, but now you know.

Certainly, you need to be technically competent and knowledgeable about engineering disciplines. You don't have to be an expert on everything, but you do have to know at least something about just about everything. You need to be familiar with technical terms, the technical life cycle and development process, and can explain them if asked. You also need to lead a team and be proficient in doing so, demonstrating many of the characteristics described in this book. And you should be ethical, moral, truthful, honest, reliable, a person of your word, and any other positive qualities and traits that demonstrate the best of any group. When you are introduced at a conference, a formal project review, a high school, or at a bar with friends or any gathering, you carry with you all that it means to be a Chief Engineer. It is more than a title; it is an expectation of excellence in our profession and in life.

Didn't know that, did you? Maybe you did, and if so, then good for those who selected you and explained all this. If they didn't, I think they should have. Am I being over-the-top and a bit overblown or excessive with that last paragraph? I don't think so. Many of those qualities and traits are items that should be demonstrated by any leader, whether a Chief Engineer or other position. But this isn't a book about other positions, so I'm trying to speak only to you. We establish and maintain our credibility, and in some cases authority, through the demonstration of excellence. It's a high standard, but Chief Engineer is a high position, and excellence is what we expect from each other.

In 2018, as we were revising NPR 7123, NASA's systems engineering policies, we decided to add a section on technical excellence using much of the wording from Chris Scolese's memo. We felt it was important to provide some sort of definition to the technical excellence term we use so often. We placed the wording in Section 1 of the NPR, right up front so that it would be understood as a description of expectations and behavior. We added it for context and to provide a common framework that everyone can use. We felt it was important enough to add to NASA policy, where today it lives.

Back to Chris's tenants of technical excellence. What are they? The memo constructs technical excellence as an edifice supported by four pillars of excellence that stand on a foundation of personal and organizational responsibility. As stated in the memo, those four pillars ensure that every NASA program and project meets the highest technical standards. They are listed below.

- **Clearly Documented Policies and Procedures:** The memo states that clear policies and procedures are essential for mission success given the complexity and uniqueness of the systems NASA develops and deploys. For engineering, these policies flow directly from the NPR 7120 series (program and project management) and from NASA Policy Directive (NPD) 1000.0, which is the Agency's strategic management and governance handbook. It goes on to say that policies and procedures are only as effective as their implementation, which is facilitated by personal and organizational responsibility (the foundation) and effective training (the next pillar). The Office of Chief Engineer (OCE) ensures that these documented policies and procedures are consistent with and reinforce NASA's organizational beliefs and values and are supplemented with handbooks and standards to facilitate optimal performance.

- **Effective Training and Development:** OCE bears the responsibility for providing NASA's technical workforce ("the most capable workforce in the world," it adds) with technical training necessary to carry out the Agency's mission. The memo mentions NASA's Academy of Program/Project and Engineering Leadership (APPEL) along with technical leadership development at many Centers. This training, while ensuring the workforce is knowledgeable about standards, specifications, processes, and procedures, is also rooted in engineering philosophy that grounds NASA's approach to technical work and decision-making, giving historical and philosophical perspectives that, again, teach and reinforce NASA's organizational values and beliefs.

CHAPTER 23 • *Ensuring Technical Excellence* 245

- **Balancing Risk:** Risk is inherent in everything NASA develops and proper risk management is a trade striking a balance between the tensions of program/project management and engineering independence. Engineering rigor cannot always be sacrificed for schedules and budget, and likewise programmatic concerns cannot always be overlooked in the development of technical approaches. ETAs are responsible for ensuring risks are considered and good engineering practices are balanced with programmatic needs.
- **Continuous Communications:** This pillar remarks that communication lies at the heart of all leadership and management challenges. It opines that every major failure in NASA's history stemmed in part from poor communication. Among our technical workforce, communication takes various forms: continuous risk management, knowledge management, dissemination of best practices and lessons learned, and continuous learning, to name just a few. It raises the importance of the empowerment of individuals at all levels to illuminate concerns without fear of adverse consequences and concludes that OCE promotes a culture of continuous communications.

These four pillars constitute both what OCE (either at HQ or the resident Center offices) can do to enable technical excellence and also what individuals who carry the responsibility (like Chief Engineers) can do as well. We'll explore that in a bit. But first, let's complete this structure that supports the edifice of Technical Excellence. The four pillars above carry the load, but they stand on two fundamental foundations without which they would collapse.

- **Personal Accountability:** The memo explains that each individual is responsible for the success of the mission. Each person, regardless of position, contributes to success and every component must work for the Agency to be successful. Personal responsibility includes the need to possess the knowledge and confidence to speak up when something is amiss in their area of responsibility.
- **Organizational Accountability:** Alternatively, NASA's technical organizations have the responsibility to provide the training, tools,

and environment for technical excellence. Providing the proper environment means establishing regular and open communications so that individuals feel comfortable exercising their personal responsibility. It also places the responsibility on the organization to ensure those who reside in the technical realm have rewarding and satisfying careers.

The theory here is that without this foundation of responsibility the four pillars cannot stand. If the individual doesn't take responsibility to contribute to the success of NASA's mission and to speak up when problems arise, and if the organization doesn't provide the tools, training, and environment to allow individuals to exercise their responsibilities, then the whole house of cards will collapse. These foundational elements are fundamental to enabling technical excellence.

So, what can you do to ensure these foundational items? Well, for example, when your team needs tools or training you can advocate for them to project leadership, or, if you are allocated a budget yourself, provide for these needs directly. More important, you have the ability to affect the environment of excellence surrounding your technical team. You can promote regular and open communication and you can create an environment in which your team members feel free to raise issues and concerns. On the individual side, you can emphasize that every member is important to the success of the effort, whether they are members of your direct team or external counterparts with whom your team interacts. You can also emphasize that any issue or concern can always be raised and that you expect nothing less than excellence from your team when situations warrant. These things are within your control.

Now back to the pillars. Again, what can you do as Chief Engineer to enable these behaviors and expectations of technical excellence in your team? We'll start with the first, Clearly Documented Policies and Processes. Your project undoubtedly has a document tree. If not, you can recommend it adopt one. A document tree is not just a listing of paper products your project uses, but a well-thought-out representation of the policies, plans, and processes your project will use and the relationships between them. The project can determine what's applicable and what's not, and which should take precedence over others. Still, the doc tree is clearly outlined and documented so that it's well understood. This can include the project SEMP and systems engineering policies, technical specifications, technical management plans, and other accoutrements you will need to design, develop, test, and operate. You will bear some responsibility for the choice and organization of the technical policies and processes and for making sure that your team understands them sufficiently so that they can be implemented.

Next is Effective Training and Development. Typically, those who are direct supervisors of your technical team members will be responsible for the members' training and career development. However, once a member is on your team you might note some absence of understanding in specific areas that could indicate the need for additional training. It would not be unreasonable for you to recommend that. Additionally, there may be technical certifications or training in operating analysis tools that would benefit the team and your team members. Again, if you see deficiencies, you can recommend training. Don't overlook the opportunity for mentorship and experiential training through details and temporary postings that could bring much-needed experience to your team. Encourage your team to purse these sorts of opportunities.

On the subject of Balancing Risk, as Chief Engineer you play a primary role in both identifying and managing your project's technical risk and also in ensuring that your team understands the trades between technical and programmatic priorities when risks decisions are made. We discussed much of this in Chapter 19, "Becoming a Master of Risk." (Hopefully, some of that stuck with you; if not, go back and take another look.) As the project ETA, you can make sure that your technical risks are acknowledged and understood by project management so that appropriate trades can be made with schedule and budget.

Finally, there's an awful lot you can do to ensure Continuous Communication. Your team should be kept well informed of developments occurring at the project manager's level that affect them (luckily, you're their primary interface with the project manager). Try to share as much as you can and only embargo information when it's absolutely necessary. Similarly, you can help your team share information among themselves. This may take some effort and constant vigilance, as sharing information may not come naturally to some people. But you can hold frequent technical team staff meetings in which you go around the table and ask for new information covering each member's responsibility. You can try weekly or monthly Activity Reports but, heck, I've never been a big fan of those, and there are other ways to collect information that are just as effective. But if you like Activity Reports, its entirely your call. Use them.

And just as you can promote technical excellence within your team, you can set high standards for yourself too. You know, talk the talk but then walk the walk. Know which technical policies, procedures, and standards are used by your project and why. Know how these flow down to your technical management plans. Get the training and preparation you need to effectively perform your job and serve as Chief Engineer (This includes leadership training). Become a master of risk, as described in Chapter 19, and know how to ensure the project balances technical with programmatic risks. And, communicate, communicate, communicate. It's expected for you to set high standards of technical excellence for your team, but it doesn't mean a thing if you don't set the same standards for yourself.

Chris Scolese's memo was followed in 2008 by a paper for an AIAA Sciences Meeting authored by William W. Vaughn titled "Technical Excellence: A Requirement for Good Engineering."* For his paper Vaughn drew from his own experience but also interviewed a number of NASA's senior engineers for their perspectives. In this paper he explored the foundation and pillars Chris highlighted, but then added a few attributes of organizational culture that he felt also reflect a commitment to

---

* William W. Vaughn, "Technical Excellence: A Requirement for Good Engineering" (AIAA-2008-1120), presented at the 47th American Institute of Aeronautics and Astronautics Aerospace Sciences Meeting in Reno, NV, January 7–11, 2008, *https://appel.nasa.gov/2011/11/27/ata_4-9_technical_excellence_systems_engineering-html*, (accessed October 9, 2019).

technical excellence. Quoting from one of his interviews, he included the following attributes.
- highest-value integrated engineering products
- continual growth, learning, and diversity of experience
- technical conscience
- responsive and technically engaged leaders at all levels
- shared accountability for successes and failures
- proactive, engaged, and predictive approach to technical content
- teams whose members complement and complete each other
- recognition that engineering requires versatility and mobility to meet the needs of the organization
- placement of the right person at the right place at the right time*

Some of these parallel what Chris stated, while others introduce new ideas; the idea of technical conscience intrigues me—I'm going to have to investigate that one further. But collectively, they espouse a prescription for the sorts of excellence we expect from our engineering staff and, as leaders, from our Chief Engineers.

All of these precepts, the collected items in this entire chapter, should be ready and ever present in every activity you perform. Through execution they should become part of your normal daily routine, intuitive behaviors you exhibit without even thinking. But if you need some help, you can jot down some of the general themes and pin them by your desk or laminate them on a card and carry them around with you as constant reminders.

In the end, just remember that the Agency and the country expect excellence from you. Achieving it is not only possible but easy if you follow a few guidelines. You can do this! This, as much as anything else in this book, is the prescription for your success.

---

* Vaughn's paper credits Teresa VanHooser from Marshall Space Flight Center for this list.

CHAPTER 24

HAVING FUN AND SHOWING IT

My guess is that you accepted your assignment as Chief Engineer because you thought it'd be great fun. Not because of the responsibility, promotion, title, or other potentially legitimate reasons, but because it'd be fun. Well, you're right, this job is fun. Damn fun! We get a unique perspective of the development of some of the most complex and complicated machinery mankind has ever built and get to oversee and shepherd it from cradle to operations. We lead teams of incredibly talented, competent, and dedicated engineers who shift quickly from strangers to colleagues to friends, and maybe even become family. We are allowed to represent this team and the project with senior leadership and to speak on their behalf. We get to use jargon and vernacular familiar to us and very few others. We are given the opportunity to become intimate with pieces and parts, components and assemblies, and really understand how they work and why they might not. And even more so, we get to deal every day with the challenges of hardware and software development that made us want to become engineers in the first place.

Heaven. What more could an engineer want? This love affair with the things we do and get to build is the essence of what keeps us coming back day after day with enthusiasm, looking forward to the moment when we walk in the door, have a cup of coffee, and get down to work. We may enter that door as just another person buying their coffee at a coffeehouse, but when we cross that threshold, we transform into a NASA Chief Engineer. Tell me, why the heck wouldn't that be fun?

Yes, there are also frustrations, hurdles, and challenges that get in the way. Not all of our best-laid plans work out, and not all of our solutions come to fruition. There are good days and there are not-so-good days. But overall, the work is enjoyable and very satisfying.

And on those days when we come face to face with frustrations and challenges, when our plans go sour and our solutions come up empty, it's important to remember that deep down the job really is fun. And you know what? It shows in our appearance, in our demeanor, in the way we conduct ourselves. And consequently, our team and everyone else can tell we're having fun. Maybe that's the greatest behavioral trait that

Chief Engineers personify—the ability to have fun with their work, regardless of whether things are going stupendously or sour.

OK, good words and a great notion, but we're still human, right? Of course, we are. We might curse (quietly) at a failure or setback, we might lose our temper (mildly) when we're faced with inappropriate behavior or incompetence, and we might get saddened or depressed (quickly) if the project faces a seemingly insurmountable problem (until we surmount it, of course). Chief Engineers are resilient people, but we can't divorce ourselves from eons of human evolution, nor can we ignore or bury negative feelings. But we can bounce back quickly because we know there's more fun to be had just around the corner and that gives us something to look forward to.

I love going to design reviews and discussions at technical milestones. There are not a lot of these at NASA HQ, where we focus more on strategic goals, budgeting, and policy. But when I do get a chance to go, I quickly take it because design reviews are just the best damn thing! There is joy in spending the day discussing development in great technical detail, looking at computer-aided design drawings and analysis results, and discussing design challenges, solutions, risks, and hazards. I find peace in enveloping myself in this PowerPoint ocean and swim happily as the charts float across the screen. I think one of the reasons I find it so enjoyable is because it all resonates with me, it's what I do, and with people who do the same, in the same language, and understand the fundamental difficulties of what we do. I find all of that empowering and comforting at the same time.

I really enjoy being given a challenge and having to find a solution. Whether it's psyching out an orbiting Shuttle's cryogenic tank in the midst of the effects destratification before the pressure becomes critical, figuring out how to get two disparate organizations in the same directorate to integrate, or developing policies where none previously existed, I get huge satisfaction and enjoyment from turning that disorder into answers. It's not just the product of this transformation that I find fun but maybe more so the process of getting there. It's the journey that I find fun, I guess.

And you know what? I think people around me can tell. I think they can see the joy I hold for my work and the contentment I get from it. Maybe folks can be just a bit happier themselves when they are around me because the joy I feel is contagious. I don't know, but I like to think that's true. I like to think that some of this joy rubs off and elevates those who are around me. If that is indeed true, then it makes me even happier.

It wouldn't surprise me if you share these feelings. Having fun as a Chief Engineer is part of the job. You won't find it in your position description or in your individual development plan, but it is nonetheless part of holding this position. It should be fun. It's supposed to be fun.

The joy we get out of being a Chief Engineer is, I believe, something inherent in all of us. It's kind of built in and flows from a common area inside of us. Our joy is a combination of responsibility, challenge, position, title, authority, activities, and topics that are personally satisfying and the people we get to interact with. That's the tangible connection. But I propose that there's an intangible part of this too, an internal passion through which we obtain personal and professional gratification. There's a part of us that just syncs with this job.

Can someone without that sort of internal passion perform the job of Chief Engineer. Sure, it can be done. There are a lot of incumbent responsibilities that can be done without passion. It is possible to be a competent and satisfactory Chief Engineer without this passion, to perform the tasks and deliver a capability on time and on cost. Many of the processes we follow are sufficiently described in our documentation to allow for this. I do know a few who fit this bill, who methodically perform the work, manage the team, and promote success of the endeavor but without much passion or joy. Many are good engineers and dedicated to NASA's mission. But I would contend those with passion and those who have fun with the job make not just good Chief Engineers but great Chief Engineers.

So have fun if you can. Be able to look past the shortcomings of the position, the frustrations and hurdles, the occasional politics and other organizational claptrap, and find ways to enjoy it all. I have noted the folks at Armstrong Flight Research Center seem to enjoy their monthly engineering technical reviews, which I join as often as I am able. At these meetings all the Center's projects provide 20 or 30 minutes of technical status on the project, along with some insight into problems and issues. Being on the East Coast at NASA HQ, I normally listen in via telecon. It could be a dry and point-of-fact discussion, but it's not. It's fun! Those presenting and those in the audience find ways to laugh and keep the spirit and atmosphere light. The laughter can be so strong sometimes that it overcomes the filters on the telecon in the meeting room and all I get is unintelligible noise on my end. These folks take their work very seriously, and they have a reputation to uphold as the world's best place to flight test experimental aircraft, but through it all they still find ways to laugh. And it's great! It makes me look forward to joining the discussion and I suspect it makes it easier for those presenting to discuss potentially uncomfortable issues in their technical progress. It's a fabulous environment in which to have an engineering review and I applaud them for it.

Another example comes again from my flight control days. A flight control team in Mission Control is, beyond anything else, professional. We dress professionally when missions are underway, we follow standard protocols of communication when discussing matters over the console voice loops, and we treat each other with utmost respect. When issues or problems arise with the orbiting spacecraft or crew, Mission Control operates similar to what I imagine it's like on a submarine on course to torpedo an enemy ship. Calls are clipped and only contain required information, acknowledgments are received in response, and it's all business! But flight controllers are human too and the team can find occasional (appropriate) ways to have fun. For instance, one particular flight director used to encourage his team to wear colorful (and outlandish, if available) ties on console, and he would give out awards each day for the best one. It was also routine for some of the flight control positions to combine resources and bring in meals for their teams. The responsibility would bounce around from group to group, but each one would try to select something that would be enjoyed by all. Sometimes it would be sandwiches or pizza, other times home cooked entrees—tuna casserole, tacos, venison barbecue, pasta dishes, you name it. And I can tell you, some of the very best Lebanese baklava I've ever had was provided by one flight controller who would spend hours at home preparing it and then bring it in to our shift on console. Delicious! But more to the point, it was all fun.

So you should have fun in your job and hopefully your team will see that you're having fun. But is your team having fun as well? A team that's having fun is likely to be a productive, cooperative, and highly functional, so be sure to monitor them as well. Periodically measure their "fun quotient." Ascertain whether they are enjoying their jobs or whether it is utter drudgery for them. They should be having fun too, and as engineers they should share the same enjoyment you get from solving tough technical problems and doing the difficult things the Agency demands of us. If they are not, there are likely signs you may be able to pick up. Look for indications of such traits as grumpiness, irritation, short temper, lethargy, lack of motivation, and a sense of being disconnected. These will not be indications that appear one day and are gone the next but rather traits that perpetuate for weeks or months at a time.

If you see your team is not having fun (as a whole or individual members), rather than trying to turn up the gain on "fun," first try to find out why they feel the way they do. Trying to turn up the gain by laughing, singing, making more jokes, having more parties, and wild-tie days would be a perfectly natural reaction, but it wouldn't get to the heart of whatever issue (or issues) is bothering them. When your team or a team member is down, talk to them. Listen deeply. Utilize that emotional intelligence we discussed way back in Chapter 1. The answers are there, although you might have to dig a bit to discover them. Once you understand the problem, fixing it may be a challenge, but at least you have a start and the simple fact of inquiring, listening, and allowing your team to talk about it will in itself be a step back to having fun again.

The opposite of this, a team or team member that is having too much fun, can be disruptive in its own way. In this I mean, of course, that they're not focused on the job but on ancillary things they'd rather be doing. Fun in this sense is not healthy fun but distracting fun, shifting their attention and effort away from the work of your project. There are lots of distractions we face in today's world, lots of opportunities to focus on other things. That's OK during, say, a lunch break, or between meetings. But when it starts to fill a significant portion of the workday, you've probably got a problem on your hands.

Now, if your team is going to have too much fun, you want it to be in the following way. As I mentioned in back in Chapter 17, "Maintaining an Awareness of Cultural Differences," at the beginning of the Constellation program I supported an effort called "CEV Smart Buyer," a short, 2-month intensive study undertaken by NASA to come up with a conceptual design of the program's planned crewed spacecraft (later called Orion) to provide a compare-and-contrast with forthcoming contractor-proposed designs. One of the astronauts on the team, through connections of his own, got us access to the Apollo 17 command module called America that was on display in the adjoining visitor center, Space Center Houston. The rationale for allowing us into the spacecraft was that it would provide us a perspective of the internal volume and layout. Orion was to be larger than the Apollo capsule, but designed to the same basic conical shape. So, we got to go inside.

About 10 of us showed up to Space Center Houston one morning and were escorted to the area where America was situated. The museum curator crawled up a ladder and entered the vehicle through the top docking hatch. He then maneuvered to the front hatch and removed the large Plexiglas barrier that allowed tourists to view the interior but not enter. Then, in pairs, we each had the opportunity to crawl inside. Those of us waiting for our turn joked about keeping all this mum from Gene Cernan, the Apollo 17 commander who still lived in Houston and who repeatedly referred to the museum piece as "his spacecraft."

Finally, it was my turn to enter. The capsule was tilted up about 10 degrees from the horizontal, a pitch that allowed better viewing of the interior to the tourists outside. But, once I swung myself in using the long handhold mounted just above the hatch opening and slid feet-first onto the center couch, I could feel myself trying to slide right back out. I continued on inside and down into the lower equipment bay deep in the spacecraft's interior where I could jump off the couch and stand on my own feet. From there, I began to explore.

The command module is, of course, littered with switches, gauges, dials, and circuit breakers covering nearly the entire interior surface. The panels create an angular environment right out of a carnival attraction meant to induce disorientation. There are no aesthetics here, only pure functionality. But inside this vehicle, I was immersed in a true deep space environment. For 10 minutes (my allotted time), I explored, crawled, investigated, inspected, all the while snapping over a hundred photographs from every perspective and vantage point I could think of. At one point I allowed myself to detach from the present and just imagined being inside this vessel, hundreds of thousands of miles from Earth, under the gravitational influence of another celestial body.

When we were finished, we returned to our respective offices. I downloaded the photographs and distributed them to the team and to my management. My boss at the time, the Chief of the Systems Division, sent me a note declaring, "Steve, thanks for the pictures. You're having way too much fun with this assignment!" In fact, I was, and it was joyous. Now that kind of having too much fun is totally acceptable!

Find out from your team what would be fun for them. Some obvious answers will have to do with work assignments and assigned tasks, and you can be creative with those such that your team get assigned the responsibilities they find most rewarding. But even within existing tasks, they may have ideas on what could be enjoyable for them to do, or in the ways in which accomplishing it would be fun. Give these your consideration. There may be good reasons not to pursue some of their ideas, but in lieu of that, why not allow them to both have fun and get the job done? It's a win-win.

I am sure when I retire or move on to a different position I will miss all of this terribly. Which brings me to the suggestion that you recognize what a fantastic job you have and enjoy it while it's yours.

EPILOGUE

We've reached the end of this journey. Are you ready for the leadership responsibilities of a NASA Chief Engineer? If you feel you're not, I hope you feel closer than when you began this book and have a better perspective for what leadership is all about as a Chief Engineer.

Think about the journey we've covered in a collective sense. Try to see how everything we've discussed comes together to form a Chief Engineer. In equation form, it would read:

> Sum (Demonstrating Emotional Intelligence
> + Representing the Voice of Many
> + Being the Box Top
> + Getting a Mentor/Being a Mentor
> + Demonstrating Knowledge of Systems Engineering
> + Being the Adult in the Room
> + Acting as the Lead Technical Integrator
> + Negotiating Solutions
> + Dealing with Engineering Change
> + Showing Enthusiasm
> + Learning Continuously
> + Serving as a Technical Authority
> + Maintaining Fairness
> + Managing Yourself
> + Employing Sound Engineering Judgement
> + Being Good at Both Tactics and Strategy
> + Maintaining an Awareness of Cultural Differences
> + Showing Accountability
> + Becoming a Master of Risk
> + Promoting Innovation
> + Building a Team
> + Having the Agility to Adapt
> + Ensuring Technical Excellence
> + Having Fun and Showing It)
> ─────────────────────────
> One Hell of a Great Chief Engineer and Leader!

You can be a good Chief Engineer by mastering portions or just a few of these. But if you want to be a great Chief Engineer, you have to include them all, and NASA wants all of you to be great! Try to get proficient in all of these, especially the ones that you find challenging. Consider it in the same category as solving one of the vexing technical challenges you've been given. You can overcome those hurdles and you can get yourself through these. You know why? Because you're a NASA Chief Engineer, that's why! *Ad Astra!*

APPENDIX 1
PRINCIPLES OF NAVAL LEADERSHIP

I mentioned the Principles of Naval Leadership in the Introduction. I'm including these principles as an Appendix for one simple reason: they constitute the best, most concise characterization of leadership principles I have ever found. In fact, I have this list, printed double-sided on a single piece of paper and laminated, hanging over my desk at NASA HQ. I refer to it often and use it frequently when anyone comes into my office asking about leadership principles.

I use this list as a check on my own leadership skills. If my behaviors are measuring up to these principles, then I'm probably doing OK. If they are not, then I need to make some adjustments.

I'd encourage you to use this as a checklist, a set of reminders, as the establishment of a bar, or however you like. But I'd encourage you to use it. These are fantastic and provide a quick reminder of how we are expected to perform as leaders.

PRINCIPLES OF NAVAL LEADERSHIP

1. **Know yourself and seek self-improvement.**
   - Make an honest evaluation of yourself to determine your strong and weak personal qualities.
   - Seek the honest opinions of your friends of superiors to show you how to improve your leadership ability.
   - Learn by studying the causes of success or failure of other leaders.
   - Develop a genuine interest in people.
   - Have specific goals and definite plans to attain them.
   - Have a systematic personal reading program that emphasizes not only professional subjects but also includes topics to help you understand people, both as individuals and in their functioning groups.

2. **Be technically and tactically proficient.**
   - Know what is expected of you and then expend time and energy on becoming proficient at those things.
   - Form an attitude early on of seeking to learn more than is necessary.

- Observe and study the actions of capable leaders.
- Spend time with those people who are recognized as technically and tactically proficient. Learn as much as you can from them.
- Seek feedback from technically and tactically competent people concerning your own performance. Be willing to change.
- Seek opportunities to apply knowledge through the exercise of command. Good leadership is acquired only through practice.
- Prepare yourself for the job of the leader at the next higher rank.

3. **Know your subordinates and look out for their welfare.**
   - Put the welfare of the women and men for whom you are accountable before your own welfare.
   - See the members of your unit and let them see you so that every one of them may know you and feel that you know them. Be approachable.
   - Let them see that you are determined to fully prepare them for the accomplishment of all missions.
   - Concern yourself with the living conditions of the members of your unit.
   - Know your unit's mental attitude; keep in touch with their thoughts.
   - Ensure fair and equal distribution of rewards.
   - Provide sufficient recreational time and insist on participation.

4. **Keep your subordinates informed.**
   - Whenever possible, explain why tasks must be done and any pertinent amplifying instruction.
   - Arrange to get sufficient feedback to assure yourself that immediate subordinates are passing on necessary information.
   - Be alert to detect the spread of rumors. Stop rumors by replacing them with the truth.
   - Build morale and esprit de corps by publicizing information concerning successes of your unit.

- Keep your unit informed about current legislation and regulations affecting their pay, promotion, privileges, and other benefits.

5. **Set the example.**
    - Show your subordinates that you are willing to do the same things you ask them to do.
    - Be physically fit, well groomed and correctly dressed.
    - Maintain an optimistic outlook.
    - Conduct yourself so that your personal habits are not open to criticism.
    - Exercise initiative and regard the spirit of initiative of your subordinates within your unit.
    - Avoid showing favoritism to any subordinate.
    - Delegate authority and avoid over supervision, in order to develop leadership among subordinates.

6. **Ensure the task is understood, supervised and accomplished.**
    - Issue every order as if it were your own.
    - Use the established chain of command.
    - Encourage subordinates to ask questions concerning any point in your orders or directives they do not understand.
    - Question subordinates to determine if there is any doubt or misunderstanding in regard to the task to be accomplished.
    - Supervise the execution of your orders.
    - Exercise care and thought in supervision. Over supervision hurts initiative and creates resentment; under supervision will not get the job done.

7. **Train your unit as a team.**
    - Study, prepare, and train thoroughly, endlessly.
    - Encourage unit participation in recreational and military events.
    - Do not publicly blame an individual for the team's failure or praise just an individual for the team's success.

- Ensure that training is meaningful, and that the purpose is clear to all members of the command.
- Train your team based on realistic conditions.
- Insist that every person understands the functions of the other members of the team and the functions of the team as a part of the unit.

8. **Make sound and timely decisions.**
   - Develop a logical and orderly thought process by practicing objective estimates of the situation.
   - When time and situation permit, plan for every possible event that can reasonably be foreseen.
   - Consider the advice and suggestions of your subordinates before making decisions.
   - Make sure your people are familiar with your policies and plans.
   - Consider the effects of your decisions on your unit.

9. **Develop a sense of responsibility among your subordinates.**
   - Operate through the chain of command.
   - Provide clear, well thought out directions.
   - Give your subordinates frequent opportunities to perform duties normally performed by senior personnel.
   - Be quick to recognize your subordinates' accomplishments when they demonstrate initiative and resourcefulness.
   - Correct errors in judgement and initiative in a way which will encourage the individual to try harder.
   - Give advice and assistance freely when it is requested by your subordinates.
   - Let your people know that you will accept honest errors without punishment in return.
   - Resist the urge to micromanage.
   - Be prompt and fair in backing subordinates.
   - Accept responsibility willingly and insist that your subordinates live by the same standard.

10. Employ your command in accordance with its capabilities.
- Avoid volunteering your unit for tasks that are beyond their capabilities.
- Be sure that tasks assigned to subordinates are reasonable.
- Assign tasks equally among your subordinates.
- Use the full capabilities of your unit before requesting assistance.

11. Seek responsibility and take responsibility for your actions.
- Learn the duties of your immediate senior and be prepared to accept the responsibilities of these duties.
- Seek a variety of leadership positions that will give you experience in accepting responsibility in different fields.
- Take every opportunity that offers increased responsibility.
- Perform every task, no matter whether it be top secret or seemingly trivial, to the best of your ability.
- Stand up for what you think is right. Have courage in your convictions.
- Carefully evaluate a subordinate's failure before taking action against that subordinate.
- In the absence of orders, take the initiative to perform the actions you believe your senior would direct you to perform if present.

APPENDIX 2

CHIEF ENGINEER'S DESK REFERENCE MATERIAL

Over the years I have come across a number of really fantastic engineering references, many originating in NASA but a few from outside the Agency. These references contain any number of engineering best practices and lessons learned obtained over decades of complex system development and a few have been elevated to technical standards. I look at this collection as a useful desk references for NASA's Corps of Chief Engineers. Some of these are easily obtained on the internet, others you have to dig a bit to obtain. However, collectively, they represent a tremendous amount of engineering knowledge. I offer them for your reference.

GENERAL

100 Questions for Technical Review
Aerospace Report No. TOR-2005(8617)-4204 (2005)
30 September 2005
Prepared by P. G. Cheng, Risk Assessment and Management Subdivision, Systems Engineering Division
Prepared for: Space and Missile Systems Center, Air Force Space Command, 2430 E. El Segundo Blvd., El Segundo, CA 90245
Contract No. FA8802-04-C-0001

Abstract
Failure reports routinely trace the underlying cause to "engineering mistakes" and lament "inadequate reviewing." Aerospace personnel participate in a variety of program reviews such as PDRs, CDRs, and MRRs. How can reviewers, in a few hours, find a mistake that has escaped years of design and quality checks by the contractor and program office?

Over the last several years we have published 100 "Space Systems Engineering Lessons Learned," each describing some past incidents and the errors that contributed to them. The following 100 questions—each hyperlinked to the relevant lessons—will help reviewers check if proper engineering practices have been followed to prevent, catch, or mitigate similar errors. For example, Question 8-1 asks "Do the tests independently confirm development results?" If a reviewer had asked

Appendix 2 • Chief Engineer's Desk Reference Material

this question about Hubble, where a flawed optical instrument was used both to guide the mirror polishing and to verify the finished product, the infamous spherical aberration might have been avoided.

These questions are open-ended and not a comprehensive checklist (which would be impossible to create), and reviewers must use their expertise to tailor the questions for a particular situation. Still, if the response is "You know, we never thought about that, we better check it," the reviewers have earned their pay!

MSFC Integrated Engineering Principles Handbook
MSFC-HDBK-3701 (2015), Baseline, Effective Date: 07/27/2015

Forward
This Handbook, produced by the Marshall Space Flight Center (MSFC) Engineering Directorate, documents a broad range of critical engineering principles needed for communication between stakeholders and the engineering community. The principles and guidance contained in this Handbook help define MSFC design practices that have become a part of our engineering excellence. These principles are required to ensure proper technical integration across the entirety of the engineering disciplines at MSFC and products that can be physically integrated during production.

This Handbook is a product of the combined MSFC engineering discipline community, including the Propulsion Systems Department, the Spacecraft and Vehicle Systems Department, the Space Systems Department, the Test Laboratory, the Mission Operations Laboratory, the Materials and Processes Laboratory, the MSFC Chief Engineer's Office, and the Safety and Mission Assurance organization.

HUMAN SPACEFLIGHT
Design Development Test and Evaluation (DDT&E) Considerations for Safe and Reliable Human Rated Spacecraft Systems
NASA/TM-2008-215126, Volumes 1 & 2
Approved 07-30-2014

Forward

Administration (NASA) to provide uniform engineering and technical requirements for processes, procedures, practices, and methods that have been endorsed as standard for NASA programs and projects, including requirements for selection, application, and design criteria of an item.

This Standard is approved for use by NASA Headquarters and NASA Centers, including Component Facilities and Technical and Service Support Centers.

This Standard establishes requirements for providing a healthy and safe environment for crewmembers and for providing health and medical programs for crewmembers during all phases of spaceflight. Requirements are established to optimize crew health and performance, thus contributing to overall mission success, and to prevent negative long-term health consequences related to spaceflight.

In this document, the Office of the Chief Health and Medical Officer establishes NASA's spaceflight crew health requirements for the pre-flight, in-flight, and post-flight phases of human spaceflight. These requirements apply to all NASA human spaceflight programs and are not developed for any specific program. However, while some of the existing programs, such as the International Space Station program, meet the intent and purpose of these requirements currently, these requirements may have implications for longer duration missions and missions with architectures and objectives outside of low Earth orbit. Although the requirements are applicable to the in-flight phase of all space missions, it is anticipated that they will be most relevant during long-duration lunar outpost and Mars exploration missions, since the combined ill effects of exposure to the space environment will be of most concern in those mission scenarios.

SCIENCE/PLANETARY

JPL Design, Verification/Validation and Operations Principles for Flight Systems
DMIE Document ID: DMIE-43913
Document Reference Number: D-17868

This document addresses the principles to be followed/utilized in the formulation and implementation processes for JPL Flight Projects, including hardware and software design/development, margins, design verification, Safety and Mission Assurance, and flight operations control and monitoring.

GSFC Rules for the Design, Development, Verification, and Operation of Flight Systems
GSFC-STD-1000G (2016)
Approved: 6/30/2016
Superseding GSFC-STD-1000F

Purpose
The Goddard Open Learning Design (GOLD) Rules specify sound engineering principles and practices, which have evolved in the Goddard community over its long and successful flight history. They are intended to describe foundational principles that "work," without being overly prescriptive of an implementation "philosophy." The GOLD Rules are a select list of requirements, which warrant special attention due either to their historical significance, or their new and rapidly evolving nature.

The formalization of key requirements helps establish the methodology necessary to consistently and efficiently achieve safety and mission success for all spaceflight products. The GOLD Rules share valuable experiences and communicate expectations to developers. Where appropriate, the rules identify typical activities across life-cycle phases with corresponding evaluation criteria. The GOLD Rules also provide a framework for the many responsible Goddard institutions to assess and communicate progress in the project's execution. The GOLD Rules ensure that GSFC Senior Management will not be surprised by late notification of noncompliance to sound and proven engineering principles that have made GSFC missions consistently successful. Each GOLD Rule specifies requirements in the form of a Rule Statement, along with supporting rationale, and guidance in the form of typical life-cycle phase activities and verifications.

Satellite Mission Operations Best Practices
Johns Hopkins Applied Physics Laboratory (2003)
April 18, 2003
Assembled by the Best Practices Working Group, Space Operations and Support Technical Committee, American Institute of Aeronautics and Astronautics

Point of Contact:
Ray Harvey
Ray.Harvey@jhuapl.edu
Johns Hopkins Applied Physics Laboratory
11100 Johns Hopkins Road
Laurel, MD 20723

Forward
The effort of compiling a collection of Best Practices for use in Space Mission Operations was initiated within a subcommittee of the American Institute of Aeronautics and Astronautics (AIAA) Space Operations and Support Technical Committee (SOSTC). The idea was to eventually post a collection of Best Practices on a website so as to make them available to the general Space Operations community. The effort of searching for available Best Practices began in the fall of 1999. As the search progressed, it became apparent that there were not many Best Practices developed that were available to the general community. Therefore, the subcommittee decided to use the SOSTC Annual Workshop on Reducing Space Mission Costs as a forum for developing Best Practices for our purpose of sharing them with a larger audience. A dedicated track at the April 2000 workshop was designed to stimulate discussions on developing such Best Practices and forming working groups made up of experienced people from various organizations to perform the development. These groups were solicited to help outside the workshop to bring this effort to fruition. Since that time, biweekly teleconferences have been held to discuss the development of the Best Practices and their posting.

One set of Best Practices that did exist was the result of a NASA Goddard Space Flight Center activity. The Satellite Operations Risk Assessment (SORA) Team produced some Best Practices based on research into a problem with SOHO operations. This set was available to us and we used it as a model. In addition to the SORA report, we started with a list of topics and functions involved in Mission Operations. Members of the Best Practices Working Group volunteered to lead the development of Best Practices for particular topics. We scheduled the telecons such that particular topics were to be discussed on particular days. The leader for that topic would send out the draft of Best Practices to the group via email. This was the basis for discussion during the telecon. Following the telecon, the leader would incorporate the various comments received. The telecons were very informal. Announcements with a proposed agenda were sent out prior to the day of the scheduled telecon (sometimes the day before) and minutes were kept and emailed to the group for those who could not attend (unfortunately not always in a timely manner). Action items were assigned as appropriate. The end results of these discussions are the sections presented within this document.

There are many reasons why this effort has been possible. One in particular was used as a selling point to the development group. First of all, we could! These are simply recommendations and rules of thumb; not declarations of what you "shall do". These are not Standards and would not go through the years of review often required of Standards. This is a way that real experienced people can do something to help their fellow Mission Operations team members and possibly help shape future Mission Operations. It is stressed in the "disclaimer" that these Best Practices are simply recommendations based on Lessons Learned. Many times when we think of our Best

Practices, we are looking at things we did right in the past and would do again the next time.

These are Lessons Learned-applied! This is our way of sharing with the community those things we did right so they may be able to take advantage of past experiences.

This effort could be construed as another attempt to foster the "Faster, Better, Cheaper" paradigm in that it may facilitate re-use of proven "processes;" but it was really put forth for another purpose. The underlying objective was to provide someone who has not done this before with some insight into what has worked in the past and give them guidance as to how they may want to implement their Space Mission Operations related application. It is this underlying principle that forms the basis of the SOSTC Best Practices Working Group (BPWG) logo. In case you have seen it (perhaps it is on the cover page) and don't quite understand: Our "Rookie" Mission Operations Manager is trying to reinvent the wheel. We don't want to see that happen. The BPWG is trying to reduce this type of occurrence by making our Best Practices available to anyone; especially to the "Rookie" Mission Operations Managers!

In closing, there is one main reason why this effort has been as successful as it has been, and it must be acknowledged here. It is the time and effort of the people on the BPWG. I was somewhat surprised at the dedication and hard work these folks put in to a "zero budget" effort. It has really made me appreciate what experienced professional people can do if they have a focused goal. My thanks go out to the members of the team who have "suffered" through the "every-other" Friday telecons. My thanks also go out to professional who have provided us feedback. As of April 2003, this effort is ongoing. We are always looking for new members to take on some of the topics we have not touched on. If you are interested in helping out or wish to comment on what we already have, please contact me at: *Ray.Harvey@jhuapl.edu*.

Whether you are considered a Ground System Administrator, Spacecraft Operator, Principal Investigator, Program Manager, Chief Scientist or, in particular, a Rookie Mission Operations Manager, we hope you find the information contained within beneficial. Please remember that these are recommendations, suggestions, and rules of thumb. They are not guaranteed to bring you success, but they may help you avoid some trouble.

AERONAUTICS

Dryden (now Armstrong) Basic Operations Manual
Volumes 1, 2 & 3, Revision 5 (1995)
This Basic Operations Manual (BOM) is the culmination of 50 years of experience in flight research. The BOM is more than a set of policies and procedures, it is a collection of lessons learned through blood, sweat, and tears on a myriad of projects and programs.

The policies, although concise, are profound in their content, and are the foundation of our operations at Dryden. These policies are not guidance. A waiver approved by the Director must be secured to deviate from the basic set of policies.

The BOM has been written to provide maximum flexibility in how the policies can be met in our activities at Dryden. The intent of the BOM is to ensure that the Risk Management process is implemented in a way to prevent injury, loss of equipment, or loss of programs important to the Unites States.

Mil-HDBK-516C, Airworthiness Certification Criteria
MIL-HDBK-516C
12 December 2014
Superseding MIL-HDBK-516B w/Change 1, 29 February 2008

Forward
1. This handbook is approved for use by all Departments and Agencies of the Department of Defense.
2. The criteria contained herein are qualitative in nature. References are provided as background for understanding the criteria, and as a basis for tailoring standards and/or methods of compliance. Also, note that each section contains a list of typical certification source data that may be referenced for evaluating system compliance with that section's criteria. Terms such as "acceptable" used in the criteria are parameters whose specific definition must be determined and documented by the implementing office in the context of each unique air system.

3. Comments, suggestions, or questions on this document should be addressed to AFLCMC/ENRS, Bldg 28, 2145 Monahan Way, Wright-Patterson AFB OH 45433-7017 or emailed to *Engineering.Standards@us.af.mil*. Since contact information can change, you may want to verify the currency of this address information using the ASSIST Online database at *https://assist.dla.mil*.

Made in the USA
Coppell, TX
28 September 2020